Miami, Fort Lauderdale, Palm Beach

Reprinted from *Fodor's Florida 1990*

Fodor's Travel Publications, Inc.
New York and London

ISBN 0-679-01771-2

Fodor's Miami, Fort Lauderdale, Palm Beach

Editor: Christopher Billy
Editorial Contributors: George Leposky, Rosalie Leposky, Fred Wright
Cartographer: David Lindroth
Illustrator: Karl Tanner
Cover Photograph: Paul Barton

Cover Design: Vignelli Associates

Special Sales

Fodor's Travel Publications are available at special discounts for bulk purchases (100 copies or more) for sales promotions or premiums. Special editions, including personalized covers, excerpts of existing guides, and corporate imprints, can be created in large quantities for special needs. For more information write to Special Marketing, Fodor's Travel Publications, 201 East 50th St., New York, NY 10022. Enquiries from the United Kingdom should be sent to Fodor's Travel Publications, 30–32 Bedford Square, London WC1B 3SG.

MANUFACTURED IN THE UNITED STATES OF AMERICA
10 9 8 7 6 5 4 3 2 1

Contents

Maps

Foreword

Greater Miami is one of the world's most popular tourist destinations. Visitors from far and near are attracted to the area's sandy beaches, warm and sunny climate and fine restaurants and accommodations. Our Florida writers have put together information on the widest possible range of activities, presenting you with selections of events and places that will be safe, worthwhile, and of good value. The descriptions we provide are just enough for you to make your own informed choices from among our selections.

This is an exciting time for Fodor's, as we continue our ambitious three-year program to rewrite, reformat, and redesign all 140 of our guides. Here are just a few of the new features:

★ Brand-new computer-generated maps locating all the top attractions, hotels, restaurants, and shops

★ A unique system of numbers and legends to help readers move effortlessly between text and maps

★ A new star rating system for hotels and restaurants

★ Restaurant reviews by major food critics around the world

★ Stamped, self-addressed postcards, bound into every guide, give readers an opportunity to help evaluate hotels and restaurants

★ Complete page redesign for instant retrieval of information

★ FODOR'S CHOICE—Our favorite museums, beaches, cafés, romantic hideaways, festivals, and more

★ HIGHLIGHTS—An insider's look at the most important developments in tourism during the past year

★ TIME OUT—The best and most convenient lunch stops along the shopping and exploring routes

★ Exclusive background essays create a powerful portrait of each destination

★ A mini-journal for travelers to keep track of their own itineraries and addresses

While every care has been taken to assure the accuracy of the information in this guide, the passage of time will always bring change, and, consequently, the publisher cannot accept responsibility for errors that may occur.

All prices and opening times quoted here are based on information available to us at press time. Hours and admission fees may change, however, and the prudent traveler will avoid inconvenience by calling ahead.

Fodor's wants to hear about your travel experiences, both pleasant and unpleasant. When a hotel or restaurant fails to live up to its billing, let us know, and we will investigate the complaint and revise our entries where the facts warrant it.

Send your letters to the editors of Fodor's Travel Publications, 201 E. 50th Street, New York, NY 10022.

Highlights '90 and Fodor's Choice

Highlights '90

The hotel boom continues throughout Florida. Palm Beach's Beach's latest and probably last hotel (due to strict zoning), the 169-room **Ocean Grand,** will open early in 1990 at 2800 S. Ocean Boulevard. The first hotel built under new zoning regulations along Fort Lauderdale Beach, unnamed at press time, is scheduled for completion in late summer. In Miami, the 40-room Miami River Inn expects to open its four historic structures along the river early in the year, and construction is just beginning on a 400-room hotel in the mixed-use Brickell Gateway development on Brickell Avenue between 14th Lane and 14th Terrace.

Two major performing arts centers are nearing completion in southeast Florida. Ft. Lauderdale's new **Performing Arts Center/Riverwalk,** which will include two theaters (one with 2,700 seats, the other with 600), will open in late 1990. By 1991 the new riverwalk with restaurants and shops will connect the theaters with Las Olas Boulevard. Also expected to open in 1991 is the 2,200-seat, $45 million Kravis Center on the Lake Worth campus of Palm Beach Community College.

For the first time since Prohibition, Florida law now allows brew-pubs and microbreweries to produce beer for on-property consumption. In 1989 **Zum Alten Fritz,** a Miami restaurant, began offering free brewery tours, and other Florida brew-pubs expect to open early in 1990.

On the sports scene, 14,000 amateur Florida athletes will participate in 32 Olympic-style events during the Sunshine State Games in July 1990 in Miami's Arena, Knight Center, Orange Bowl Stadium, Tropical Park, and the North and South campuses of Miami-Dade Community College. Homestead's 186-acre baseball complex will open late in 1990 and will welcome a major-league team for spring training in 1991.

Fodor's Choice

No two people will agree on what makes a perfect vacation, but it's fun, and it can be helpful, to know what others think. Here, then, is a very personal list of Fodor's Choices. We hope you'll have a chance to experience some of them yourself while visiting the Greater Miami area.

Special Moments

Sunrise on the beach at Key Biscayne
Sunset on the Anhinga Trail in Everglades National Park
Coconut Grove Arts Festival
King Orange Jamboree Parade in downtown Miami
Fort Lauderdale's Winterfest Holiday Boat Parade
Strolling Fort Lauderdale's Riverwalk
Cycling the Palm Beach bike trail along Lake Worth

Taste Treats

Stone crabs at Joe's Stone Crab on Miami Beach
Cuban fare at Islas Canarias in Miami
Chocolate concoctions at Chef Allen's in North Miami Beach
Tropical fruits at Robert Is Here in Florida City
Alligator tail at Shirttail Charlie's in Fort Lauderdale
Soft-shelled crabs in Bonaventure Resort and Spa
Fresh heart-of-palm salad at Cafe Max in Pompano Beach
Tropical fruit sorbets at La Vielle Maison in Boca Raton
Sunday brunch at The Breakers Beach Club in Palm Beach

Off the Beaten Track

Weeks Air Museum in South Dade
Little Haiti in Miami
Elliott Key in Biscayne National Park
Davie Rodeo Grounds
Gumbo Limbo Nature Center in Boca Raton
Loxahatchee Wildlife Refuge in Palm Beach County
Lion Country Safari in Palm Beach County
Blowing Rocks Preserve in Martin County

After Hours

Tobacco Road in Miami
Churchill's Hideaway in Little Haiti
The Island Club on Miami Beach
Biscayne Baby in Coconut Grove
Taurus Steak House in Coconut Grove
Musician Exchange Downtown Cafe in Fort Lauderdale

Pier Top Lounge at Pier 66 Hotel & Marina in Fort Lauderdale
Doherty's in Palm Beach

Hotels

Grand Bay Hotel, Coconut Grove *(Very Expensive)*

Grove Isle, Coconut Grove *(Very Expensive)*

Hyatt Coral Gables at the Alhambra *(Very Expensive)*

Inter-Continental Miami, Miami *(Very Expensive)*

Sonesta Beach Hotel, Key Biscayne *(Very Expensive)*

Turnberry Isle Yacht and Country Club, North Miami
Beach *(Very Expensive)*

Alexander Hotel, Miami Beach *(Expensive)*

Cavalier Hotel, Miami Beach *(Expensive)*

Jupiter Beach Hilton, Jupiter *(Expensive)*

Riverside Hotel, Fort Lauderdale *(Expensive)*

Casa Alhambra Bed & Breakfast, Fort Lauderdale *(Moderate)*

Place St. Michel, Coral Gables *(Moderate)*

Restaurants

Cafe Chauveron, Miami Beach *(Very Expensive)*

The Dining Room, Palm Beach *(Very Expensive)*

The Pavillion Grill, Miami *(Very Expensive)*

Cafe Max, Pompano Beach *(Expensive)*

Casa Juancho, Miami *(Expensive)*

Casa Vecchia, Fort Lauderdale *(Expensive)*

Chef Allen's, North Miami Beach *(Expensive)*

Grand Cafe, Coconut Grove *(Expensive)*

La Vieille Maison, Boca Raton *(Expensive)*

House of India, Coral Gables *(Moderate)*
Hy-Vong Vietnamese Cuisine, Miami *(Moderate)*

Joe's Stone Crab, Miami Beach *(Moderate)*

Shirttail Charlie's, Fort Lauderdale *(Moderate)*

Captain Bob's, Florida City *(Inexpensive)*

Richard Accursio's Capri Restaurant, Florida City *(Inexpensive)*

The Florida Peninsula

GEORGIA

Amelia Island

St. Mary's R.

95

Jacksonville

ATLANTIC OCEAN

N

10

River

Osceola National Forest

St. Augustine

St. John's River

Santa Fe R.

Suwannee

Gainesville

41

75

301

1

Ocala

Ocala National Forest

40

Daytona Beach

Cedar Keys

27

4

98

19

50

50

Titusville

John F. Kennedy Space Center

528

Cape Canaveral

Walt Disney World

Orlando

Meritt Island

75

4

Tarpon Springs

Winter Haven

Florida's Turnpike

Melbourne

Sebastian Inlet Recreation Area

Clearwater

Tampa

95

Tampa Bay

St. Petersburg

Manatee R.

27

Kissammee R.

Vero Beach

Fort Pierce

Bradenton

Hutchinson Island

Sarasota

Peace R.

Venice

70

75

Lake Okeechobee

West Palm Beach

Singer Island

Caloosahatchee R.

Cape Coral

80

Palm Beach

Captiva Island

Fort Myers

27

Sanibel Island

Boca Raton

Naples

84

Big Cypress National Preserve

Fort Lauderdale

41

Miami Beach

Gulf of Mexico

Miami

Biscayne Bay

Everglades National Park

Cape Sable

Florida Bay

0   50 miles

0   75 km

Key West

1

Florida Keys

World Time Zones

Numbers below vertical bands relate each zone to Greenwich Mean Time (0 hrs.).
Local times may differ, as indicated by lightface numbers on the map.

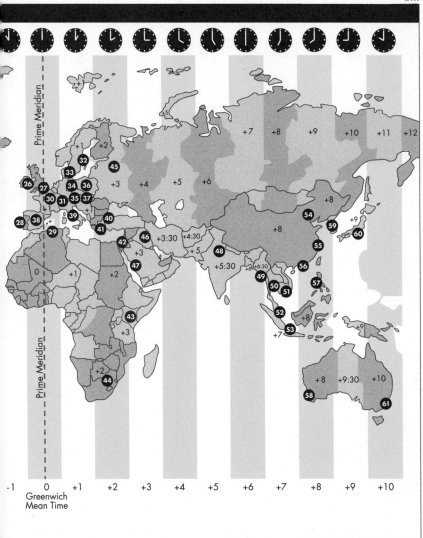

Prime Meridian

+7 +8 +9 +10 +11 +12

+1 +2

32

45

33

26 27 34 36 +3 +4 +5 +6

30 31 35 37

28 38 39

29 40 +8 54

41 59

60

42 46 +3:30 +4:30 55

+3 +5

47 48 56

+5:30 +6:30 57

0 +1 49

+2 50 51

52 +8

53

43 +7

+3

+2

44 +8 +9:30 +10

58

61

Prime Meridian

-1 0 +1 +2 +3 +4 +5 +6 +7 +8 +9 +10

Greenwich
Mean Time

Mecca, **47**	Ottawa, **14**	San Francisco, **5**	Toronto, **13**
Mexico City, **12**	Paris, **30**	Santiago, **21**	Vancouver, **4**
Miami, **18**	Perth, **58**	Seoul, **59**	Vienna, **35**
Montreal, **15**	Reykjavík, **25**	Shanghai, **55**	Warsaw, **36**
Moscow, **45**	Rio de Janeiro, **23**	Singapore, **52**	Washington, DC, **17**
Nairobi, **43**	Rome, **39**	Stockholm, **32**	Yangon, **49**
New Orleans, **11**	Saigon, **51**	Sydney, **61**	Zürich, **31**
New York City, **16**		Tokyo, **60**	

1 Essential Information

Before You Go

Visitor Information

Contact the **Florida Division of Tourism** for information on tourist attractions and answers to questions about traveling in the state.

In Florida: 126 Van Buren Street, Tallahassee 32301, tel. 904/487–1462 or 1463.

In Canada: 150 W. Bloor Street, Suite 310, Toronto, Ontario M5S1M62X9, tel. 800/268–3791 or 416/928–3111.

In the United Kingdom: 18/24 Westbourne Grove, 1st floor, London W25RH, tel. 01/727–1661. British travelers can also get assistance from the **U.S. Travel and Tourism Administration** (22 Sackville St., London W1X2EA, tel. 01/439–7433).

For additional information, contact the regional tourist bureaus and chambers of commerce in the areas you wish to visit (*see* individual chapters for listings).

Tour Groups

If you prefer to leave the driving to someone else, consider a package tour. Although you will have to march to the beat of a tour guide's drum rather than your own, you are likely to save money on airfare, hotels, and ground transportation. For the more experienced or adventurous traveler, a variety of special-interest and independent packages are available. Listed below is a sampling of available options. Check with your travel agent or the Florida Division of Tourism (904/487–1462) for additional resources.

When considering a tour, be sure to find out exactly what expenses are included (particularly tips, taxes, side trips, additional meals, and entertainment); ratings of all hotels on the itinerary and the facilities they offer; cancellation policies for you and for the tour operator; and, if you are traveling alone, the cost for a single supplement. Most tour operators request that bookings be made through a travel agent; there is no additional charge for doing so.

General-Interest Tours **Cosmos/Globus Gateway** (150 S. Los Robles Ave., Suite 860, Pasadena, CA 91101, tel. 818/449–0919 or 800/556–5454) offers an Orlando/Bahamas tour. **American Express Vacations** (Box 5014, Atlanta, GA 30302, tel. 800/241–1700 or in GA 800/282–0800) offers packages to Orlando/Disney World and Miami/Key Biscayne. **Maupintour** (Box 807, Lawrence, KA 66044, tel. 913/843–1211 or 800/255–4266) sells sunny Florida packages during the winter months. **Domenico Tours** (751 Broadway, Bayonne, NJ 07002, tel. 800/554–TOUR) offers packages to Orlando, Miami Beach, Palm Beach, St. Petersburg, Ft. Lauderdale, and Miami Beach/Bahamas/Walt Disney World.

Special-Interest Tours

Adventure **Sobek's International Explorers Society** (Box 1089, Angels Camp, CA 95222, tel. 209/736–4524) will take you canoeing through the Florida Everglades or island-hopping by sailboat off the gulf coast of Florida in their "Adventure Sail Escape."

Wilderness Southeast (711 Sandtown Rd., Savannah, GA 31410, tel. 912/897–5108) runs rugged trips through the Everglades and places like the Okefenokee Swamp in Georgia. Also available is a four-day trip through Central Florida, beginning with canoeing excursions in Ocala National Forest and ending with a snorkeling expedition on the Gulf Coast—this is the only location in the state where the tourist can legally swim with the manatees.

Nature Visit the loggerhead turtle on Sanibel Island, off Florida's gulf coast, with conservationists in an outing arranged by **Smithsonian Associates Travel Program** (1100 Jefferson Dr. SW, Washington, DC 20560, tel. 202/357–4700). You must pay a $20 fee to become a member of the Smithsonian to take any of the trips offered in the program.

Package Deals for Independent Travelers

American Fly AAway Vacations (tel. 800/433–7300) offers city packages with discounts on hotels and car rentals. The airline offers a "Fly and Drive" package throughout the entire state. **Delta Air Lines** (tel. 800/872–7786) offers nine different packages in Florida, including trips to Ft. Lauderdale, Miami, and Key West. **American Express** has similar city packages, with half-day sightseeing tours, available from any American Express office.

Tips for British Travelers

Government Tourist Offices
The **United States Travel and Tourism Administration** (22 Sackville St., London W1X 2EA, tel. 01/439–7433) will send brochures and give you advice on your trip to Florida.

Passports and Visas
You will need a valid passport (£15) and a U.S. Visitors Visa that you can get either through your travel agent or by post from the **United States Embassy** (Visa and Immigration Dept., 5 Upper Grosvenor St., London W1A 2JB, tel. 01/499–3443). The embassy no longer accepts visa applications made by personal callers. No vaccinations are required.

Customs
Visitors of 21 or over can take in 200 cigarettes or 50 cigars or three pounds of tobacco; one U.S. liter of alcohol; and duty-free gifts to a value of $100. Be careful not to try to take in meat or meat products, seeds, plants, fruits, etc. Avoid illegal drugs like the plague.

Returning to Britain you may bring home: (1) 200 cigarettes or 100 cigarillos or 50 cigars or 250 grams of tobacco; (2) two liters of table wine with additional allowances for (a) one liter of alcohol over 22% by volume (38.8° proof, most spirits), (b) two liters of alcohol under 22% by volume (fortified or sparkling wine), or (c) two more liters of table wine; and (3) 50 grams of perfume and ¼ liter of toilet water; and (4) other goods up to a value of £32.

Insurance
We recommend that you insure yourself to cover health and motoring mishaps through **Europ Assistance** (252 High St., Croydon, Surrey CRO 1NF, tel. 01/680–1234).

It is also wise to take out insurance to cover loss of luggage (though check that this isn't already covered in any existing home-owner's policy). Trip-cancellation insurance is another wise buy. **The Association of British Insurers** (Aldermary

House, Queen St., London EC4N 1TT, tel. 01/248–4477) will give comprehensive advice on all aspects of vacation insurance.

Tour Operators Numerous tour operators offer packages to Florida. Here we list just a few; contact your travel agent to find companies best suited to your needs and pocketbook.

Albany Travel (Manchester) Ltd. (190 Deansgate, Manchester M3 3WD, tel. 061/833–0202) offers an eight-day "Florida Resorts" tour featuring southern Florida and the Florida Keys. Prices start from £1,049 per person.

Jetlife Holidays (169–171 High St., Orpington, Kent BR6 0LW, tel. 0689/77061) has a wide range of vacations to various destinations in Florida.

Poundstretcher (Airlink House, Hazelwick Ave., Three Bridges, Sussex RH10 1YS, tel. 0293/548241) offers seven nights in Fort Lauderdale from £599 and seven nights in Miami from £575. It also offers a wide range of fly-drive vacations, golf and tennis vacations, and cruises.

Speedbird (Alta House, 152 King St., London W6 0QU, tel. 01/741–8041) has excellent fly-drive offers and motor-camper vacations that are particularly flexible. Ask for the brochure.

Airfares If you want to make your own way to Florida and need a reasonably priced ticket, try the small ads in the daily or Sunday newspapers or in magazines such as *Time Out*. You should be able to pick up something at rock-bottom prices. Be prepared to be flexible about your dates of travel and book as early as possible.

Also check out the APEX tickets offered by the major airlines, which are another good option. As we went to press, round-trip tickets to Miami cost £199. Be sure to ask if there are any hidden extras, since airport taxes and supplements can increase the price dramatically.

Car Rental There are offices of the major car rental companies in most large towns, and you can either make your arrangements before you leave or when you get to your destination.

Avis (Hayes Gate House, Uxbridge Rd., Hayes, Middlesex UB4 0JN, tel. 01/848–8733) offers seven days' rental of, say, a Chevrolet at about £92; extra days start at £23 per day.

Hertz (Radnor House, 1272 London Rd., London SW16 4XW, tel. 01/679–1799) offers an "Affordable America" program. At press time, seven days rental of a Ford Escort, for example, cost about $135; extra days run about $37 a day. Most rental offers include unlimited mileage, but don't forget to budget for the price of gas, local taxes, and collision insurance. Also check out the fly-drive offers from tour operators and airlines; some good bargains are usually available.

When to Go

Florida is a state for all seasons, although most visitors prefer October-April, particularly in southern Florida.

Winter is the height of the tourist season, when southern Florida is crowded with "snowbirds" fleeing the cold weather in the North. Hotels, bars, discos, restaurants, shops, and attractions are all crowded. Hollywood and Broadway celebrities appear in sophisticated supper clubs, and other performing artists hold the stage at ballets, operas, concerts, and theaters.

Summer in Florida, as smart budget-minded visitors have discovered, is often hot and very humid, but the season is made bearable along the coast by ocean breezes. Besides, many hotels lower their prices considerably during summer.

For the college crowd, spring vacation is still the time to congregate in Florida, especially in the Fort Lauderdale beach area.

Climate What follows are average daily maximum and minimum temperatures for major cities in Florida.

Key West (The Keys)								
Jan.	76F	24C	**May**	85F	29C	**Sept.**	90F	32C
	65	18		74	23		77	25
Feb.	76F	24C	**June**	88F	31C	**Oct.**	83F	28C
	67	19		77	25		76	24
Mar.	79F	26C	**July**	90F	32C	**Nov.**	79F	26C
	68	20		79	26		70	21
Apr.	81F	27C	**Aug.**	90F	32C	**Dec.**	76F	24C
	72	22		79	26		67	19

Miami								
Jan.	74F	23C	**May**	83F	28C	**Sept.**	86F	30C
	63	17		72	22		76	24
Feb.	76F	24C	**June**	85F	29C	**Oct.**	83F	28C
	63	17		76	24		72	22
Mar.	77F	25C	**July**	88F	31C	**Nov.**	79F	26C
	65	18		76	24		67	19
Apr.	79F	26C	**Aug.**	88F	31C	**Dec.**	76F	24C
	68	20		77	25		63	17

Current weather information for over 500 cities around the world may be obtained by calling **WeatherTrak** information service at 900/370–8728 or in TX, 900/575–8728. A taped message will tell you to dial the three-digit access code for the destination you're interested in. The code is either the area code (in the United States) or the first three letters of the foreign city. For a list of all access codes, send a stamped, addressed envelope to Cities, Box 7000, Dallas, TX 75209. For further information, phone 214/869–3035 or 800/247–3282.

Festivals and Seasonal Events

Top seasonal events in Florida include Miami Film Festival in February; Florida Derby Festival from March through April; Sunfest in Palm Beach in May; and Key West's celebration of Hemingway Days in July. For exact dates and details about the following events, contact the Florida Department of Commerce, Division of Tourism (126 Van Buren St., Tallahassee 32399, tel. 904/487–1462 or 1463).

Jan.: Hollywood Sun 'n Fun Festival includes celebrity entertainment and top-notch food (tel. 305/920–3330).

Early Jan.: Polo Season opens at the Palm Beach Polo and Country Club (13198 Forest Hill Blvd., West Palm Beach 33414, tel. 407/793–1440).

Mid Jan.: Art Deco Weekend spotlights Miami Beach's historic district with an Art Deco street fair, a 1930s-style Moon Over

Miami Ball, and live entertainment (661 Washington Ave., Bin L, Miami Beach 33119, tel. 305/672–2014).

Mid Jan.: Taste of the Grove Food and Music Festival is a popular fund-raiser put on in Coconut Grove's Peacock Park by area restaurants (tel. 305/442–2001).

Late Jan.: South Florida Fair and Exposition takes place in West Palm Beach (General Office, 9067 Southern Blvd., West Palm Beach 33411, tel. 407/793–0333).

Late Jan. or early Feb.: Key Biscayne Art Festival is an annual juried show of 175 talented artists at the entrance to Cape Florida State Park (Richard Maloy, Key Biscayne Rotary Club, Box 490174, Key Biscayne 33149, tel. 305/361–0775).

Feb.–Mar.: Winter Equestrian Festival includes more than 1,000 horses and three grand-prix equestrian events at the Palm Beach Polo and Country Club in West Palm Beach (tel. 407/798–7000).

Early Feb.: Scottish Festival and Games features a variety of events in Key Biscayne (tel. 305/757–6730).

Mid-Feb.: Miami Film Festival is 10 days of international, domestic, and local films sponsored by the Film Society of America (7600 Red Rd., Penthouse Suite, Miami 33157, tel. 305/444–FILM).

Mid-Feb.: Islamorada Sportfishing Festival features a weekend of fishing, arts and crafts, races, and prizes (tel. 305/664–4503).

Mid-Feb.: Coconut Grove Art Festival is the state's largest (tel. 305/447–0401).

Early Mar.–early Apr.: Florida Derby Festival is a series of cultural, social, artistic, and athletic events in Broward, Dade, and Palm Beach counties (Festival, Box 705, Hallandale 33008, tel. 305/454–8544).

Early Mar.: Carnaval Miami is a carnival celebration staged by the Little Havana Tourist Authority (970 S.W. First St., Miami 33130, tel. 305/324–7349).

Early Apr.: Bounty of the Sea Seafood Festival in Miami includes a limbo contest, a chowder competition, an Underwater Film Festival, and more (International Oceanographic Foundation/Planet Ocean, 3979 Rickenbacker Causeway, Miami 33149, tel. 305/361–5786).

Early Apr.–late May: Addison Mizner Festival in Boca Raton celebrates the 1920s in Palm Beach County (tel. 800/242–1774).

Late Apr.: River Cities Festival is a three-day event in Miami Springs and Hialeah that focuses attention on the Miami River and the need to keep it clean (tel. 305/887–1515).

Late Apr.–early May: Conch Republic Celebration in Key West honors the founding fathers of the Conch Republic, "the small island nation of Key West" (tel. 305/294–4440).

First weekend in May: Sunfest includes a wide variety of cultural and sporting events in West Palm Beach (tel. 407/659–5980).

Mid–May: Arabian Nights Festival in Opa-locka is a mix of contemporary and fantasy-inspired entertainment (tel. 305/686–4611).

Mid–May: Pompano Seafood Festival includes one of the nation's premier billfish tournaments, plus area restaurants that showcase their offerings (tel. 305/941–2940).

Mid–July: Hemingway Days Festival in Key West includes plays, short-story competitions, and a Hemingway look-alike contest (tel. 305/294–4440).

Month of Aug.: Boca Festival Days includes many educational, cultural, and recreational activities in Boca Raton (tel. 407/ 395–4433).

Mid–to late Sept.: Festival Miami is three weeks of performing and visual arts sponsored by the University of Miami. (University of Miami School of Music, Box 248165, Coral Gables 33124, tel. 305/284–3941).

Late Sept.: Miami Boat Show in the Grove draws up to 200,000 people to Coconut Grove in Miami (tel. 305/579–3310).

Mid–Oct.: Florida State Chili Cookoff Champtionship at Port of the Islands Resort in the Everglades means all the chili you can eat (25000 Tamiami Trail East, Naples 33961, tel. 800/237–4173 or in FL 800/282–3011).

Late Oct.: Fantasy Fest in Key West is an unrestrained Halloween costume party, parade, and town fair (tel. 305/294–4440).

Early–late Dec.: Winterfest and Boat Show in Fort Lauderdale has a rodeo, shoreline competitions, a Fun Fest for children, and a boat parade and ends with a "Light Up Lauderdale" New Year's Eve bash (tel. 305/522–3983).

Late Dec.: Coconut Grove King Mango Strut is a parody of the Orange Bowl Parade (tel. 305/858–6253).

What to Pack

Pack light, because porters and luggage trolleys are hard to find. Luggage allowances on domestic flights vary slightly from airline to airline. Most allow three checked pieces and one carry-on. In all cases, check-in luggage cannot weight more than 70 pounds each or be larger than 62 inches (length + width + height) and must fit under the seat or in the overhead luggage compartment.

The northern part of the state is much cooler in the winter than is the southern part. Temperatures can dip to the 50s, even in the Keys, so take a sweater or jacket, just in case.

The Miami area is warm year-round and often extremely humid during the summer months. Be prepared for sudden summer storms, but leave the plastic raincoats at home because they're uncomfortable in the high humidity.

Dress is casual throughout the state, with sundresses, jeans, or walking shorts appropriate during the day. A few of the better restaurants request that men wear jackets and ties, but most do not. Be prepared for air-conditioning bordering on the glacial, especially in the Miami/Fort Lauderdale areas.

You can swim in Florida year-round. Be sure to take a sun hat and a good sunscreen because the sun can be fierce, even in the winter.

Cash Machines

Virtually all U.S. banks belong to a network of ATMs (automatic teller machines), which dispense cash 24 hours a day in cities throughout the country. There are some eight major networks in the United States, the largest of which are **Cirrus**, owned by MasterCard, and **Plus**, affiliated with Visa. Some banks belong to more than one network. These cards are not automatically issued; you have to ask for them. Cards issued by American Express, Visa, and MasterCard may also be used in the ATMs, but

the fees are usually higher than the fees on bank cards, and
there is a daily interest charge on the "loan," even if monthly
bills are paid on time. Each network has a toll-free number you
can call to locate machines in a given city. The Cirrus number is
800/424–7787; the Plus number is 800/843–7587. Check with
your bank for fees and for the amount of cash you can withdraw
per day.

Traveling with Film

If your camera is new, shoot and develop a few rolls before leaving home. Pack some lens tissue and an extra battery for your
built-in light meter. Invest about $10 in a skylight filter and
screw it onto the front of your lens; it will protect the lens and
also reduce haze.

Film doesn't like hot weather. If you're driving in summer,
don't store film in the glove compartment or on the shelf under
the rear window. Put it behind the front seat on the floor, on
the side opposite the exhaust pipe.

On a plane trip, never pack unprocessed film in check-in luggage; if your bags get X-rayed, say goodbye to your pictures.
Always carry undeveloped film with you through security and
ask to have it inspected by hand. (It helps to isolate your film in
a plastic bag, ready for quick inspection.) Inspectors at American airports are required by law to honor requests for hand
inspection.

The newer airport scanning machines used in all U.S. airports
are safe for anything from five to 500 scans, depending on the
speed of your film. The effects are cumulative; you can put the
same roll of film through several scans without worry. After
five scans, though, you're asking for trouble.

If your film gets fogged and you want an explanation, send it to
the National Association of Photographic Manufacturers (600
Mamaroneck Ave., Harrison, NY 10528). It will try to deter-
mine what went wrong. The service is free.

Car Rentals

Florida is a car renter's bazaar, with more discount companies
offering more bargains—and more fine print—than anywhere
else in the nation. If you're planning to rent a car in Florida,
shop around for the best combination rate for car and airfare.
Jacksonville, for example, is often somewhat cheaper to fly into
than Miami, but Miami's car-rental rate are usually lower than
Jacksonville's. In major Florida cities, peak-season rates for a
subcompact average around $110 a week, often with unlimited
mileage. Some companies advertise peak-season promotional
rates as low as $59 a week with unlimited mileage, but only a
few cars are available at this rate, and you may have to pay
twice as much if you keep the car less than seven days! Some of
these companies require you to keep the car in the state and are
quick to charge for an extra day when you return a vehicle late.

Avis (800/331–1212), **Budget** (tel. 800/527–0700), **Dollar** (tel.
800/421–6868), **Hertz** (tel. 800/654–3131), **National** (tel. 800/
328–4567), **Sears** (tel. 800/527–0770), and **Thrifty** (tel. 800/367–
2277) maintain airport and city locations throughout Florida.
So do **Alamo** (tel. 800/327–9633) and **General** (tel. 800/327–

7607), which offer some of the state's lowest rates. **Rent-A-Wreck** (tel. 800/221–8282) and **Ugly Duckling** (tel. 800/365–4357) rent used cars throughout the state, usually with more stringent mileage restrictions.

Besides the national rental companies, several regional and local firms offer good deals in major Florida cities. These include **Auto Host** (tel. 800/527–4678), **Payless** (tel. 800/237–2804), **Lindo's** (tel. 800/237–8396), **USA** (tel. 800/872–2277), and **Value** (tel. 800/327–2501). In Fort Lauderdale, local companies include **Aapex Thompson** (tel. 305/566–8663) and **Air and Sea** (tel. 305/764–1008). In Miami, **A-OK** (tel. 305/633–3313) and **Dolphin** (tel. 305/871–5553) are local budget companies, while **AutoExotica** (tel. 305/871–3686) and **Cars of the Rich and Famous** (tel. 305/945–2737) rent cars fit for a "Miami Vice" set. Down in Key West, try **Tropical Rent-a-Car** (tel. 305/294–8136).

It's always best to know a few essentials *before* you arrive at the car-rental counter. Find out what the collision damage waiver (CDW), usually an $8–$12 daily surcharge, covers and whether your corporate or personal insurance already covers damage to a rental car (if so, bring a photocopy of the benefits section along). More and more companies are now holding renters responsible for theft and vandalism damages if they don't buy the CDW; in response, some credit card and insurance companies are extending *their* coverage to rental cars. These include **Access America** (tel. 800/851–2800), **Chase Manhattan Bank Visa Cards** (tel. 800/645–7352), and **Dreyfus Consumer Bank Gold and Silver MasterCards** (tel. 800/847–9700). Find out, too, if you must pay for a full tank of gas whether you use it or not, and make sure you get a reservation number.

Traveling with Children

Publications *Family Travel Times,* an 8- to 12-page newsletter published 10 times a year by Travel with Your Children (80 Eighth Ave., New York, NY 10011, tel. 212/206–0688). The $35 subscription includes access to back issues and twice-weekly opportunities to call in for specific advice. Send $1 for a sample issue.

Great Vacations with Your Kids: The Complete Guide to Family Vacations in the U.S. by Dorothy Ann Jordon and Marjorie Adoff Cohen (E. P. Dutton, 2 Park Ave., New York, NY 10016; $9.95) details everything from city vacations to adventure vacations to child-care resources.

Bimonthly publications for parents that are filled with listings of events, resources, and advice are available free at such places as libraries, supermarkets, and museums: *Florida Parent* (4331 N. Federal Hwy., Ft. Lauderdale 33060, tel. 305/776–3305) covers Palm Beach, Broward, and Dade counties.

Hotels Florida may have the highest concentration of hotels with organized children's programs in the United States. The following list gives examples of the kinds of services and activities offered by some of the major chains. It is by no means exhaustive. Be sure to ask about children's programs when you make a reservation.

Guest Quarters Suite Hotels (Ft. Lauderdale, tel. 800/424–2900) offers the luxury of two-room suites with kitchen facilities and children's menus in the restaurant. It also allows children under 18 to stay free in the same suite with their parents. **Sonesta International Hotels** (tel. 800/343–7170) have a children's program at Sonesta Beach Hotel Key Biscayne. Also look for children's programs at **Marriott's Harbor Beach Resort** (3030 Holiday Dr., Ft. Lauderdale 33316, tel. 305/525–4000 or 800/228–9290). Most **Days Inn** hotels (tel. 800/325–2525) charge only a nominal fee for children under 18 and allow kids 12 and under to eat free (many offer efficiency-type apartments, too).

Condo Rentals   See *The Condo Lux Vacationer's Guide to Condominium Rentals in the Southeast* by Jill Little (Vintage Books/Random House, New York; $9.95).

Home Exchange   See *Home Exchanging: A Complete Sourcebook for Travelers at Home or Abroad* by James Dearing (Globe Pequot Press, Box Q, Chester, CT 06412, tel. 800/243–0495 or in CT 800/962–0973; $9.95).

Getting There   On domestic flights, children under 2 who do not occupy a seat travel free. Various discounts apply to children 2–12. Reserve a seat behind the bulkhead of the plane, which offers more legroom and can usually fit a bassinet (supplied by the airline). At the same time, inquire about special children's meals or snacks, offered by most airlines. (See "TWYCH's Airline Guide," in the Feb. 1988 issue of *Family Travel Times,* for a rundown on the services offered by 46 airlines; an update is planned for February 1990.) Ask the airline in advance if you can bring aboard your child's car seat. (For the booklet "Child/ Infant Safety Seats Acceptable for Use in Aircraft," write Community and Consumer Liaison Division, APA-400 Federal Aviation Administration, Washington, DC 20591, tel. 202/267–3479.)

Hints for Disabled Travelers

The **Information Center for Individuals with Disabilities** (Fort Point Place, 1st floor, 27–43 Wormwood St., Boston, MA 02117, tel. 617/727–5540) offers useful problem-solving assistance, including lists of travel agents that specialize in tours for the disabled.
Moss Rehabilitation Hospital Travel Information Service (12th St. and Taber Rd., Philadelphia, PA 19141, tel. 215/329–5715) provides information on tourist sights, transportation, and accommodations in destinations around the world. The fee is $5 for up to three destinations. Allow one month for delivery.
Mobility International (Box 3551, Eugene, OR 97403, tel. 503/343–1284) is a membership organization with a $20 annual fee offering information on accommodations, organized study, and so forth.
The **Society for the Advancement of Travel for the Handicapped** (26 Court St., Penthouse Suite, Brooklyn, NY 11242, tel. 718/858–5483) offers access information. Annual membership costs $40, or $25 for senior travelers and students. Send $1 and a stamped, self-addressed envelope.
The **National Park Service** provides a **Golden Access Passport** free of charge to those who are medically blind or have a permanent disability; the passport covers the entry fee for the holder and anyone accompanying the holder in the same private, noncommercial vehicle and a 50% discount on camping, boat launching, and parking. All charges are covered except lodging. Apply for the passport in person at any national recreation facility that charges an entrance fee; proof of disability is re-

quired. For additional information, write to the National Park Service (U.S. Dept. of Interior, 18th and C Sts. NW, Washington, DC 20240).

"Information/Referral Numbers for Physically Challenged Visitors" is a useful booklet available without charge from the Florida Bureau of Visitor Services (101 E. Gaines St., Fletcher Bldg., Room 422, Tallahassee 32399, tel. 904/488–7300).

Greyhound/Trailways (tel. 800/531–5332) will carry a disabled person and companion for the price of a single fare.

Amtrak (tel. 800/USA–RAIL) requests 72 hours' notice to provide redcap service, special seats, or wheelchair assistance at stations equipped to provide this service. All handicapped and elderly passengers are entitled to a 25% discount on regular, discounted coach fares. A special children's handicapped fare is also available, offering qualifying children ages 2–11 a 25% discount on their already discounted children's fare. It should be noted that there are exceptions to these discounts on certain prescribed days with various routes. Always check with Amtrak first. For a free copy of *Access Amtrak,* a guide to its services for elderly and handicapped travelers, write to Amtrak (National Railroad Corporation, 400 N. Capitol St. NW, Washington, DC 20001).

Publications *The Itinerary* (Box 1084, Bayonne, NJ 07002, tel. 201/858–3400) is a bimonthly travel magazine for the disabled. Call for a subscription ($10 for a year, $18 for two); it's not available in stores.

Access to the World: A Travel Guide for the Handicapped, by Louise Weiss, offers tips on travel and accessibility around the world. It is available from Henry Holt & Co. for $12.95 (tel. 800/247–3912, the order number is 0805 001417).

Twin Peaks Press (Box 129, Vancouver, WA 98666, tel. 206/694–2462 or 800/637–2256 for orders only) specializes in books for the disabled. *Travel for the Disabled* ($9.95) offers helpful hints as well as a comprehensive list of guidebooks and facilities geared to the disabled. *Directory of Travel Agencies for the Disabled* ($12.95) lists more than 350 agencies throughout the world. *Wheelchair Vagabond* ($9.95) helps independent travelers plan for extended trips in cars, vans, or campers. Twin Peaks also offers a "Traveling Nurse's Network," which provides registered nurses trained in all medical areas to accompany and assist disabled travelers.

Access Travel, published in 1985 by the U.S. Office of Consumer Affairs, is a free brochure that lists design features, facilities, and services for the handicapped at 519 airport terminals in 62 countries. Order publication 570V by writing S. James, Consumer Information Center-K, Box 100, Pueblo, CO 81002.

Access America: An Atlas and Guide to the National Parks for Visitors with Disabilities (published by Northern Cartographic, Box 133, Burlington, VT 05402, tel. 801/655–4321) contains detailed information about access for the 37 largest and most visited national parks in the United States. It costs $67.45 plus $5 shipping if ordered directly from the publisher.

Hints for Older Travelers

The **American Association of Retired Persons** (AARP, 1909 K St. NW, Washington, DC 20049, tel. 202/872–4700) has two programs for independent travelers: (1) the Purchase Privilege

Program, which offers discounts on hotels, airfare, car rentals, and sightseeing, and (2) the AARP Motoring Plan, which offers emergency aid (road service) and trip-routing information for an annual fee of $33.95 per person or per married couple. The **AARP Travel Service** also arranges group tours in conjunction with two companies: Olson-Travelworld (100 N. Sepulvedo Blvd., El Segundo, CA 90245, tel. 800/227–7737) and RFD, Inc. (4401 West 110th St., Overland Park, KS 66211, tel. 800/448–7010). AARP members must be 50 or older. Annual dues are $5 per person or per married couple.

If you're planning to use an AARP or other senior-citizen identification card to obtain a reduced hotel rate, mention it at the time you make your reservation, not when you check out. At restaurants, show your card to the maître d' before you're seated, because discounts may be limited to certain set menus, days, or hours. When renting a car, remember that economy cars, priced at promotional rates, may cost less than cars that are available with your ID card.

Travel Industry and Disabled Exchange (TIDE, 5435 Donna Ave., Tarzana, CA 91356, tel. 818/343–6339) is an industry-based organization with a $15-per-person annual membership fee. Members receive a quarterly newsletter and information on travel agencies and tours.

National Council of Senior Citizens (925 15th St. NW, Washington, DC 20005, tel. 202/347–8800) is a nonprofit advocacy group with some 4,000 local clubs across the country. Annual membership is $10 per person or $14 per couple. Members receive a monthly newspaper with travel information and an ID for reduced rates on hotels and car rentals.

Mature Outlook (6001 N. Clark St., Chicago, IL 60660, tel. 800/336–6330), a subsidiary of Sears Roebuck & Co., is a travel club for people over 50, offering discounts at Holiday Inns and a bimonthly newsletter. Annual membership is $9.95 per person or per married couple. Instant membership is available at participating Holiday Inns.

Golden Age Passport is a free lifetime pass to all parks, monuments, and recreation areas run by the federal government. People over 62 should pick one up in person at any national park that charges admission. A driver's license or other proof of age is required.

September Days Club (tel. 800/241–5050) is run by the moderately priced **Days Inns of America.** The $12 annual membership fee for individuals or couples over 50 entitles them to reduced car rental rates and reductions of 15%–50% at 95% of the chain's more than 350 motels. Members also receive *Travel Holiday Magazine Quarterly* for updated information and travel articles.

Elderhostel (80 Boylston St., Suite 400, Boston, MA 02116, tel. 617/426–7788) is an innovative program for people age 60 or over (only one member of a traveling couple needs to qualify). Participants live on dorms on 1,200 campuses in the United States and around the world. Mornings are devoted to lectures and seminars, afternoons to sightseeing and field trips. The fee includes room, board, tuition (in the United States and Canada) and round-trip transportation (overseas). Special scholarships are available for those who qualify financially.

Publications "Travel Tips for Senior Citizens" (U.S. Dept. of State Publication 8970, revised Sept. 1987) is available for $1 from the Superintendent of Documents (U.S. Government Printing Office, Washington, DC 20402). *The Discount Guide for Travelers Over 55,* by Caroline and Walter Weintz, lists helpful addresses, package tours, reduced-rate car rentals, etc., in the United States and abroad. To order, send $7.95 plus $3 shipping and handling to NAL/Cash Sales (Bergenfield Order Dept., 120 Woodbine St., Bergenfield, NJ 07021, tel. 800/526–0275).

The Senior Citizen's Guide to Budget Travel in the United States and Canada is available for $4.95 plus shipping from Pilot Books (103 Cooper St., Babylon, NY 11702, tel. 516/422–2225).

Although Florida probably attracts more elderly people than any other state, the state publishes no booklet addressed directly to senior citizens.

Senior-citizen discounts are common throughout Florida, but there are no set standards. Some discounts, like those for prescriptions at the Eckerd Drug chain, require that you fill out a card and register. The best bet is simply to ask whether there is a senior-citizen discount available on your purchase, meal, or hotel stay.

Further Reading

Suspense novels that are rich in details about Florida include Elmore Leonard's *La Brava*, John D. MacDonald's *The Empty Copper Sea*, and Joan Higgins's *A Little Death Music*. Pat Frank's *Alas Babylon* describes a fictional nuclear disaster in Florida.

Look for *Snow White and Rose Red* and *Jack and the Beanstalk*, Ed McBain's novels about Matthew Hope, an attorney who practices law in a Florida gulf city. Pat Booth's novel *Palm Beach* describes the glittering Palm Beach scene of sun and sex.

Other recommended novels include Evelyn Mayerson's *No Enemy But Time; To Have and Have Not,* by Ernest Hemingway; and *The Day of the Dolphin*, by Robert Merle.

Among the recommended nonfiction books are *Key West Writers and Their Homes*, Lynn Kaufelt's tour of homes of Hemingway, Wallace Stevens, Tennessee Williams, and others; *The Everglades: River of Grass,* by Marjory S. Douglas; *Florida*, by Gloria Jahoda, published as part of the Bicentennial observance; *Miami Alive*, by Ethel Blum; and *Florida's Sandy Beaches*, University Press of Florida.

Arriving and Departing

By Plane

Most major U.S. airlines schedule regular flights into Florida, and some, such as Delta, serve the Florida airports extensively.

Delta and Piedmont have regular service into West Palm Beach, Fort Lauderdale, Miami, and Key West.

Other major airlines that serve the Florida airports include Continental, American, USAir, American Trans Air, Northwest, Pan Am, United, and TWA. Many foreign airlines also fly into some of the major airports in Florida; the smaller, out-of-the-way airports are usually accessible through the commuter flights of major domestic carriers.

When booking reservations, keep in mind the distinction between nonstop flights (no stops and no changes), direct flights (no changes of aircraft, but one or more stops), and connecting flights (one or more changes of planes at one or more stops). Connecting flights are often the least expensive, but they are the most time-consuming, and the biggest nuisance.

Smoking If cigarette smoke bothers you, request a seat *far away from* the smoking section. Remember, FAA regulations require airlines to find seats for all nonsmokers.

Carry-on Luggage Under new rules in effect since January 1988, passengers are usually limited to two carry-on bags. For bags stored under your seat, the maximum dimensions are $9'' \times 14'' \times 22''$. For bags that can be hung in a closet, the maximum dimensions are $4'' \times 23'' \times 45''$. For bags stored in an overhead bin, the maximum dimensions are $10'' \times 14'' \times 36''$. Any item that exceeds the specified dimensions will generally be rejected as a carryon and handled as checked baggage. Keep in mind that an airline can adapt these rules to circumstances; on an especially crowded flight, don't be surprised if you are allowed only one carry-on bag.

In addition to the two carryons, passengers may also bring aboard: a handbag (pocketbook or purse), an overcoat or wrap, an umbrella, a camera, a reasonable amount of reading material, an infant bag, crutches, cane, braces, or other prosthetic device upon which the passenger is dependent, and an infant/child safety seat.

Note that these regulations are for U.S. airlines only. Foreign airlines generally allow one piece of carry-on luggage in tourist class, in addition to handbags and bags filled with duty-free goods. Passengers in first and business class are also allowed to carry on one garment bag. It is best to check with your airline ahead of time to find out what their exact rules are regarding carry-on luggage.

Checked Luggage Luggage allowances vary slightly from airline to airline. Many carriers allow three checked pieces; some allow only two. It is best to check before you go. In all cases, check-in luggage cannot weigh more than 70 pounds per piece or be larger than 62 inches (length + width + height).

Lost Luggage On domestic flights, airlines are responsible for lost or damaged property only up to $1,250 per passenger. If you're carrying valuables, either take them with you on the airplane or purchase additional insurance for lost luggage. Some airlines will issue additional luggage insurance when you check in, but many do not. Insurance for lost, damaged, or stolen luggage is available through travel agents or directly through various insurance companies. Two that issue luggage insurance are **Tele-Trip** (tel. 800/228–9792), a subsidiary of Mutual of Omaha, and **The Travelers Insurance Co.** (Ticket and Travel Dept., 1 Tower Sq., Hartford, CT 06183, tel. 800/243–3174 or 203/277–2318). Tele-Trip operates sales booths at airports, and it also issues insurance through travel agents. Tele-Trip will insure checked luggage for up to 180 days at $500–$3,000 valuation. For 1–3 days, the rate for a $500 valuation is $8.25; for 180 days, $100. The Travelers will insure checked or hand luggage at $500–$2,000 valuation per person, also for a maximum of 180 days. Rates for 1–5 days for $500 valuation are $10; for 180 days, $85.

Other companies with comprehensive policies include **Access America Inc.**, a subsidiary of Blue Cross-Blue Shield (Box 807, New York, NY 10163, tel. 800/851–2800); **Near, Inc.** (1900 N. MacArthur Blvd., Suite 210, Oklahoma City, OK 73127, tel. 800/654–6700); and **Travel Guard International** (*see* Health and Accident Insurance).

Before you go, itemize the contents of each bag in case you need to file an insurance claim. Be certain to put your home address on each piece of luggage, including carry-on bags. If your luggage is stolen and later recovered, the airline must deliver the luggage to your home free of charge.

By Car

Three major interstates lead to Florida from various parts of the country. I–95 begins in Maine, runs south through New England and the Mid-Atlantic states, and enters Florida just north of Jacksonville. It continues south past Daytona Beach, Vero Beach, Palm Beach, and Fort Lauderdale, eventually ending in Miami.

I–75 begins at the Canadian border in Michigan and runs south through Ohio, Kentucky, Tennessee, and Georgia before entering Florida. The interstate moves through the center of the state before veering west into Tampa. It follows the west coast south to Naples, then crosses the state and ends in Miami.

California and all the most southern states are connected to Florida by I–10. This interstate originates in Los Angeles and moves east through Arizona, New Mexico, Texas, Louisiana, Mississippi, and Alabama before entering Florida at Pensacola on the west coast. I–10 continues straight across the northern half of the state until it terminates in Jacksonville.

Speed Limits In Florida the speed limits are 55 mph on the state highways, 30 mph within city limits and residential areas, 55–65 mph on the interstates. These limits may vary, so be sure to watch road signs for any changes.

By Train

Amtrak (tel. 800/USA-RAIL) provides service to Miami and several other major cities in Florida.

By Bus

Greyhound-Trailways passes through practically every major city in Florida, including West Palm Beach, Fort Lauderdale, Miami, and Key West. For information about bus schedules and fares, contact your local Greyhound Information Center.

Staying in Florida

Tourist Information

The **Florida Division of Tourism** operates **welcome centers** on I–10, I–75, I–95, U.S. 231 (near Graceville), U.S. 1 and 301 (near Boulogne) and in the lobby of the new Capitol in Tallahassee (Department of Commerce, 126 Van Buren St., Tallahassee 32399, tel. 904/487–1462).

Shopping

Malls in Florida are full of nationally franchised shops, major department-store chains, and one-of-a-kind shops catering to a mass audience. Small shops in out-of-the-way places, however, often have the best souvenirs and most special gift items.

Indian Artifacts Indian crafts are abundant, particularly in the southern part of the state, where you'll find billowing dresses and shirts, hand-sewn in striking colors and designs. At the Miccosukee Indian Village, 25 miles west of Miami on the Tamiami Trail (U.S. 41), as well as at the Seminole and Miccosukee reservations in the Everglades, you can also find handcrafted dolls and beaded belts.

Seashells While the best shelling in Florida is on the beaches of Sanibel Island off Fort Myers, shell shops, selling mostly kitsch items, abound throughout Florida.

Citrus Fruit Orange juice—Florida's "liquid gold"—is a staple throughout the state. The welcome centers greet visitors with a fresh glass of it and many restaurants squeeze it for you while you watch. Fresh citrus is available most of the year, except in summer. Some groves still give free samples of juice and fruit slices, but many now charge a small fee for a taste.

Don't expect to roam the groves picking your own fruit. Public access was prohibited to limit the spread of a disastrous canker blight which threatened Florida's citrus industry in the mid-1980s.

Two kinds of citrus grow in Florida: the sweeter and more costly Indian River fruit from a thin ribbon of groves along the east coast, and the less-costly fruit from the interior. After killer freezes in 1984 and 1985 ruined many groves in the Orlando area, the interior growers began planting in warmer areas south and west of Lake Okeechobee.

Citrus is sold in quarter, half, three-quarter, and full bushels. Many shippers offer special gift packages with several varieties of fruit, jellies, and other food items. Some prices include U.S. postage, others may not. Shipping may exceed the cost of the fruit. If you have a choice of citrus packaged in boxes or bags, take the boxes. They are easier to label, are harder to squash, and travel better than the bags.

Malls and Boutiques The Greater Miami area has many look-alike shopping strips and malls with the same retail and discount shops. You'll find finer boutiques in specialty malls such as Mayfair Shops in the Grove and the Bal Harbor Shops (9700 Collins Ave., Bal Harbour 33154, tel. 305/866–0311). The half mile of Flagler Street in the heart of downtown Miami is the nation's most important import-export center, where bargain items for international travelers include cameras, electronics, and jewelry.

Fort Lauderdale's finest shops cluster along six blocks of Las Olas Boulevard and at the 150-store Galleria At Fort Lauderdale (2414 E. Sunrise Blvd., tel. 305/564-1015).

For the ultimate Florida shopping experience, stroll Palm Beach's Worth Avenue. Here you'll find shops like Gucci and Ralph Lauren tucked between galleries selling ancient Chinese art or Oriental rugs, gourmet restaurants, one-of-a-kind jewelry stores, and chocolatiers.

Beaches

No point in Florida is more than 60 miles from saltwater. This long, lean peninsula is bordered by a 526-mile Atlantic coast from Fernandina Beach to Key West and a 792-mile coast along the Gulf of Mexico and Florida Bay from Pensacola to Key West. If you were to stretch Florida's convoluted coast in a straight line, it would extend for about 1,800 miles. What's more, if you add in the perimeter of every island surrounded by saltwater, Florida has about 8,500 miles of tidal shoreline— more than any other state except Alaska. Sand beaches comprise about 1,016 miles of Florida's coastline.

Visitors unaccustomed to strong subtropical sun run a risk of sunburn and heat prostration on Florida beaches, even in winter. The natives go to the beach early in the day or in the late afternoon. If they must be out in direct sun at midday, they limit their sun exposure and strenuous exercise and drink plenty of liquids.

The state owns all beaches below the mean high-tide line, even in front of hotels and private resorts, but gaining access to the public beach can be a problem along much of Florida's coastline. You must pay to enter and/or park at most state, county, and local beachfront parks. Where hotels dominate the beach frontage, public parking may be limited or nonexistent.

From the Treasure Coast south, erosion has been gnawing away at the beaches. Major beach rehabilitation projects have been completed in Fort Lauderdale, the Sunny Isles area of north Dade County, Miami Beach, and Key Biscayne.

In the Florida Keys, coral reefs and prevailing currents prevent sand from building up to form beaches. The few Keys beaches are small, narrow, and generally have little or no sandy bottom.

Participant Sports

Bicycling Bicycling is popular throughout Florida. The terrain is flat in the south and gently rolling along the central ridge and in much of the Panhandle. Most cities of any size have bike-rental shops, which are good sources of information on local bike paths.

Florida's Department of Transportation (DOT) publishes free bicycle trail guides which you can request from the state bicycle-pedestrian coordinator (605 Suwannee St., Mail Room Station 19, Tallahassee 32399-0450, tel. 904/488-4640). DOT also sells seven maps for bicycle trips of 35 to 300 miles. *Maps and Publications, 605 Suwannee St., Mail Room Station 12,*

Tallahassee 32399–0450, tel. 904/488–9220. Cost: $1 plus 6% sales tax per map.

For information on local biking events and clubs, contact **Florida Bicycle Associations** (Box 16652, Tampa 33687–6652, tel. 800/FOR BIKE). In Greater Miami, contact Dade County's bicycle-pedestrian coordinator (Office of the County Manager, Metro-Dade Government Center, 111 N.W. 1st St., Suite 910, Miami 33128, tel. 305/375–4507).

Canoeing The best time to canoe in Florida is winter, the dry season, when you're less likely to get caught in a torrential downpour or be eaten alive by mosquitos.

The Everglades has areas suitable for flat-water wilderness canoeing that are comparable to spots in the Boundary Waters region of Minnesota. Other popular canoeing rivers include the Crystal, Peace, St. Johns, Suwannee, Wakulla, Wekiva, and Withlacoochee. A free guide issued by the Florida Department of Natural Resources (DNR), *Florida Recreational Trails System Canoe Trails,* describes nearly 950 miles of designated canoe trails along 36 Florida creeks, rivers, and springs (Office of Communications, Marjory Stoneman Douglas Building, 3900 Commonwealth Blvd., Tallahassee 32399, tel. 904/488–6327). Contact individual national forests, parks, monuments, reserves, and seashores for information on their canoe trails. Local chambers of commerce have information on canoe trails in county parks.

Two Florida canoe outfitter organizations publish free lists of canoe outfitters who organize canoe trips, rent canoes and canoeing equipment, and help shuttle canoeists' boats and cars. *Canoe Outpost System* is a brochure listing eight independent outfitters serving 11 Florida rivers (Rte. 7, Box 301, Arcadia 33821, tel. 813/494–1215). The **Florida Association of Canoe Liveries and Outfitters (FACLO)** publishes a free list of 26 canoe outfitters who organize trips on 28 creeks and rivers (Box 1764, Arcadia 33821).

Fishing When President Bush made his pre-inaugural bonefishing trip to Islamorada in 1989, he was following a time-honored angling tradition. Other celebrities who have come to Florida to cast a hook and line include President Theodore Roosevelt, British statesman Winston Churchill, and novelists Zane Grey and Ernest Hemingway.

In Atlantic and Gulf waters, fishing seasons and other regulations vary by location, and by the number and size of fish of various species that you may catch and retain. For a free copy of the annual *Florida Fishing Handbook,* write to the **Florida Game and Fresh Water Fish Commission** (620 Meridian St., Tallahassee 32399–1600, tel. 904/488–1960).

Opportunities for salt-water fishing abound from the Keys all the way up the Atlantic Coast to Georgia and up the Gulf Coast to Alabama. Many seaside communities have fishing piers that charge admission to fishermen (and usually a lower rate to watchers). These piers usually have a bait-and-tackle shop. Write the **Florida Sea Grant Extension Program** for a free list of Florida fishing piers (Rm. G-022, McCarty Hall, University of Florida, Gainesville 32611, tel. 904/392–1771).

Inland, there are more than 7,000 fresh-water lakes to choose from. The largest—448,000-acre **Lake Okeechobee,** the fourth-largest natural lake in the United States—is home to bass, bluegill, speckled perch, and succulent catfish (which the locals call "sharpies"). In addition to the state's many natural fresh-water rivers, South Florida also has an extensive system of flood-control canals. In 1989 scientists found high mercury levels in largemouth bass and warmouth caught in parts of the Everglades in Palm Beach, Broward, and Dade counties, and warned against eating fish from those areas.

It's easy to find a boat-charter service that will take you out into deep water. The Keys are dotted with charter services, and Key West has a sportfishing and shrimping fleet that you would expect to find in large cities. Depending on your taste, budget, and needs, you can charter anything from an old wooden craft to a luxurious, waterborne palace with state-of-the-art amenities.

Licenses are required for both freshwater and saltwater fishing. The fees for a saltwater fishing license are $30 for nonresidents and $12 for residents. Nonresidents can purchase freshwater fishing licenses good for 10 days ($15) or for one year ($30); residents pay $12 for an annual license. Combined annual freshwater fishing and hunting licenses are also available at $66 for nonresidents and $150 for residents.

Golf Except in the heart of the Everglades, you'll never be far from one of Florida's 930 golf courses. Palm Beach County, the state's leading golf locale with 130 golf courses, also hosts the home offices of the National Golf Foundation and the Professional Golfers Association of America.

Many of the best golf courses in Florida allow visitors to play without being members or hotel guests. Thus, you can pretend that you're playing in the annual Doral Ryder Open when you play the deadly 18th hole on the Blue Monster course at the Doral Resort and Country Club in Miami.

Especially in winter, you should reserve tee-off times in advance. Ask about golf reservations when you make your lodging reservations.

Hunting Hunters in Florida stalk a wide variety of resident game animals and birds, including deer, wild hog, wild turkey, bob white quail, ducks, and coots. A plain hunting license costs $11 for Florida residents, $50 for nonresidents.

Each year in June, the **Florida Game and Fresh Water Fish Commission** announces the dates and hours of the fall hunting seasons for public and private wildlife-management areas. Hunting seasons vary across the state. Where hunting is allowed, you need the landowner's written permission—and you must carry that letter with your hunting license in the field. Trespassing with a weapon is a felony. For a free copy of the annual *Florida Hunting Handbook,* contact the game commission (620 Meridian St., Tallahassee 32399–1600, tel. 904/488–1960).

Jogging, Running, and Walking All over Florida, you'll find joggers, runners, and walkers on bike paths and city streets—primarily in the early morning and after working hours in the evening. Some Florida hotels have set up their own running trails; others provide guests with information on measured trails in the vicinity. The first time you run in Florida, be prepared to go a shorter distance than normal because of higher heat and humidity.

Two major Florida festivals include important running races. Each year in January the **Capital Bank Orange Bowl 10K,** the state's best-known running event, brings world-class runners to Miami. In April, as part of the Florida Keys' annual Conch Republic Days, runners congregate near Marathon on one of the world's most spectacular courses for the **Seven Mile Bridge Run.**

Local running clubs all over the state sponsor weekly public events for joggers, runners, and walkers. For a list of local clubs and events throughout the state, call or send a self-addressed stamped envelope to the **Florida Athletics Congress** (1330 N.W. 6th St., Gainesville 32601, tel. 904/336–2120). For information about events in South Florida contact the 1,500-member **Miami Runners Club** (7920 S.W. 40th St., Miami 33155, tel. 305/227–1500).

Scuba Diving and Snorkeling
South Florida and the Keys attract most of the divers and snorkelers, but the more than 300 dive shops throughout the state schedule drift, reef, and wreck-diving trips for scuba divers all along Florida's Atlantic and Gulf coasts. The low-tech pleasures of snorkeling can be enjoyed all along the Overseas Highway in the Keys and elsewhere where shallow reefs hug the shore.

Contact the **Dive Industry Association** for a free directory of Florida dive shops. (Teall's Inc., 111 Saguaro La., Marathon 33050, tel. 305/743–3942).

Tennis
Many Florida hotels have a resident tennis pro and offer special tennis packages with lessons. Many local park and recreation departments throughout Florida operate modern tennis centers like those at country clubs, and most such centers welcome nonresidents, for a fee. In the Miami area, you can play at the **Biltmore Tennis Center** in Coral Gables, home of the *Rolex/ Orange Bowl International Tennis Championship* or Dade County's **International Tennis Center** on Key Biscayne, home of the *Lipton International Players Championships.*

For general information and schedules for amateur tournaments, contact the **Florida Tennis Association** (801 N.E. 167th St., Suite 301, North Miami Beach 33162, tel. 305/652–2866).

Parks and Nature Preserves

Although Florida is the fourth most-populous state in the nation, more than 5,550 square miles of undeveloped land—almost 10% of the state's total area—have been set aside in national forests, parks, monuments, reserves, and seashores; state forests and parks; county parks; and nature preserves owned and managed by private conservation groups.

On holidays and weekends, crowds flock to Florida's most popular parks—even some on islands that are accessible only by boat. Come early or risk being turned away. Write ahead to ask rangers in the parks, sanctuaries, and preserves about the best season to visit. In winter, northern migratory birds descend on the state. Many resident species breed in the warm summer months, but others (such as the wood stork) time their breeding cycle to the winter dry season. In summer, mosquitos are voracious and daily afternoon thundershowers add to the state's humidity, but this is when the sea turtles come ashore to lay their eggs and when you're most likely to see frigate birds and other tropical species.

Federal Parks The federal government maintains no centralized information service for its natural and historic sites in Florida. You must contact each site directly for information on current recreational facilities and hours. To obtain a copy of **Guide and Map of National Parks of U.S.,** which provides park addresses and facilities lists, write to *U.S. Government Printing Office, Washington, DC 20402. GPO No. 024005008527. Cost: $1.25 (no tax or postage).*

In 1908 the federal government declared the keys around what is now **Fort Jefferson National Monument** in the Dry Tortugas a wildlife sanctuary to protect the sooty tern. **Everglades National Park** was established in 1947. Another site in Florida under federal management is the **Big Cypress National Preserve** and **Biscayne National Park** in the Everglades.

Federal wildlife refuges in Florida include the **Great White Heron National Wildlife Refuge** and **National Key Deer Refuge** (in the Keys) and **Loxahatchee National Wildlife Refuge** near Palm Beach. The federal government also operates the **Key Largo National Marine Sanctuary** and **Looe Key National Marine Sanctuary.**

State Parks The **Florida Department of Natural Resources** is responsible for hundreds of historic buildings, landmarks, nature preserves, and an expanding state park system. When you request a free copy of the *Florida State Park Guide,* mention which parts of the state you plan to visit. For information on camping facilities at the state parks, ask for the free *Florida State Parks, Fees and Facilities* and *Florida State Parks Camping Reservation Procedures* brochures (Marjory Stoneman Douglas Building, Room 613, 3900 Commonwealth Blvd., Tallahassee 32399, tel. 904/488-7326).

Private Nature Preserves In 1905, Audubon Society warden Guy Bradley died while protecting the egrets nesting at Cuthbert Rookery, in what is now Everglades National Park. Private efforts to preserve Florida's fragile ecosystems continue today, as the **National Audubon Society** and the **Nature Conservancy** acquire and manage sensitive natural areas.

On Big Pine Key, Audubon has leased acreage without charge to the U.S. Fish and Wildlife Service in the **National Key Deer Refuge.** Audubon also controls more than 65 other Florida properties, including islands, prairies, forests, and swamps. Visitation at these sites is limited. For information, contact *National Audubon Society, Sanctuary Director* (Miles Wildlife Sanctuary, RR 1, Box 294, West Cornwall Road, Sharon CT 06069, tel. 203/364-0048).

Dining

Florida regional cuisine changes as you move across the state, based on who settled the area and who now operates the restaurants. South Florida's diverse assortment of Latin American restaurants offer the distinctive national fare of Argentina, Brazil, Colombia, Cuba, El Salvador, Mexico, Nicaragua, and Puerto Rico as well as West Indian delicacies from the Bahamas, Haiti, and Jamaica.

The influence of earlier Latin settlements remains in Key West, but look for traditional Miccosukee and Seminole Indian fried bread, catfish, and frog legs at tribe-owned restaurants in the Everglades.

All over Florida, Asian cuisine no longer means just Chinese. Indian, Japanese, Pakistani, Thai, and Vietnamese specialties are now available. Continental cuisine (French, German, Italian, Spanish, and Swiss) is also well represented all over Florida. Many of these restaurants have excellent wine lists.

Although the better restaurants in all price categories pride themselves on using fresh seafood, in some cases the fish is imported from quite a long distance. Two South Florida seafood pioneers, Joe's Stone Crab Restaurant in Miami Beach and East Coast Fisheries in Miami, still have a steady local supply from their own fish houses in Marathon. In the Florida Keys, many small restaurants specialize in chowder, fritters, salads, and other dishes made with conch (a large shellfish, pronounced "konk").

Every Florida restaurant claims to make the best Key-lime pie. Pastry chefs and restaurant managers take the matter very seriously—they discuss the problems of getting good lime juice and maintaining top quality every day. Traditional Key-lime pie is yellow, not green, with an old-fashioned Graham cracker crust and meringue top. The filling should be tart, and chilled but not frozen. Some restaurants serve their Key-lime pie with a pastry crust; most substitute whipped cream for the more temperamental meringue. Each pie will be a little different. Try several, and make your own choice.

Ratings	**Category**	**Cost*:Major City**	**Cost*:Other Areas**
	Very Expensive	over $50	over $40
	Expensive	$30–$50	$25–$40
	Moderate	$15–$30	$10–$25
	Inexpensive	under $15	under $10

per person, excluding drinks, service, and 6% state sales tax

Lodging

Hotels and Motels All the major hotel and motel chains, including Days Inn, Econo Lodge, Hyatt, Hilton, Holiday Inn, Knight's Inn, Marriott, Motel 6, Peabody, Pickett, Quality Inns, Radisson, Ramada, Sheraton, Stouffer, and Westin are represented in Florida. Holiday Inn, Marriott, and Quality Inns operate under a variety of brand names offering varying levels of amenities and prices.

Although many hotels in Florida have affiliated with a chain to get business from its central reservation system, some fine hotels and resorts still remain independent. They include the Don Cesar Beach Resort on St. Petersburg Beach, Governors Inn in Tallahassee, and Pier House in Key West.

The Florida Hotel & Motel Association publishes an *Annual Travel Directory* which you can obtain without charge at Florida Welcome Centers or by contacting the **Florida Division of Tourism** (Department of Commerce, 126 Van Buren St., Talla-

hassee 32399, tel. 904/487–1462). You can also order it from the
FH&MA if you send them a stamped, addressed No. 10 envelope and $1 for postage and handling (117 W. College Ave., Box
1529, Tallahassee 32301–1529, tel. 904/224–2888 or in FL, 800/
432–2004).

Alternative Lodgings Small inns and guest houses are becoming increasingly numerous and popular in Florida. Many offer the convenience of bed-
and-breakfast accommodations in a homelike setting; many, in
fact, are in private homes, and the owners treat you almost like
a member of the family. **Inn Route, Inc.** (225 W. 5th Ave.,
Mount Dora 32757, tel. 904/383–8397), a new statewide association of small, architecturally distinctive historic inns, planned
to publish a free brochure late in 1989. You can also order *Guide
to the Small and Historic Lodgings of Florida,* a paperback
book updated every two years (Pineapple Press Inc., Drawer
16008, Sarasota 34239, tel. 813/952–1085. Cost: $12.95 plus 6%
sales tax).

Bed-and-breakfast referral and reservation agencies in Florida
include: **A & A Bed & Breakfast of Florida, Inc.** (Box 1316, Winter Park 32790, tel. 407/628–3222), **Bed'n Breakfast—Central
Gulf Coast** (Box 9515, Pensacola 32513–9515, tel. 904/438–
7968), **Bed & Breakfast Co., Tropical Florida** (Box 262, Miami
33243, tel. 305/661–3270). **Bed & Breakfast East Coast** (Box
1373, Marathon 33050, tel. 305/743–4118), **Bed & Breakfast of
Volusia County** (Box 573, De Leon Springs 32028, tel. 904/985–
5068), **Suncoast Accommodations of Florida** (8690 Gulf Blvd.,
St. Petersburg Beach 33706, tel. 813/360–1753) and **Tallahassee Bed & Breakfast, Inc.** (3023 Windy Hill Lane, Tallahassee
32308, tel. 904/385–3768).

Camping and RV Facilities Contact directly the national parks and forests you plan to visit
for information on camping facilities (*see* Federal Parks, above).
For information on camping facilities in state parks, contact the
Florida Department of Natural Resources (*see* State Parks,
above).

The free annual *Florida Camping Directory* lists 200 commercial campgrounds in Florida with 50,000 sites. It's available at
Florida Welcome Centers, from the Florida Division of Tourism, and from the **Florida Campground Association** (1638 N.
Plaza Dr., Tallahassee 32308–5323, tel. 904/656–8878).

Ratings

Category	Cost*:Major City	Cost*:Other Areas
Very Expensive	$150 peak season $100 off-peak	$100
Expensive	$120–$150 peak season $80–$100 off-peak	$70–$100
Moderate	$80–$120 peak season $50–$80 off-peak	$40–$70
Inexpensive	under $80 peak season under $50 off-peak	under $40

*All prices are for a standard double room, excluding 6% state
sales tax and nominal (1%–3%) tourist tax.*

Vacation Ownership Resorts Vacation ownership resorts sell hotel rooms, condominium apartments, or villas in weekly, monthly, or quarterly increments. The weekly arrangement is most popular; it's often referred to as "interval ownership" or "time sharing." Of 1,100 vacation ownership resorts in the U.S., 300 are in Florida, with the heaviest concentration in the Disney World/Orlando area. Most vacation ownership resorts are affiliated with one of two major exchange organizations—**Interval International** *(6262 Sunset Dr., Penthouse One, South Miami, 33143, tel. 305/666–1861; 800/828–8200)* or **Resort Condominiums International** *(3502 Woodview Trace, Indianapolis, IN 46268–3131, tel. 317/876–8899, 800/338–7777).* As an owner, you can join your resort's exchange organization and swap your interval for another someplace else in any year when you want a change of scene. Even if you don't own an interval, you can rent at many vacation ownership resorts where unsold intervals remain and/or owners have placed their intervals in a rental program. For rental information, contact the exchange organizations (Interval International, tel. 800/722–1861; Resort Condominiums International, tel. 800/654–5000), the individual resort, or a local real estate broker in the area where you want to rent.

2 Miami

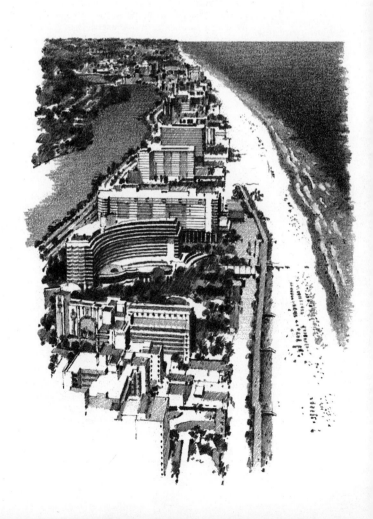

Introduction

by George and Rosalie Leposky

A husband-wife team, George and Rosalie Leposky are veteran Florida travel writers. Their articles have appeared in some 100 newspapers and consumer magazines throughout North America. They also write for trade publications in the travel and hospitality field, including Hotel & Resort Industry *and* Lodging. *The Leposkys live in the Coconut Grove section of Miami.*

What they say about Miami is true. The city *is* different. Miami is different from what it once was and it's different from other cities. Once a sleepy southern resort town, Miami today is a burgeoning giant of international commerce and finance as well as a place to find pleasure and relaxation. Like all big cities, Miami inspires the first-time visitor with hopes and dreams. Also as in other cities, many of these hopes and dreams can be sidetracked by crime and violence.

Miami's natural difference can be detected when you fly into the city. Clinging to a thin ribbon of dry land between the marshy Everglades and the Atlantic Ocean, Miami remains vulnerable to its perennial mosquitoes, periodic flooding, and potential devastation by hurricanes. These perils give life in Miami a flavor of urgency, a compulsion to prosper and party before the dream ends.

Miami may be the wrong place for a city, but it's the right place for a crossroads. Long before Spain's gold-laden treasure ships passed offshore in the Gulf Stream, the Calusa Indians who lived here had begun to trade with their mainland neighbors to the north and their island brethren to the south. Repeating this prehistoric pattern, many U.S. and multinational companies now locate their Latin American headquarters in Greater Miami because no other city can match its airline connections to the Western Hemisphere.

That same ease of access, coupled with a congenial climate, attracts hordes of Latin tourists—especially in Miami's steamy summer months (South America's winter), when domestic visitors from the northern United States are less in evidence.

Access and climate also explain why Miami has become what *Newsweek* calls "America's Casablanca." Whenever a Latin American or Caribbean government erupts in revolution and economic chaos, the inevitable refugees flock inexorably to Miami (and open restaurants). Even without a revolution, Miami's cosmopolitan character and entrepreneurial spirit attract other immigrants from all over the world.

Today, more than 45% of Greater Miami's population is Hispanic—the majority from Cuba, with significant populations from Colombia, El Salvador, Nicaragua, and Panama. About 150,000 French- and Creole-speaking Haitians also live in Greater Miami, as do Brazilians, Germans, Greeks, Iranians, Israelis, Italians, Jamaicans, Lebanese, Malaysians, Russian Jews, Swedes, and more—a veritable Babel of tongues. Most either know or are trying to learn English. You can help them by speaking slowly and distinctly.

Try not to think of Miami as a "melting pot." Where ethnic and cultural diversity are the norm, there's less pressure to conform. Miamians practice matter-of-factly the customs they brought here—much to the consternation of other Miamians whose customs differ. The community wrestles constantly with these tensions and sensitivities.

As a big city, Miami has its share of crime, violence, and drug trafficking—but not the pervasive lawlessness portrayed on the "Miami Vice" TV show. You probably won't find the city's seamy underside unless you go looking for it.

What you will find just by coming to Miami is a multicultural metropolis that works and plays with vigor and that welcomes you to share its celebration of diversity.

Arriving and Departing by Plane

Airport   **Miami International Airport (MIA),** six miles west of downtown Miami, is Greater Miami's only commercial airport. MIA has the nation's second-largest volume of international passenger and cargo traffic. MIA's busiest hours, when flight delays may occur, are 11 AM—8 PM.

MIA contains 108 aircraft gates along seven concourses. During 1990, expect to encounter renovation on concourse H.

When you fly out of MIA, plan to check in 55 minutes before departure for a domestic flight and 90 minutes before departure for an international flight. Services for international travelers include 24-hour multilingual information and paging phones and foreign currency conversion booths throughout the terminal. An information booth with multilingual staff and 24-hour currency exchange are at Concourse E.

Between the Airport and Center City By Bus   **Metrobus.** The county's Metrobus system has one benefit—its modest cost—if you're willing to put up with the inconveniences of infrequent service, scruffy equipment, and the circuitous path that many routes follow. *Fare $1 (exact change), transfers 25 cents.*

Greyhound. You can take a Greyhound bus from the Metrobus depot at MIA to Homestead and the Florida Keys or to other Greyhound stations in Greater Miami *(see* By Bus).

By Taxi   For trips originating at MIA or the Port of Miami, a $1 toll is added to the meter fare—except for the flat-fare trips described below. You'll pay a $12 flat fare between MIA and the Port of Miami, in either direction.

For taxi service from the airport to destinations in the immediate vicinity, ask a uniformed county taxi dispatcher to call an **ARTS (Airport Region Taxi Service)** cab for you. These special blue cabs will offer you a short-haul flat fare.

SuperShuttle vans transport passengers between MIA and local hotels, the Port of Miami, and even individual residences on a 24-hour basis. The company's service area extends from Palm Beach to Monroe County (including the Lower Keys). Drivers provide narration en route. It's best to make reservations 24 hours before departure, although the firm will try to arrange pick-ups within Dade County on as little as four hours' notice. *For information and reservations from inside MIA, tel. 305/871–8488. Reservations outside MIA, tel. 305/871–2000 (Dade and Monroe counties) or 305/674–1700 (Broward and Palm Beach counties). Pet transport fee: $5. Lower rate for 2nd passenger in same party for many destinations. Children under 3 ride free with parents. Credit cards: AE, MC, V.*

By Limousine   **Bayshore Limousine** has chauffeur-driven four-door town cars and stretch limousines available on demand at MIA or through the 24-hour reservation service. It serves Miami, Fort Lauderdale, Palm Beach, and the Keys. *11485 S.W. 87th Ave., Miami, tel. 305/253–9046, 325–3851, or 858–5888. AE, MC, V.*

Arriving and Departing by Car, Train, and Bus

By Car   The main highways into Greater Miami from the north are Florida's Turnpike (toll) and I–95. In Broward County (the next county north), you'll encounter major delays throughout 1990 from construction to widen the highway.

Delays on roads into Miami from other directions are most likely on weekends, when recreational traffic is the heaviest. From the northwest, take I–75 or U.S. 27 into town. From the Everglades to the west, use the Tamiami Trail (U.S. 41). From the south, use U.S. 1 and the Homestead Extension of Florida's Turnpike.

Rental Cars   Six rental-car firms—Avis **Rent-a-Car, Budget Rent-a-Car, Dollar Rent-a-Car, Hertz Rent-a-Car, National Rent-a-Car,** and **Value Rent-a-Car**—have booths near the baggage claim area on MIA's lower level—a convenience when you arrive.

By Train   **Amtrak's** two trains between Miami and New York City, the *Silver Meteor* and *Silver Star*, make different stops along the way. Each has a daily Miami arrival and departure.

Amtrak's "All Aboard" fare is the most economical way to travel to Florida, if you have time to meet the length-of-stay requirements. Trains run full all year, except in October and May. For the best fare, contact Amtrak as soon as you decide to take a trip. Ask for Amtrak's 1990 travel planner. *Amtrak Station, 8303 N.W. 37th Ave., Miami 33147. General office tel. 305/835–1200, passenger service tel. 305/835–1225. Advance reservations required. Reservations: Amtrak Customer Relations, 400 N. Capitol St., NW, Washington, DC 20001, tel. U.S. 800/USA-RAIL, Canada 800/4AMTRAK.*

Tri-Rail commuter trains connect Miami with Broward and Palm Beach weekdays. Call for schedule and details on weekly and monthly passes. *Tel. 305/728–8445 or 800/TRI–RAIL. Suite 801, 1 River Plaza, 305 S. Andrews Ave., Fort Lauderdale, FL 33301.*

By Bus   **Greyhound/Trailways** buses (tel. 305/374–7222 or 305/373–6561) stop at seven bus stations in Greater Miami. No reservations.

Getting Around Miami

Greater Miami resembles Los Angeles in its urban sprawl and traffic congestion. You'll need a car to visit many of the attractions and points of interest listed in this book. Some are accessible via public transportation.

A department of county government, the Metro-Dade Transit Agency, runs the public transportation system. It consists of 450 Metrobuses on 67 routes, the 21-mile Metrorail elevated rapid transit system, and the 1.9-mile Metromover in downtown Miami. Free maps, schedules, and a First-Time Rider's Kit are available. *111 N.W. 1st St., Miami 33128. Maps by Mail, tel. 305/638–6137. Route information tel. 305/638–6700 daily 6 AM–11 PM. Fare $1, transfers 25 cents, exact change only.*

By Train   Metrorail runs from downtown Miami north to Hialeah and south along U.S. 1 to Dadeland. *Service every 7 minutes in peak hours, 15–30 minutes other times. Weekdays 6AM–midnight, weekends 6:30 AM–6:30 PM. Runs until midnight for special events such as the Orange Bowl Parade. Fare: $1.*

Metromover's two loops circle downtown Miami, linking major hotels, office buildings, and shopping areas *(see* Exploring Downtown Miami). *Service every 90 seconds. Weekdays 6:30 AM–midnight, weekends 8:30 AM–midnight. Later for special events. Fare 25 cents.*

By Bus   Metrobus stops are marked by blue-and-green signs with a bus logo and route information. The frequency of service varies widely. Obtain specific schedule information in advance for the routes you want to ride.

By Taxicab   There are 1,709 taxicabs in Dade County. Fares are $1 for the first ⅓ mile, 20 cents for each additional 1/6 mile; waiting time 20 cents for the first 1 3/5 minutes, 20 cents for each additional 4/5 minute. No additional charge for extra passengers, luggage, or road and bridge tolls. Taxi companies with dispatch service are **Central Taxicab Service** (tel. 305/534–0694), **Diamond Cab Company** (tel. 305/545–7575), **Magic City Cab Company** (tel. 305/757–5523), **Metro Taxicab Company** (tel. 305/888–8888), **Society Cab Company** (tel. 305/757–5523), **Super Yellow Cab Company** (tel. 305/885–5555), **Tropical Taxicab Company** (tel. 305/945–1025), and **Yellow Cab Company** (tel. 305/444–4444).

By Car   Finding your way around Greater Miami is easy if you know how the numbering system works. Miami is laid out on a grid with four quadrants—northeast, northwest, southeast, and southwest—which meet at Miami Avenue and Flagler Street. Miami Avenue separates east from west and Flagler Street separates north from south. *Avenues* and *courts* run north-south; *streets, terraces,* and *ways* run east-west. *Roads* run diagonally, northwest-southeast.

Many named streets also bear numbers. For example, Unity Boulevard is N.W. and S.W. 27th Avenue, LeJeune Road is N.W. and S.W. 42nd Avenue. However, named streets that depart markedly from the grid, such as Biscayne Boulevard and Brickell Avenue, have no corresponding numerical designations. Dade County and most other municipalities follow the Miami numbering system.

In Miami Beach, *avenues* run north-south; *streets,* east-west. Numbers rise along the beach from south to north and from the Atlantic Ocean in the east to Biscayne Bay in the west.

In Coral Gables, all streets bear names. Coral Gables uses the Miami numbering system for north-south addresses but begins counting east-west addresses westward from Douglas Road (S.W. 37th Ave.).

Hialeah has its own grid. Palm Avenue separates east from west; Hialeah Drive separates north from south. *Avenues* run north-south and *streets* east-west. Numbered streets and avenues are designated west, east, or southeast.

Important Addresses and Numbers

Information Centers The Greater Miami Convention and Visitors Bureau plans to open tourist information centers in downtown Miami, Miami Beach, Homestead-Florida City, and Miami International Airport. Contact the bureau for locations and hours or to request information by mail.

Visitor Services, Greater Miami Convention and Visitors Bureau (701 Brickell Ave., Suite 2700, Miami 33131, tel. 305/539–3040).

Chambers of Commerce Greater Miami has more than 20 local chambers of commerce, each promoting its individual community. Most maintain racks of brochures on tourist information in their offices and will send you information about their community.

Coconut Grove Chamber of Commerce (2820 McFarland Rd., Coconut Grove 33133, tel. 305/444–7270).
Coral Gables Chamber of Commerce (50 Aragon Ave., Coral Gables 33134, tel. 305/446–1657).
Gold Coast Chamber of Commerce (1100 Kane Concourse, Suite 210, Bay Harbor Islands 33154, tel. 305/866–6020). Serves the beach communities of Bal Harbour, Bay Harbor Islands, Golden Beach, North Bay Village, Sunny Isles, and Surfside.
Key Biscayne Chamber of Commerce (Key Biscayne Bank Bldg., 95 W. McIntyre St., Key Biscayne 33149, tel. 305/361–5207).
Miami Beach Chamber of Commerce (1920 Meridian Ave., Miami Beach 33139, tel. 305/672–1270).
South Miami Chamber of Commerce (6410 S.W. 80th St., South Miami 33143, tel. 305/661–1621).

Tickets **Ticketmaster.** You can use this service to order tickets for performing arts and sports events by telephone. A service fee is added to the price of the ticket. *Tel. 800/446–3939 or tel. 305/654–3309 (Dade), 305/523–3309 (Broward), or 407/588–3309 (Palm Beach). MC, V.*

Emergencies Dial 911 for **police** and **ambulance.** You can dial free from pay phones.

Telecommunication lines for the hearing impaired are used by hearing-impaired travelers with telecommunication devices (TDD) to reach TDD-equipped public services:

Fire/Police/Medical/Rescue (tel. 305/595–4749 TDD)
Operator and Directory Assistance (tel. 800/855–1155 TDD)
Deaf Services of Miami (4800 W. Flagler St., Room 213, Miami, tel. 305/444–2211 TDD or voice 305/444–2266). Operates daily 6 AM–midnight. Relays calls to help the hearing-impaired contact people who hear and speak normally.

Ambulance **Randle Eastern Ambulance Service Inc.** Serves all of Greater Miami. Meets air ambulances and takes patients to hospitals. Services include advanced life-support systems. *35 S.W. 27th Ave., Miami 33135, tel. 305/642–6400. Open 24 hrs. AE, MC, V.*

Hospitals The following hospitals have 24-hour emergency rooms:

Miami Beach: *Mt. Sinai Medical Center* (4300 Alton Rd., Miami Beach, tel. 305/674–2121; physician referral, tel. 674–2273). Just off Julia Tuttle Causeway (I–195).

St. Francis Hospital (250 W. 63rd St., Miami Beach, tel. 305/868–5000; physician referral, tel. 305/868–2728). Near Collins Ave. and north end of Alton Rd.

Central: *University of Miami/Jackson Memorial Medical Center.* Includes Jackson Memorial Hospital, a county hospital with Greater Miami's only trauma center. Near Dolphin Expressway. Metrorail stops a block away. *1611 N.W. 12th Ave., Miami, tel. 305/325–7429. Emergency room, tel. 305/549–6901. Interpreter service, tel. 305/549–6316. Patient relations, tel. 305/549–7341. Physician referral, tel. 305/547–5757.*
Mercy Hospital (3663 S. Miami Ave., Coconut Grove, tel. 305/854–4400; physician referral, tel. 305/285–2929). Greater Miami's only hospital with an emergency boat dock.
Miami Children's Hospital (6125 S.W. 31st St., tel. 305/666–6511; physician referral, ext. 2563).

South: *Baptist Hospital of Miami* (8900 N. Kendall Dr., Miami, tel. 305/596–1960; physician referral, tel. 305/596–6557).

24-Hour Pharmacies Of the 287 pharmacies in Greater Miami, only three are open 24 hours a day. Most pharmacies open at 8 or 9 AM and close between 9 PM and midnight. Many pharmacies offer local delivery service.

Eckerd Drugs. 1825 Miami Gardens Dr. N.E. (185th St.), North Miami Beach, tel. 305/932–5740 and 9031 S.W. 107th Ave., Miami, tel. 305/274–6776.

Walgreens. 5731 Bird Rd., Miami, tel. 305/666–0757.

Physician Referral Services **24-Hour Doctors House Calls.** Many Greater Miami hotels use this referral service, which will send a physician to you. Medical services available include general medicine, pediatrics, and geriatrics. In-office dental referrals. Translators available. *3801 N. University Dr., Suite 507, Sunrise, tel. 305/945–6325.*

East Coast District Dental Society. Office open weekdays 9 AM–4:30 PM for dental referral. Services include general dentistry, endodontics, periodontics, and oral surgery. *420 S. Dixie Hwy., Suite 2E, Coral Gables, tel. 305/667–3647.*

Guided Tours

Orientation Tours **Miami Vision** (2699 Collins Ave., Suite 113, Miami Beach, tel. 305/532–0040). Several packages combine city tours with attractions. Prices include admission to attractions. Both minivan and private-car tours are available. Well-informed, congenial guides speak English, French, German, Italian, Portuguese, and Spanish. Phone for hotel pickup time or ask your concierge.

Old Town Trolley of Miami. Narrated tours of Miami and Miami Beach leave Bayside Marketplace every half hour. *Box 12985, Miami 33101, tel. 305/374–8687. Miami tour: $11 adults, $4 children 3–15. Miami Beach: $7 adults, $4 children 3–15. No credit cards.*

Special-Interest Tours Boat Tours ***Heritage of Miami II.*** Miami's official tall ship, an 85-foot steel traditional sailing schooner docks at Bayside Marina. Carries up to 49 passengers for day sailing, sleeps 16; children and cameras welcome. Ice and ice chest on board, soft drinks for sale; bring your own food. Standard Biscayne Bay day trip lasts two hours. Reservations recommended. *Dinner Key Marina, Mi-*

ami, tel. 305/858–6264. Sails daily, weather permitting. Cost: $20 adults, $15 seniors, $10 armed forces personnel and children under 12.

Island Queen. 90-passenger tour boat docks at the Hyatt Regency Hotel's patio dock, 400 S.E. 2nd Ave., Miami. Two-hour narrated tours of Port of Miami and Millionaires' Row. Transportation to and from Island Queen available from Miami Vision. *8265 S.W. 179th Ter., Miami 33157, tel. 305/379–5119. Tours daily. Cost: $9 adults, $4.50 children.*

Nikko Gold Coast Cruises. Three 150-passenger boats based at Haulover Park Marina specialize in water tours to major Greater Miami attractions. *10800 Collins Ave., Miami Beach, tel. 305/945–5461. Tours daily. Bayside Marketplace, $8 adults, $4.50 children under 12.*

History Tours **Art Deco District Tour.** Meet your guide at 10:30 AM Saturday at 661 Washington Avenue, the **Miami Design Preservation League's** Welcome Center, for a 90-minute tour. Wear comfortable shoes and bring a hat. Also available is the League's *Art Deco District Guide,* a book with 6 detailed walking or driving tours of the square-mile Art Deco District on Miami Beach. *Bin L, Miami Beach 33119, tel. 305/672–2014. Cost: $5.*

Historical Museum of Southern Florida. Guided tours available in English or Spanish. **Museum Tour** covers the exhibits, which survey 10,000 years of Miami-area history; includes 15-minute slide show. The **Curator's Cabinet Tour** combines the Museum Tour with a look behind the scenes at departments that visitors seldom see, including a research center with 500,000 photos and the cataloging and conservation departments. The museum also conducts tours throughout the Greater Miami area. *101 W. Flagler St., Miami, tel. 305/375–1492.*

Prof. Paul George. Explore Miami's history with a professional historian on a four-hour walking tour of downtown. Paul George is a history professor at Florida Atlantic University and the University of Miami and president of the Florida Historical Society. Tour begins on the north bank of Miami River behind the Hyatt Regency Hotel, 400 S.E. 2nd Ave. Wear comfortable walking shoes and a hat. Sat. 9 AM–1 PM by appointment. George also gives 3½-hour walking tours of historic Coconut Grove, Coral Gables, Little Havana, Miami's old city Cemetery, the Miami Beach Art Deco District, and downtown Fort Lauderdale. *1345 S.W. 14th St., Miami, tel. 305/858–6021. Cost: $8 adults, $6 children 7–14, under 7 free.*

Rickshaw Tours **Royal Rickshaw.** Look for rickshaws along Main Highway in Coconut Grove's Village Center (Box 0174 Coconut Grove 33233–0174, tel. 305/443–6571). Nightly 8 PM–2 AM in Coconut Grove. Rickshaw holds two adults. $3 per person for 10-minute ride through Coconut Grove, $6 per person for 20-minute lovers' moonlight ride down to Biscayne Bay. No credit cards.

Exploring Downtown Miami

Numbers in the margin correspond with points of interest on the Downtown Miami map.

Orientation From a distance you see downtown Miami's future—a 21st-century skyline already stroking the clouds with sleek fingers of steel and glass. By day, this icon of commerce and technology sparkles in the strong subtropical sun; at night, it basks in the man-made glow of floodlights.

On the streets downtown, you encounter a polyglot present. Staid-suited lawyers and bankers share the sidewalks with Hispanic merchants wearing open-neck, intricately embroidered shirts called *guayaberas*. Fruit merchants sell their wares from pushcarts. European youths with backpacks stroll the streets. Foreign businessmen haggle over prices in import-export shops. You hear Arabic, Chinese, Creole, French, German, Hebrew, Hindi, Japanese, Portuguese, Spanish, Swedish, Yiddish, and even a little English now and then.

With effort, you can find remnants of downtown Miami's past. Most of the city's "old" downtown buildings date from only the 1920s and 1930s—an incongruity if you're from someplace that counts its past in centuries. Remember that Miami is a young city, incorporated in 1896 with just 3,000 residents. A Junior League book, *Historic Downtown Miami*, locates and describes 27 elderly structures in and near downtown, including 21 you can see in a two-hour self-guided walking tour of slightly more than a mile.

Touring Downtown Miami Parking downtown is inconvenient and expensive. If you're staying elsewhere in the area, leave your car at an outlying Metrorail station and take the train downtown. Metromover, a separate light-rail mass-transit system, circles the heart of the city on twin elevated loops.

No part of downtown is more than two blocks from one of Metromover's nine stations. We've organized the downtown Miami tour around those stations, so you can ride Metromover directly to the attractions downtown that interest you most.

1 2 When you get off the Metrorail train at **Government Center Station,** notice the **Dade County Courthouse** (73 W. Flagler St.). It's the building to the east with a pyramid at its peak, where turkey vultures roost in winter. Built in 1928, it was once the tallest building south of Washington, D.C.

3 As you leave the Metrorail station, you'll enter **Metro-Dade Center,** the county government's 30-story office building. Designed by architect Hugh Stubbins, it opened in 1985.

4 Across N.W. 1st Street from Metro-Dade Center stands the **Metro-Dade Cultural Center** (101 W. Flagler St.), opened in 1983. The 3.3-acre complex is a Mediterranean expression of architect Philip Johnson's postmodern style. An elevated plaza provides a serene haven from the city's pulsations and a superb setting for festivals and outdoor performances.

The Center for the Fine Arts is an art museum in the tradition of the European *kunsthalle* (exhibition gallery). With no permanent collection, it organizes and borrows temporary exhibitions on many artistic themes. Shows scheduled for 1990 include geometric abstract paintings since 1945 and "Soul and Form." *Tel. 305/375–1700. Open Tues.–Sat. 10–5, Thurs. 10–9, Sun. noon–5. Admission: $3 adults, $2.50 senior citizens, $2 children 6–12, under 6 free. Donations Tues.*

The Historical Museum of Southern Florida is a regional museum that interprets the human experience in southern Florida from prehistory to the present. Artifacts on permanent display include Tequesta and Seminole Indian ceramics, clothing, and tools; a 1920 streetcar; and an original edition of Audubon's *Birds of America*. *Tel. 305/375–1492. Open Mon.–Sat. 10–5,*

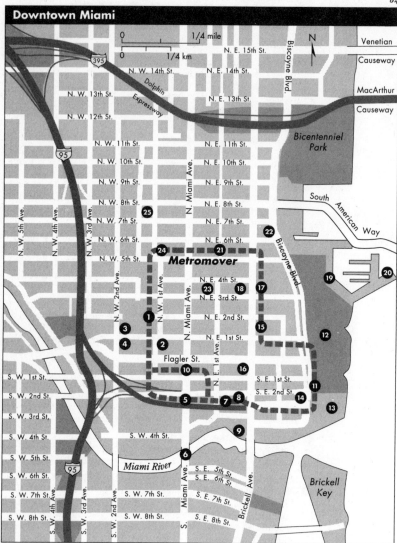

Downtown Miami

Bayfront Park, **12**

Bayfront Park Station, **11**

Bayside Marketplace, **19**

CenTrust Tower, **8**

College Station, **17**

Dade County Courthouse, **2**

Edcom Station, **21**

First St. Station, **15**

Ft. Dallas Park Station, **5**

Freedom Tower, **22**

Government Center Station, **1**

Gusman Center, **16**

HMS *Bounty*, **20**

Hotel Inter-Continental Miami, **13**

James Knight Center, **9**

Metro-Dade Center, **3**

Metro-Dade Cultural Center, **4**

Miami Arena, **25**

Miami Ave. Bridge, **6**

Miami Ave. Station, **10**

Miami-Dade Community College, **18**

State/Plaza Station, **24**

Southeast Financial Center, **14**

U.S. Courthouse, **23**

World Trade Center Station, **7**

Thurs. 10–9, Sun. noon–5. Admission: $3 adults, $2 children 6–12, under 6 free. Donations Mon.

The Main Public Library has 700,000 volumes and a computerized card catalog. Inside the entrance, look up at the rotunda mural, where artist Edward Ruscha interpreted a quotation from Shakespeare: "Words without thought never to heaven go." You'll find art exhibits in the auditorium and second-floor lobby. *Tel. 305/375–BOOK. Open Mon.–Sat. 9–5, Thurs. 9–9, Sun. 1–5. Closed Sun. May–Sept.*

At Government Center Station, you can also transfer to Metromover's inner and outer loops through downtown. We've listed the stations and their attractions in sequence along the outer loop.

⑤
⑥ The first stop is **Ft. Dallas Park Station.** If you disembark here, you're a block from the **Miami Ave. Bridge,** one of 11 bridges on the river that open to let ships pass. From the bridge approach, watch freighters, tugboats, research vessels, and luxury yachts ply this busy waterway.

Time Out Stroll across the bridge to **Tobacco Road** for some liquid refreshment and a sandwich or snack. Built in 1912, this friendly neighborhood pub was a speakeasy during Prohibition. *626 S. Miami Ave., tel. 305/374–1198. Open weekdays 11:30 AM–5 AM, weekends 1 PM–5 AM. Lunch weekdays 11:30–2:30. Dinner served Sun.–Thurs. AE, DC.*

⑦
⑧ The next Metromover stop, **Knight Center Station,** nestles in a niche inside the **CenTrust Tower** (100 S.E. 1st St.), a wedge-shape 47-story skyscraper designed by I. M. Pei & Partners. The building is brilliantly illuminated at night. Inside the
⑨ CenTrust Tower, follow signs to the **James L. Knight International Center** (400 S.E. 2nd Ave., tel. 305/372–0929), a convention and concert hall adjoining the Hyatt Regency Hotel.

At the Knight Center Station, you can transfer to the inner loop
⑩ and ride one stop to the **Miami Avenue Station,** a block south of **Flagler Street,** downtown Miami's commercial spine. Like most such thoroughfares, Flagler Street lost business in recent years to suburban malls—but unlike most, it found a new lease on life. Today, the half-mile of Flagler Street from Biscayne Boulevard to the Dade County Courthouse is the most important import-export center in the United States. Its stores and arcades supply much of the world with automotive parts, audio and video equipment, medical equipment and supplies, photographic equipment, clothing, and jewelry.

⑪ If you stay on the outer loop, you'll come next to **Bayfront Park Station,** opposite **Claude and Mildred Pepper Bayfront Park,**
⑫ which extends from Biscayne Boulevard east to the edge of the bay. Japanese sculptor Isamu Noguchi redesigned the park just before his death in 1989; it now includes a memorial to the *Challenger* astronauts, an amphitheater, and a fountain honoring the late Florida Congressman Claude Pepper and his wife.
⑬ Just south of Bayfront Park, the lobby of the **Hotel Inter-Continental Miami** (100 Chopin Plaza) contains *The Spindle,* a huge sculpture by Henry Moore.

West of Bayfront Park Station stands the tallest building in
⑭ Florida, the 55-story **Southeast Financial Center** (200 S. Bis-

cayne Blvd.), with towering royal palms in its one-acre Palm
Court plaza beneath a steel-and-glass space frame.

⑮ The next Metromover stop, **First Street Station,** places you a
block north of Flagler Street and the **Gusman Center for the**
⑯ **Performing Arts,** an ornate former movie palace restored as a
concert hall. Gusman Center resembles a Moorish courtyard
with twinkling stars in the sky. Performances there include the
Miami City Ballet, under the direction of Edward Villella, and
the New World Symphony, a unique, advanced-training orchestra led by Michael Tilson Thomas. *Gusman Center: 174 E.*
Flagler St., Miami 33131. Box office tel. 305/372–0925; Ballet:
905 Lincoln Rd., Miami Beach, 33139, tel. 305/532–4880; Sym-
phony: 555 Lincoln Rd., Miami Beach, 33139, tel. 305/371–
3005.

⑰ The **College/Bayside Station** Metromover stop serves the down-
⑱ town campus of **Miami-Dade Community College,** where you'll
enjoy browsing through two fine galleries. The Francis Wolfson
Art Gallery on the fifth floor houses traveling exhibitions of
contemporary art. *300 N.E. 2nd Ave., tel. 305/347–3278. Week-*
days 9–5:30. Free. The Mitchell Wolfson, Jr., Collection of
Decorative and Propaganda Arts on the third floor displays
works from Mr. Wolfson's personal holdings. *Tel. 305/347–*
3429. Open weekdays 10–5. Admission free.

College/Bayside Station is also the most convenient Metro-
⑲ mover stop for **Bayside Marketplace,** a waterside mall built by
The Rouse Company, between Bayfront Park and the entrance
to the Port of Miami. Bayside's 235,000 square feet of retail
space include 81 specialty shops, pushcarts in the mall's Pier 5
area, conventional restaurants, and a fast-food court with some
30 vendors. The mall adjoins the 208-slip Miamarina, where
you can see luxurious yachts moored and ride in an authentic
36-foot-long Venetian gondola. *401 Biscayne Blvd., tel. 305/*
577–3344, for gondola rides 305/529–7178. Open Mon.–Sat. 10
–10, Sun. noon–8.

⑳ While you're at Bayside, tour the **H.M.S. *Bounty,*** a fully rigged
reproduction of an 18th-century armed merchant ship. Built in
Nova Scotia for the 1962 MGM film *Mutiny on the Bounty*, the
ship has since participated in the Bicentennial tall-ships parade
and Statue of Liberty celebration in New York Harbor. *Tel.*
305/375–0486. Open Sun.–Thurs. noon–8, Fri. noon–10, Sat.
10–10. Admission: $3.50 adults, $2 seniors, $1.50 children 4–
12, under 4 free. The Bounty may leave on tour June–Oct.

As Metromover rounds the curve between College/Bayside
㉑ ㉒ Station and **College North Station,** look northeast to see **Free-**
dom Tower (600 Biscayne Blvd.), where the Cuban Refugee
Center processed more than 500,000 Cubans who entered the
United States to flee Fidel Castro's regime in the 1960s. Built
in 1925 for the *Miami Daily News*, this imposing Spanish-
baroque structure was inspired by the Giralda, an 800-year-old
bell tower in Seville, Spain. After years as a derelict, Freedom
Tower was renovated in 1988. To see it up close, walk north
from College North Station to N.E. 6th Street, then two blocks
east to Biscayne Boulevard.

A two-block walk south from College North Station will bring
㉓ you to the **U.S. Courthouse,** a handsome keystone building
erected in 1931 as Miami's main post office. Go to the second-
floor central courtroom to see *Law Guides Florida Progress*, a

huge depression-era mural by artist Denman Fink. *300 N.E. 1st Ave. Building open weekdays 8:30–5; during those hours, security guards will open courtroom on request. No cameras or tape recorders allowed in building.*

㉔
㉕ From **State Plaza/Arena Station,** walk two blocks north on N.W. 1st Avenue to the new **Miami Arena** (721 N.W. 1st Ave., tel. 305/374–6877), home of the Miami Heat, a National Basketball Association team. Other sports and entertainment events also take place there.

Just across the Miami River from downtown, a canyon of tall buildings lines **Brickell Avenue,** a southward extension of S.E. 2nd Avenue that begins in front of the Hyatt Regency Hotel (400 S.E. 2nd Ave.). For the best views, drive Brickell Avenue from north to south. You'll pass the largest concentration of international banking offices in the United States.

South of S.E. 15th Street, several architecturally interesting condominiums rise between Brickell Avenue and Biscayne Bay. Israeli artist Yacov Agam painted the rainbow-hued exterior of **Villa Regina** (1581 Brickell Ave.). Arquitectonica, a nationally prominent architectural firm based in Miami, designed three of these buildings: **The Palace** (1541 Brickell Ave.), **The Imperial** (1617 Brickell Ave.), and **The Atlantis** (2025 Brickell Ave.). The 20-story Atlantis, where a palm tree grows in a hole in the building between the 12th and 16th floors, forms a backdrop for the opening credits of the television show "Miami Vice."

At S.E. 25th Road, turn right, follow signs to **I–95,** and return to downtown Miami on one of the world's most scenic urban highways. I–95 parallels Brickell Avenue and soars 75 feet above the Miami River, offering a superb view of the downtown skyline. At night, the CenTrust Tower is awash with light, and, on the adjoining Metrorail bridge, a neon rainbow glows— Rockne Krebs's 3,600-foot-long light sculpture, *The Miami Line.* Just beyond the river, take the Biscayne Boulevard exit back to S.E. 2nd Avenue in front of the Hyatt Regency Hotel.

Exploring Miami Beach

Numbers in the margin correspond with points of interest on the Miami Beach map.

Orientation Most visitors to the Greater Miami area don't realize that Miami and Miami Beach are separate cities. Miami, on the mainland, is south Florida's commercial hub. Miami Beach, on 17 islands offshore in Biscayne Bay, is sometimes considered America's Riviera, luring refugees from winter to its warm sunshine, sandy beaches, and graceful palms.

In 1912, what would become Miami Beach was little more than a sandspit in the bay. Then Carl Graham Fisher, a millionaire promoter who built the Indianapolis Speedway, began to pour much of his fortune into developing the island city.

Ever since, Miami Beach has experienced successive waves of boom and bust—thriving in the early 1920s and the years just after World War II, but also enduring the devastating 1926 hurricane, the Great Depression, travel restrictions during World War II, and an invasion of criminals released from Cuba during the 1980 Mariel boatlift.

Today, a renaissance is under way as Miami Beach revels in the architectural heritage of its mile-square Art Deco District. About 650 significant buildings in the district are listed on the National Register of Historic Places.

The term "Art Deco" describes the modern architecture that emerged in the 1920s and 1930s. Its forms are eclectic, drawn from nature (including birds, butterflies, and flowers); from ancient Aztec, Mayan, Babylonian, Chaldean, Egyptian, and Hebrew designs; and from the streamlined, aerodynamic shapes of modern transportation and industrial machinery. For detailed information on touring the Art Deco District, contact the Miami Design Preservation League *(see* Guided Tours).

Driving Tour of Miami Beach In our exploration, we direct you from the mainland to Miami Beach and through a cross section of the Art Deco District, and the elegant residential neighborhood surrounding the La Gorce Country Club.

From the mainland, cross the **MacArthur Causeway** (Rte. 41) to Miami Beach. To reach the causeway from downtown Miami, turn east off Biscayne Boulevard north of N.E. 11th Street. From I–95, turn east onto I–395. The eastbound Dolphin Expressway (Rte. 836) becomes I–395 east of the I–95 interchange. As you approach the MacArthur Causeway bridge across the Intracoastal Waterway, *The Miami Herald* building looms above Biscayne Bay on your left.

1 Cross the bridge to **Watson Island,** created by dredging in 1931. Make the first left turn to the **Japanese Garden,** which has stone lanterns, a rock garden, and an eight-ton, eight-foot-tall statue of Hotei, Japanese god of prosperity. Industrialist Kiyoshi Ichimura gave the one-acre garden to the City of Miami in 1961 as an expression of friendship. It was restored in 1988.

East of Watson Island, the causeway leaves Miami and enters **2** Miami Beach. On the left, you'll pass the bridge to **Palm and 3** **Hibiscus islands** and then the bridge to **Star Island.** Past and present celebrities who have lived on these islands include Al Capone (93 Palm Ave., Palm Island), author Damon Runyon (271 Hibiscus Island), and TV star Don Johnson (8 Star Island).

East of Star Island, the causeway mounts a high bridge. Look **4** left to see an island with an obelisk, the **Flagler Memorial Monument.** The memorial honors Henry M. Flagler, who built the Florida East Coast Railroad to Miami, opening south Florida to tourism and commerce.

5 Just beyond the bridge, turn right onto Alton Road past the **Miami Beach Marina** (300 Alton Rd., tel. 305/673–6000), where dive boats depart for artificial reefs offshore in the Atlantic Ocean.

Continue to the foot of Alton Road, turn left on Biscayne **6** Street, then go right at Washington Avenue to enter **South Pointe Park** (1 Washington Ave.). From the 50-yard Sunshine Pier, which adjoins the mile-long jetty at the mouth of Government Cut, you can fish while watching huge ships pass. No bait or tackle is available in the park. Other facilities include two observation towers, and volleyball courts.

When you leave the park, take Washington Avenue north. On the northwest corner of Washington Avenue and 5th Street, Cassius Clay (now Muhammad Ali) prepared for his champion-

Art Deco District, **8**
Bass Museum of Art, **15**
Espanola Way, **9**
Fifth Street Gym, **7**
Flagler Memorial, **4**
Fontainebleau
Hilton, **16**
Hibiscus Island, **3**
Hotel National, **14**
Jackie Gleason
Theater, **13**
La Gorce Country
Club, **17**
Lincoln Rd. Arts
District, **10**
Miami Beach City
Hall, **11**
Miami Beach Marina, **5**
Palm Island, **2**
South Pointe Park, **6**
Stephen Muss
Convention Center, **12**
Watson Island, **1**

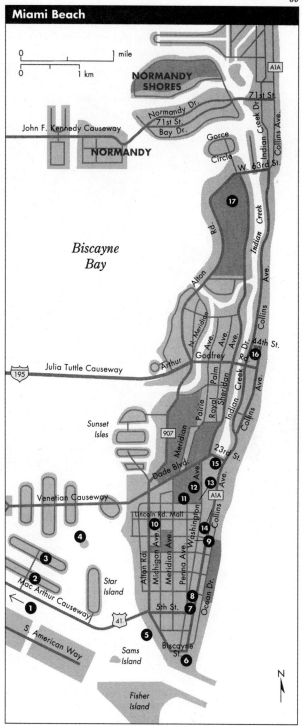

Miami Beach

7 ship bouts in the **Fifth Street Gym.** You can visit to watch young boxers train. *501 Washington Ave., tel. 674–8481. Open Mon.– Sat. 8–7, Sun. 8–2. Admission: $1 to look, $3 to train.*

Time Out A block east on 5th Street and a block north on Collins Avenue, Albert Starr's **Nature's Garden Bakery** makes delicious kosher special-diet breads and cakes. Try the millet cookies and the apple strudel without salt, sweetener, eggs, or yeast. *600 Collins Ave., tel. 305/534–1877. Closed Fri. afternoon and Sat.*

Return to 5th Street, go a block east to Ocean Drive, and turn **8** left. A block north at 6th Street, the **Art Deco District** begins. Take Ocean Drive north past a line of pastel-hued Art-Deco hotels on your left and palm-fringed Lummus Park and the beach on your right. Turn left on 15th Street, and left again at the next corner onto Collins Avenue.

Now drive along the Art Deco District's two main commercial streets. Take Collins Avenue south, turn right at 5th Street, and right again at the next corner onto **Washington Avenue,** an intriguing mixture of delicatessens, produce markets, and stores selling Jewish religious books and artifacts.

Go north on Washington Avenue and you'll come to the **Art Deco District Welcome Center** (661 Washington Ave., tel. 305/ 672–2014, open weekdays 10–6, Sat. 10–1; for more information, *see* Guided Tours). Continuing on Washington Avenue, go **9** past 14th Street to **Espanola Way,** a narrow street of Mediterranean-revival buildings constructed in 1925 and frequented through the years by artists and writers. In the 1930s, Cuban bandleader Desi Arnaz performed in the Village Tavern, now part of the **Clay Hotel & International Youth Hostel** (406 Espanola Way, tel. 305/534–2988). The hostel caters to young visitors from all over the world who seek secure, inexpensive lodgings within walking distance of the beach.

Turn left onto Espanola Way, go five blocks to Jefferson Avenue, and turn right. Three blocks north of Espanola Way is **Lincoln Road Mall,** a landscaped shopping thoroughfare known during its heyday in the 1950s as "Fifth Avenue of the South." Trams shuttle shoppers along the mall, which is closed to all other vehicular traffic between Washington Avenue and Alton Road.

Park in the municipal lot a half-block north of the mall to stroll **10** through the **Lincoln Road Arts District,** where three blocks of storefronts on Lincoln Road from Meridian Avenue to Lenox Avenue have been transformed into galleries, studios, classrooms, and art-related boutiques and cafes.

The arts district also includes the 500-seat **Colony Theater** (1040 Lincoln Rd., tel. 305/673–7486), a former movie house. Now it's a city-owned performing arts center featuring dance, drama, music, and experimental cinema.

From the parking lot, go to the first main street north of Lincoln Road Mall and turn right. You're on 17th Street, recently renamed **Hank Meyer Boulevard** for the local publicist who encouraged comedian Jackie Gleason to broadcast his TV show from Miami Beach in the 1950s. Two blocks east on your left, **11** beside the entrance to **Miami Beach City Hall** (1700 Convention

Center Dr., tel. 305/673-7030), stands *Red Sea Road*, a huge red sculpture by Barbara Neijna.

⓬ Also to your left is the **Stephen Muss Convention Center** (1901 Convention Center Dr., tel. 305/673-7311), doubled in size in 1988 to 1.1 million square feet of exhibit space.

⓭ Continuing two more blocks east, admire another large sculpture, *Mermaid*, by Roy Lichtenstein, in front of **Jackie Gleason Theater of the Performing Arts** (1700 Washington Ave., tel. 305/673-8300), where Gleason's TV show once originated. Now the 3,000-seat theater hosts touring Broadway shows and classical concert performers. Near the sculpture, stars appearing in the theater since 1984 have left their footprints and signatures in concrete. This **Walk of the Stars** includes George Abbott, Julie Andrews, Leslie Caron, Carol Channing, and Edward Villela.

Go two more blocks east on Hank Meyer Boulevard to Collins Avenue, toward three of the largest Art Deco hotels, built in the 1940s with streamlined tower forms reflecting the 20th century's transportation revolution:

⓮ The round dome atop the tower of the 11-story **Hotel National** (1677 Collins Ave., tel. 305/532-2311) resembles a balloon. The tower at the 12-story **Delano Hotel** (1685 Collins Ave., tel. 305/538-7881) sports fins suggesting the wings of an airplane or a Buck Rogers spaceship. The 11-story **Ritz Plaza** (1701 Collins Ave., tel. 305/531-6881) rises to a cylindrical tower resembling a submarine periscope.

⓯ Turn left on Collins Avenue. At 21st Street, turn left beside the Miami Beach Public Library in Collins Park, go two blocks to Park Avenue, and turn right. You're approaching the **Bass Museum of Art,** with a diverse collection of European art, including *The Holy Family*, a painting by Peter Paul Rubens; *The Tournament*, a 16th-century Flemish tapestry; and works by Albrecht Dürer and Henri de Toulouse-Lautrec. Park behind the museum and walk around to the entrance past massive tropical baobab trees. *2121 Park Ave., tel. 305/673-7530. Open Tues.–Sat. 10–5, Sun. 1–5. Admission: $2 adult, $1 students with ID, children 16 and under free. Donations Tues.*

⓰ Return on 21st Street or 22nd Street to Collins Avenue and turn left. As you drive north, a triumphal archway looms ahead, framing a majestic white building set in lush vegetation beside a waterfall and tropical lagoon. This vista is an illusion—a 13,000-square-foot outdoor mural on an exterior wall of the **Fontainebleau Hilton Resort and Spa** (4441 Collins Ave., tel. 305/538-2000). Artist Richard Haas designed the mural to illustrate how the hotel and its rock-grotto swimming pool would look behind the wall. Locals call the 1,206-room hotel "Big Blue." It's the giant of Miami Beach, with 190,000 square feet of meeting and exhibit space.

⓱ Go left on 65th Street, turn left again at the next corner onto Indian Creek Drive, and right at 63rd Street, which leads into Alton Road, a winding, landscaped boulevard of gracious homes styled along Art Deco lines. You'll pass the **La Gorce Country Club** (5685 Alton Rd. tel. 305/866-4421), which developer Carl Fisher built and named for his friend Oliver La Gorce, then president of the National Geographic Society.

To return to the mainland on the MacArthur Causeway, stay on
Alton Road south to 5th Street, then turn right.

Exploring Little Havana

*Numbers in the margin correspond with points of interest on
the Miami, Coral Gables, and Key Biscayne map.*

Orientation Thirty years ago, the tidal wave of Cubans fleeing the Castro
regime flooded an elderly neighborhood just west of downtown
Miami with refugees. This area became known as Little Havana. Today, with a half-million Cubans widely dispersed
throughout Greater Miami, Little Havana remains a magnet
for Cubans and Anglos alike. They come to experience the flavor of traditional Cuban culture.

That culture, of course, functions in Spanish. Many Little Havana residents and shopkeepers speak almost no English. If
you don't speak Spanish, point and smile to communicate.

Touring Little Begin this tour in downtown Miami, westbound on Flagler
Havana Street. Cross the Miami River to Little Havana, and park near
Flagler Street and Ronald Reagan Avenue (S.W. 12th Ave.) to
explore a thriving commercial district.

❶ Continue west on Flagler Street to Teddy Roosevelt Avenue
(S.W. 17th Ave.) and pause at **Plaza de la Cubanidad,** on the
southwest corner. Red-brick sidewalks surround a fountain
and monument with a quotation from José Martí, a leader in
Cuba's struggle for independence from Spain: *"Las palmas son
novias que esperan."* (The palm trees are girlfriends who will
wait.)

❷ Turn left at Douglas Road (S.W. 37th Ave.), drive south to
Calle Ocho (S.W. 8th St.), and turn left again. You are now on
the main commercial thoroughfare of Little Havana.

Time Out For a total sensory experience, have a snack or meal at **Ver-
sailles,** a popular Cuban restaurant. Etched-glass mirrors
lining its walls amplify bright lights and the roar of rapid-fire
Spanish. Most of the servers don't speak English; you order by
pointing to a number on the menu (choice of English or Spanish
menus). Specialties include *palomilla*, a flat beefsteak; *vieja
ropa* (literally, old clothes), a shredded-beef dish in tomato
sauce; and *arroz con pollo*, chicken and yellow rice. *3555 S.W.
8th St., tel. 305/445–7614. Open Sun.–Thurs. 8 AM–2 AM, Fri. 8
AM–3:30 AM, Sat. 8 AM–4:30 AM. AE, CB, DC, MC, V.*

East of Unity Boulevard (S.W. 27th Ave.), Calle Ocho becomes
a one-way street eastbound through the heart of Little Havana, where every block deserves exploration. If your time is
limited, we suggest the three-block stretch from S.W. 14th Avenue to S.W. 11th Avenue. Parking is more ample west of
Ronald Reagan Avenue (S.W. 12th Ave.).

❸ At Calle Ocho and Memorial Boulevard (S.W. 13th Ave.) stands
the **Brigade 2506 Memorial,** commemorating the victims of the
unsuccessful 1961 Bay of Pigs invasion of Cuba by an exile
force. An eternal flame burns atop a simple stone monument
with the inscription: *"Cuba—A Los Martires de La Brigada de
Asalto Abril 17 de 1961."* The monument also bears a shield
with the Brigade 2506 emblem, a Cuban flag superimposed on a
cross. Walk a block south on Memorial Boulevard from the Bri-

gade 2506 Memorial to see other monuments relevant to Cuban history, including a statue of José Martí.

❹ When you return to your car, drive five blocks south on Ronald Reagan Avenue to the **Cuban Museum of Art and Culture.** Created by Cuban exiles to preserve and interpret the cultural heritage of their homeland, the museum has expanded its focus to embrace the entire Hispanic art community. It has a small permanent collection and mounts temporary exhibitions. *1300 S.W. 12th Ave., tel. 305/858-8006. Open weekdays 10-5, weekends 1-5. Admission: donation requested.*

To return to downtown Miami, take Ronald Reagan Avenue back north to S.W. 8th Street, turn right, go east to Miami Avenue or Brickell Avenue, turn left, and go north across the Miami River.

Exploring Coral Gables/Coconut Grove/ South Miami

Orientation This tour directs you through three separate communities, each unique in character. Two of them, Coral Gables and South Miami, are independent suburbs. The third, Coconut Grove, was annexed to the City of Miami in 1925 but still retains a distinctive personality.

Coral Gables, a planned community of broad boulevards and Spanish Mediterranean architecture, justifiably calls itself "The City Beautiful." Developer George E. Merrick began selling Coral Gables lots in 1921 and incorporated the city in 1925. He named most of the streets for Spanish explorers, cities, and provinces. Street names are at ground level beside each intersection on whitewashed concrete cornerstones.

The 1926 hurricane and the Great Depression prevented Merrick from fulfilling many aspects of his plan. The city languished until after World War II but then grew rapidly. Today, Coral Gables has a population of about 43,000. In its bustling downtown, many multinational companies maintain headquarters or regional offices.

A pioneer farming community that grew into a suburb, South Miami today retains small-town charm. Its main attraction for visitors is an architecturally impressive mall, The Bakery Centre, constructed on the former site of Holsum Bakery. Samples of the old bakery's architectural ornamentation are on display.

Coconut Grove is south Florida's oldest settlement, inhabited as early as 1834 and established by 1873, two decades before Miami. Its early settlers included Bahamian blacks, "conchs" from Key West, and New England intellectuals. They built a community that attracted artists, writers, and scientists to establish winter homes. By the end of World War I, more people listed in *Who's Who* gave addresses in Coconut Grove than anyplace else.

To this day, Coconut Grove reflects the pioneers' eclectic origins. Posh estates mingle with rustic cottages, modest frame homes, and starkly modern dwellings—often on the same block. To keep Coconut Grove a village in a jungle, residents lavish affection on exotic plantings while battling to protect remaining native vegetation.

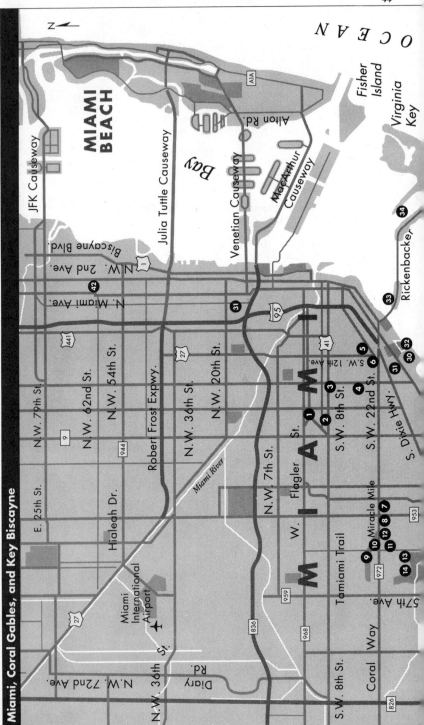

Miami, Coral Gables, and Key Biscayne

44

OCEAN

MIAMI BEACH

Bay

JFK Causeway

Julia Tuttle Causeway

Venetian Causeway

MacArthur Causeway

Fisher Island

Virginia Key

Alton Rd.

A1A

Biscayne Blvd.

N.W. 2nd Ave.

N. Miami Ave.

42

1

31

95

41

33

Rickenbacker

34

441

27

5
6
S.W. 12th Ave.

30
32
31

E. 25th St.

N.W. 79th St.

N.W. 62nd St.

N.W. 54th St.

N.W. 36th St.

N.W. 20th St.

9

944

Robert Frost Expwy.

Hialeah Dr.

27

Miami River

N.W. 7th St.

Flagler St.

M I A M I

1
2
3
4

S.W. 8th St.

S.W. 22nd St.

S. Dixie Hwy.

953

N.W. 36th Ave.

N.W. 72nd Ave.

Dinary Rd.

Miami International Airport

836

959

968

W. Flagler St.

M I A M I

Tamiami Trail

972

9
10 Miracle Mile
11
12
8
7
13
14

57th Ave.

Coral Way

S.W. 8th St.

826

N

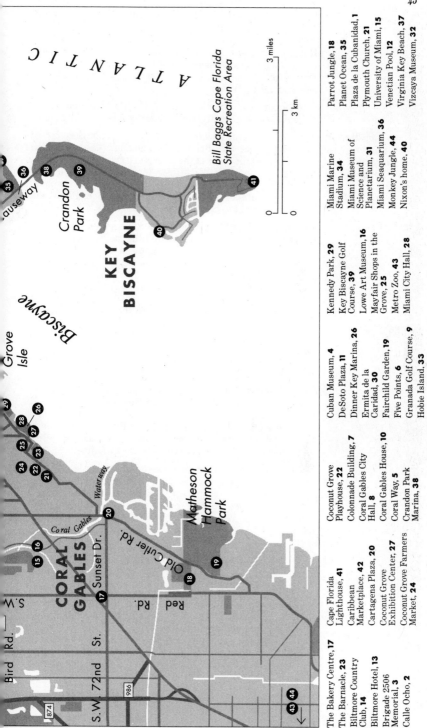

ATLANTIC

Causeway

Biscayne

KEY
BISCAYNE

*Grove
Isle*

Crandon
Park

*Bill Baggs Cape Florida
State Recreation Area*

3 miles

3 km

Matheson
Hammock
Park

Coral Gables

Sunset Dr.

CORAL
GABLES

Red Rd.

Old Cutler Rd.

Waterway

Bird Rd.

S.W. 72nd St.

The Bakery Centre, **17**
The Barnacle, **23**
Biltmore Country
Club, **14**
Biltmore Hotel, **13**
Brigade 2506
Memorial, **3**
Calle Ocho, **2**

Cape Florida
Lighthouse, **41**
Caribbean
Marketplace, **42**
Cartagena Plaza, **20**
Coconut Grove
Exhibition Center, **27**
Coconut Grove Farmers
Market, **24**

Coconut Grove
Playhouse, **22**
Colonnade Building, **7**
Coral Gables City
Hall, **8**
Coral Gables House, **10**
Coral Way, **5**
Crandon Park
Marina, **38**

Cuban Museum, **4**
DeSoto Plaza, **11**
Dinner Key Marina, **26**
Ermita de la
Caridad, **30**
Fairchild Garden, **19**
Five Points, **6**
Granada Golf Course, **9**
Hobie Island, **33**

Kennedy Park, **29**
Key Biscayne Golf
Course, **39**
Lowe Art Museum, **16**
Mayfair Shops in the
Grove, **25**
Metro Zoo, **43**
Miami City Hall, **28**

Miami Marine
Stadium, **34**
Miami Museum of
Science and
Planetarium, **31**
Miami Seaquarium, **36**
Monkey Jungle, **44**
Nixon's home, **40**

Parrot Jungle, **18**
Planet Ocean, **35**
Plaza de la Cubanidad, **1**
Plymouth Church, **21**
University of Miami, **15**
Venetian Pool, **12**
Virginia Key Beach, **37**
Vizcaya Museum, **32**

The historic center of the Village of Coconut Grove went through a hippy period in the 1960s, laid-back funkiness in the 1970s, and a teenybopper invasion in the early 1980s. Today, the tone is increasingly upscale, mellow, and sophisticated—a congenial mix of art-cinema and legitimate theaters, galleries, boutiques, elegant restaurants, and bars and sidewalk cafes where the literati hang out.

Two Junior League books, *Historic Coral Gables* and *Historic Coconut Grove*, give directions for self-guided walking tours.

Driving Tour of Coral Gables/ Coconut Grove/ South Miami
❺
❻
This tour begins in downtown Miami. Go south on S.E. 2nd Avenue, which becomes Brickell Avenue and crosses the Miami River. Half a mile south of the river, turn right onto **Coral Way**, which at this point is S.W. 13th Street. Within half a mile, Coral Way doglegs left under I–95 and becomes S.W. 3rd Avenue. It continues another mile to a complex intersection, **Five Points**, and doglegs right to become S.W. 22nd Avenue.

Along the S.W. 3rd Avenue and S.W. 22nd Avenue segments of Coral Way, banyan trees planted in the median strip in 1929 arch over the roadway. The banyans end at the Miami/Coral Gables boundary, where **Miracle Mile** begins. This four-block stretch of Coral Way, from Douglas Road (37th Ave.) to Le Jeune Road (42nd Ave.) in the heart of downtown Coral Gables, is really a half-mile long. To stroll the full mile, walk up one side and down the other. Miracle Mile's 160 shops range from chain restaurants and shoe stores to posh boutiques and beauty salons. The stores are numbered from 1 to 399. As you go west, numbers and quality both increase. Request a complete directory from the Miracle Mile Merchants' Association (220 Miracle Mile, Suite 218, Coral Gables, tel. 305/445–0591).

❼ **The Colonnade Building** (133–169 Miracle Mile, Coral Gables) on Miracle Mile once housed George Merrick's sales office. Its rotunda bears an ornamental frieze and a Spanish-tile roof 75 feet above street level. The Colonnade Building has been restored and connected to the new 13-story Colonnade Hotel and an office building that echoes the rotunda's roofline.

❽ The ornate Spanish Renaissance structure facing Miracle Mile just west of Le Jeune Road is **Coral Gables City Hall,** opened in 1928. It has a three-tier tower topped with a clock and a 500-pound bell. Inside the bell tower, a mural by artist Denman Fink depicts the four seasons. *405 Biltmore Way, Coral Gables, tel. 305/442–6400. Open weekdays 8–5.*

❾ Follow Coral Way west of Le Jeune Road to the right of City Hall. You'll pass the **Granada Golf Course** (2001 Granada Blvd., Coral Gables, tel. 305/442–6484), one of two public courses in Coral Gables.

❿ One block west of the golf course, turn right on Toledo Street to park behind **Coral Gables House**, George Merrick's boyhood home. The city acquired the dwelling in 1976 and restored its 1920s appearance. It contains many Merrick family furnishings and artifacts. *907 Coral Way, Coral Gables, tel. 305/442–6593. Open Sun. and Wed. 1–4. Admission: $1 adults, 50 cents children.*

⓫ Return to Coral Way, turn right, then left at the first stoplight. Now you're southbound on Granada Boulevard, approaching **De Soto Plaza and Fountain,** a classical column on a pedestal with water flowing from the mouths of four sculptured faces. The closed eyes of the face looking west symbolize the day's end. Denman Fink designed the fountain in the early 1920s.

Follow the traffic circle almost completely around the fountain to northeast-bound De Soto Boulevard. On your right in the ⑫ next block is **Venetian Pool,** a unique municipal swimming pool transformed from a rock quarry. *2701 De Soto Blvd., Coral Gables, tel. 305/442–6483. Summer hours: weekdays 11–7:30, weekends 10–4:30; winter hours: Tues.–Fri. 11–4, weekends 10–4:30. Admission (nonresident): $2.85 adults, $1.14 children under 13. Free parking across De Soto Blvd.*

From the pool, go around the block with right turns onto Almeria Avenue, Toledo Street, and Sevilla Avenue. You'll return to the De Soto Fountain and take De Soto Boulevard southeast to ⑬ emerge in front of **The Biltmore Hotel** (1200 Anastasia Ave., Coral Gables, tel. 305/445–1926). Like the Freedom Tower in downtown Miami, the Biltmore's 26-story tower is a replica of the Giralda Tower in Seville, Spain.

The opulent Biltmore opened in January 1926 as the centerpiece of George Merrick's planned city. It suffered financially during the Great Depression, became a veterans' hospital during World War II, and stood vacant from 1968 to 1986. After extensive restoration and renovation, it has reopened as a 279-unit hotel.

Go inside the Biltmore to admire the lobby's vaulted ceiling and gargoyles, the two ballrooms' impressive chandeliers and intricately painted ceilings, and the open courtyard's fountain and gracious proportions. A second-floor promenade overlooks the 18-hole Biltmore Golf Course, now a public course known for its scenic and competitive layout, and the largest hotel pool in the United States, with a capacity of 1.25 million gallons.

Just west of The Biltmore Hotel stands a separate building, ⑭ **The Biltmore Country Club,** which the city restored in the late 1970s. It's a richly ornamented beaux arts-style structure with a superb colonnade and courtyard. On its ground floor are facilities for golfers. In the former club lounge, Le Biltmore Restaurant occupies a lofty room paneled with veneer from 60 species of trees.

From the hotel, turn right on Anastasia Avenue, go east to Granada Boulevard, and turn right. Continue south on Granada Boulevard over a bridge across the **Coral Gables Waterway,** which connects the grounds of The Biltmore Hotel with Biscayne Bay. In the hotel's heyday, Venetian gondolas plied the waterway, bringing guests to a bayside beach.

At Ponce de León Boulevard, turn right. On your left is Metrorail's Stonehenge-like concrete structure, and on your ⑮ right, the **University of Miami**'s 260-acre main campus. With nearly 20,000 students, UM is the largest private university in the Southeast.

Turn right at the first stoplight to enter the campus and park in ⑯ the lot on your right designated for visitors to UM's **Lowe Art Museum.** The Lowe's permanent collection of 8,000 works includes Renaissance and Baroque art, American paintings, Latin American art, and Navajo and Pueblo Indian textiles and baskets. The museum also hosts traveling exhibitions. *1301*

Stanford Dr., Coral Gables, tel. 305/284–3535 for recorded information, 305/284–3536 for museum office. Open all year Sun. and Tues.–Fri. noon–5, Sat. 10–5. Admission: $2 adults, $1 students and seniors, children under 16 free.

Now exit the UM campus on Stanford Drive, pass under Metrorail, and cross Dixie Highway. Just beyond the Burger King on your right, bear right onto Maynada Street. Turn right at the next stoplight onto **Sunset Drive.** Fine old homes and mature trees line this officially designated "historic and scenic road" that leads to and through downtown South Miami.

On the northwest corner of Sunset Drive and Red Road (57th Ave.), note the pink building with a mural on which an alligator seems ready to devour a horrified man. This trompe l'oeil fantasy, *South Florida Cascade,* by illusionary artist Richard Haas, highlights the main entrance to **The Bakery Centre.** *5701 Sunset Dr., South Miami, tel. 305/662–4155.*

On the third level of The Bakery Centre, the **Miami Youth Museum** features cultural arts exhibits, hands-on displays, and activities to enhance a child's creativity and inspire interest in artistic careers. *5701 Sunset Dr., South Miami, tel. 305/661–ARTS. Open weekdays 10–5, weekends noon–5. Admission: $3 adults, children under 2 free.*

Go south on Red Road and turn right just before Killian Drive (S.W. 112th St.) into the grounds of **Parrot Jungle,** where more than 1,100 exotic birds are on display. Many of the parrots, macaws, and cockatoos fly free, but they'll come to you for seeds that you can purchase from old-fashioned gumball machines. Attend a trained-bird show, watch baby birds in training, and pose for photos with colorful macaws perched on your arms. The "jungle" is a natural hammock surrounding a sinkhole. Stroll among orchids and other flowering plants nestled among ferns, bald-cypress trees, and massive live oaks. Also see the cactus garden and Flamingo Lake, with a breeding population of 75 Caribbean flamingos. Opened in 1936, Parrot Jungle is one of Greater Miami's oldest and most popular commercial tourist attractions. *11000 S.W. 57th Ave., Miami, tel. 305/666–7834. Open daily 9:30–5. Admission: $9.75 adults, $4 children 3–12.*

From Parrot Jungle, take Red Road ⅓ mile south and turn left at Old Cutler Road, which curves north along the uplands of South Florida's coastal ridge. Visit 83-acre **Fairchild Tropical Garden,** the largest tropical botanical garden in the continental United States. *10901 Old Cutler Rd., Coral Gables, tel. 305/667–1651. Open daily except Christmas 9:30–4:30. Admission: $4 adults, children under 12 free with parents. Hourly tram rides, $1 adults, 50 cents children 12 & under.*

North of the garden, Old Cutler Road traverses Dade County's oldest and most scenic park, **Matheson Hammock Park.** The Civilian Conservation Corps developed the 100-acre tracts of upland and mangrove swamp in the 1930s on land donated by a local pioneer, Commodore J. W. Matheson. The park's most popular feature is a bathing beach, where the tide flushes a saltwater "atoll" pool through four gates. *9601 Old Cutler Rd., Coral Gables, tel. 305/666–6979. Park open 6 AM–sundown. Pool lifeguards on duty winter 7:30 AM–6 PM, summer 7:30 AM–7 PM. Parking fee for beach and marina $2 per car, $5 per car with trailer. Limited upland parking free.*

⑳ Continue north on Old Cutler Road to **Cartagena Plaza,** cross the Le Jeune Road bridge over the waterway, and turn right at the first stoplight onto Ingraham Highway. Four blocks later, you're back in the City of Miami, at the south end of Coconut Grove. Follow Ingraham Highway to Douglas Road and turn right at the next stoplight onto Main Highway. You're following old pioneer trails that today remain narrow roads shaded by a canopy of towering trees.

㉑ One block past the stoplight at Royal Palm Avenue, turn left onto Devon Road in front of **Plymouth Congregational Church.** Opened in 1917, this handsome coral-rock structure resembles a Mexican mission church. The front door, of hand-carved walnut and oak with original wrought-iron fittings, came from an early 17th-century monastery in the Pyrenees. A hole in the lower right side of the door gives the church cat access to mice. *3429 Devon Rd., Coconut Grove, tel. 305/444–6521. Ask at the office to go inside the church, weekdays 9–4:30. Services Sun. 10 AM.*

When you leave the church, go around the block opposite the church. Turn left from Devon Road onto Hibiscus Street, left again onto Royal Palm Avenue, and left at the stoplight onto Main Highway.

You're now headed for the historic **Village of Coconut Grove,** a trendy commercial district with red-brick sidewalks and more than 300 restaurants, stores, and art galleries.

Parking can be a problem in the village—especially on weekend evenings, when police direct traffic and prohibit turns at some intersections to prevent gridlock. Be prepared to walk several blocks from the periphery into the heart of the Grove.

㉒ As you enter the village center, note the apricot-hued Spanish rococo **Coconut Grove Playhouse** to your left. Built in 1926 as a movie theater, it became a legitimate theater in 1956 and is now owned by the State of Florida. The playhouse presents Broadway-bound plays and musical reviews and experimental productions in its 1,100-seat main theater and 100-seat cabaret-style Encore Room. *3500 Main Hwy., Coconut Grove, tel. 305/442–4000 to box office; tel. 305/442–2662 to administrative office. Parking lot: $2 during the day, $4 at night.*

㉓ Benches and a shelter opposite the playhouse mark the entrance to **The Barnacle,** a pioneer residence that is now a state historic site. Commodore Ralph Munroe built The Barnacle in 1891. Its broad, sloping roof and deeply recessed verandas channel sea breezes into the house. A central stairwell and rooftop vent allow hot air to escape. Many furnishings are original. While living at The Barnacle, Munroe built shoal-draft sailboats. One such craft, the ketch *Micco*, is on display. *3485 Main Hwy., Coconut Grove, tel. 305/448–9445. Open for tours only Thurs.–Mon. 9, 10:30, 1, and 2:30; closed Tues. and Wed. Admission: $1 adults, 50 cents children under 12. Reservations for groups of 8 or more; others meet ranger at entrance gate.*

Time Out Turn left at the next street, Commodore Plaza, and pause. **To Market/To Market,** a French gourmet cafe, features 16 kinds of muffins and a superb Greek-style salad bulging with brine-soaked olives and feta cheese. Other fare includes quiches, pâtés, sandwiches, cheeses, French pastries, American-style breakfasts, wine, beer, and soft drinks. On weekend mornings, locals bicycle in for a croissant-and-eggs brunch and a chat with the neighbors. *3195 Commodore Plaza, Coconut Grove, tel. 305/446–6090. Open Sun.–Thurs. 7 AM–10PM, Fri. and Sat. 7 AM–midnight. Inside and outdoors service and carryouts available. AE, CB, DC, MC, V.*

24 If your timing is right, visit the **Coconut Grove Farmers Market,** a laid-back, Brigadoon-like happening that appears as if by magic each Saturday on a vacant lot. To get there from Commodore Plaza, go north to Grand Ave., cross McDonald Ave. (S.W. 32nd Ave.), and go a block west to Margaret Street. Vendors set up outdoor stands to offer home-grown tropical fruits and vegetables (including organic produce), honey, seafoods, macrobiotic foods, and ethnic fare from the Caribbean, the Middle East, and Southeast Asia. Nonfood items for sale include plants, handicrafts, candles, jewelry, and homemade clothing. A masseur plies his trade, musicians play, and the Hare Krishnas come to chant. People-watching is half the fun. Open Saturday 8–3.

Now return to the heart of the village center. Then take Grand
25 Avenue a block east to Virginia Street and enter **Mayfair Shops in the Grove,** an exclusive open-air mall with a small branch of high-fashion Burdines department store and 74 other upscale shops. The 181 rooms of Mayfair House, a luxury hotel, surround the mall's southern section. As you stroll through Mayfair, admire its fountains, copper sculptures, and lavish Romanesque ornamentation formed in concrete. The design recalls a classic building in Chicago, The Rookery—with good reason. Frank Lloyd Wright, who remodeled The Rookery in 1905, taught Mayfair's architect, Kenneth Treister. *2911 Grand Ave., Coconut Grove, tel. 305/448–1700. Open Mon., Thurs., and Fri. 10–9; Tues., Wed., and Sat. 10–7; Sun. noon–5:30.*

Leaving the village center, take McFarlane Road east from its intersection with Grand Avenue and Main Highway. Peacock Park, site of the first hotel in Coconut Grove, is on your right.
26 Ahead, seabirds soar and sailboats ride at anchor in **Dinner Key Marina** (3400 Pan American Dr., Coconut Grove, tel. 305/579–6980), named for a small island where early settlers held picnics. With 575 moorings, it's Greater Miami's largest marina.

McFarlane Road turns left onto South Bayshore Drive. Turn right at the first stoplight onto Unity Boulevard (S.W. 27th Ave.), and go east into a parking lot that serves the marina and
27 the 105,000-square-foot **Coconut Grove Exhibition Center** (3360 Pan American Dr., Coconut Grove, tel. 305/579–3310), where antique, boat, and home-furnishings shows are held.

28 At the northeast corner of the lot is **Miami City Hall,** which was built in 1934 as the terminal for the Pan American Airways seaplane base at Dinner Key. The building retains its nautical-style art-deco trim. *3500 Pan American Dr., Coconut Grove, tel. 305/579–6325. Open weekdays 8–5.*

From City Hall, drive west on Pan American Drive toward South Bayshore Drive, with its pyramidlike Grand Bay Hotel.
29 Turn right on South Bayshore Drive, and go north past **Kennedy Park.** Leave your car in the park's lot north of Kirk Street

and walk toward the water. From a footbridge over the mouth of a small tidal creek, you'll enjoy an unobstructed view across Biscayne Bay to Key Biscayne. Film crews use the park often to make commercials and Italian westerns.

Continue north on South Bayshore Drive to Fair Isle Street and turn right. You're approaching **Grove Isle,** a 26-acre island with a 49-room hotel, high-rise apartments, and a private club. Developer Martin C. Margulies displays selections from his extensive private art collection in the lobbies. Along a walk beside the bay stand massive sculptures by modern luminaries, including Alexander Calder, Jean Dubuffet, Willem de Kooning, Alexander Liberman, and Isamu Noguchi. *4 Grove Isle Dr., Coconut Grove, tel. 305/250-4000. Phone the club's membership office, weekdays 9–5, and mention Fodor's Florida 1990 to obtain a free guest pass.*

Return to South Bayshore Drive, turn right, and go north past the entrance to Mercy Hospital, where South Bayshore Drive becomes South Miami Avenue. At the next stoplight beyond the hospital, turn right on a private road that goes past St. Kieran's Church to **Ermita de La Caridad**—Our Lady of Charity Shrine—a conical building 90 feet high and 80 feet wide overlooking the bay so worshipers face toward Cuba. A mural above the shrine's altar depicts the history of Cuba. *3609 S. Miami Ave., Coconut Grove, tel. 305/854-2404. Open daily 9–9.*

Return to South Miami Avenue, turn right, go about three-tenths of a mile, and turn left to the **Miami Museum of Science and Space Transit Planetarium.** This is a participatory museum, chock-full of sound, gravity, and electricity displays for children and adults alike to manipulate and marvel at. A wildlife center behind the museum houses native Florida snakes, turtles and tortoises, birds of prey, and large wading birds. *3280 S. Miami Ave., Miami, tel. 305/854-4247; 24-hour Cosmic Hotline for planetarium show times and prices, 305/854-2222. Open daily 10–6. Admission to museum: $4 adults, $2.50 children; to planetarium shows $5 adults, $2.50 children and seniors; to laser light shows $6 adults, $3 children and seniors.*

Across South Miami Avenue is the entrance to **Vizcaya Museum and Gardens,** an estate with an Italian Renaissance-style villa built in 1912–16 as the winter residence of Chicago industrialist James Deering. The house and gardens overlook Biscayne Bay on a 30-acre tract that includes a native hammock and more than 10 acres of formal gardens and fountains. You can leave your car in the Museum of Science lot and walk across the street or drive across and park in Vizcaya's own lot.

The house contains 34 rooms of antique furniture, plus paintings, sculpture, and other decorative arts. These objects date from the 15th through the 19th centuries, representing the Renaissance, Baroque, Rococo, and Neoclassic styles. *3251 S. Miami Ave., Miami, tel. 305/579-2813 (recording) or 305/579-2808. House open 9:30–4:30; ticket booth open to 4:30, garden to 5:30. Admission: $6.50 adults, $4.50 children 5–18. Guided tours available, group tours by appointment.*

As you leave Vizcaya, turn north (left from the Museum of Science lot, right from the Vizcaya lot) onto South Miami Avenue.

You may follow South Miami Avenue all the way downtown or turn right at the first stoplight onto Federal Highway, which runs into Brickell Avenue one long block north, in front of the entrance to the Rickenbacker Causeway to Key Biscayne.

Exploring Virginia Key and Key Biscayne

Orientation Government Cut and the Port of Miami separate the dense urban fabric of Miami Beach from Greater Miami's playground islands, Virginia Key and Key Biscayne. Parks occupy much of both keys, providing congenial upland with facilities for basking on the beach, golf, tennis, softball, and picnicking—plus uninviting but ecologically valuable stretches of dense mangrove swamp. Also on the keys are several marinas, an assortment of water-oriented tourist attractions, and the laidback village where Richard Nixon set up his presidential vacation compound.

Driving Tour of Virginia Key and Key Biscayne To reach Virginia Key and Key Biscayne, take the **Rickenbacker Causeway** across Biscayne Bay from the mainland at Brickell Avenue and S.W. 26th Road, about two miles south of downtown Miami. A fitness pathway for biking and jogging parallels the causeway. *Toll: $1 per car, bicycles and pedestrians free.*

㉝ About 200 feet east of the toll gate (just across the first low bridge), you can rent windsurfing equipment on **Hobie Island.** *Sailboards Miami, Box 16, Key Biscayne, tel. 305/361–SAIL, open daily 9:30–dusk. Cost: $12/hour; $39 for 2-hr windsurfing lesson.*

The **Old Rickenbacker Causeway Bridge,** built in 1947, is now a fishing pier. The west stub begins about a mile from the toll gate. Park near its entrance and walk past fishermen tending their lines to the gap where the center draw span across the Intracoastal Waterway was removed. There you can watch boat traffic pass through the channel, pelicans and other seabirds soar and dive, and porpoises cavort in the bay.

The new high-level **William M. Powell Bridge** rises 75 feet above the water to eliminate the need for a draw span. The panoramic view from the top encompasses the bay, keys, port, and downtown Miami Beach and the Atlantic Ocean in the distance. The speed limit is 45 mph, and you can't stop on the bridge, so park in the fishing pier lot and walk up.

㉞ Next along the causeway stands the 6,538-seat **Miami Marine Stadium** (3601 Rickenbacker Causeway, Miami, tel. 305/361–6732), where summer pops concerts take place and name entertainers perform throughout the year. You can join the audience on land in the stadium or on a boat anchored just offshore. Fourth of July concertgoers enjoy a spectacular fireworks display that is visible for miles up and down the bay.

㉟ Adjoining the stadium is **Planet Ocean,** the world's largest marine science museum. Most of its displays invite your participation. Touch an iceberg; walk through the eye of a hurricane; and measure yourself against the smallest sailing vessel ever to cross the Atlantic, *April Fool*—an inch under six feet long. *3979 Rickenbacker Causeway, Miami, tel. 305/361–5786; recorded program information, 305/361–9455. Open daily 10–6. Admission: $7.50 adults, $6 senior citizens, $4 children 6–12.*

③⑥ Down the causeway from Planet Ocean at the **Miami Seaquarium,** Lolita, a killer whale, cavorts in a huge tank. She performs three times a day, as do sea lions and dolphins in separate shows. Exhibits include a shark pool, 250,000-gallon tropical reef aquarium, and manatees. *4400 Rickenbacker Causeway, Miami, tel. 305/361-5705; recorded program information, 305/361-5703. Open daily 9:30-6:30. Admission: $13.95 adults, $11.95 senior citizens, $9.95 children 4-12.*

③⑦ Opposite the causeway from the Seaquarium, a road leads north to **Virginia Key Beach,** a City of Miami park, with a two-mile stretch of ocean frontage, shelters, barbecue grills, ball fields, nature trails, and a fishing area. Ask for directions at the entrance gate. Cost is $2 per car.

③⑧ From Virginia Key, the causeway crosses **Bear Cut** to the north end of Key Biscayne, where it becomes Crandon Boulevard. The **Crandon Park Marina,** behind Sundays on the Bay Restaurant, sells bait and tackle. *4000 Crandon Blvd., Key Biscayne, tel. 361-1161. Open 7-6.*

Beyond the marina, Crandon Blvd. bisects 1,211-acre **Crandon Park.** Turnouts on your left lead to four parking lots, adjacent picnic areas, ball fields, and 3.3 miles of beach. *Open all year 8 AM-sunset. Parking: $2 per car.*

③⑨ On your right are entrances to the **Key Biscayne Golf Course,** and the **International Tennis Center.**

④⓪ From the traffic circle at the south end of Crandon Park, Crandon Boulevard continues for two miles through the developed portion of Key Biscayne. You'll come back that way, but first detour to the site of **President Nixon's home** (485 W. Matheson Dr.). Turn right at the first stoplight onto Harbor Drive, go about a mile, and turn right at Matheson Drive. A later owner enlarged and totally changed Nixon's home.

Emerging from West Matheson Drive, turn right onto Harbor Drive and go about a mile south to Mashta Drive, and follow Mashta Drive east past Harbor Drive to Crandon Boulevard, and turn right.

You are approaching the entrance to **Bill Baggs Cape Florida State Recreation Area,** named for a crusading newspaper editor whose efforts prompted the state to create this 406-acre park. The park includes 1¼ miles of beach and a seawall along Biscayne Bay where fishermen catch bonefish, grouper, jack, snapper, and snook. There is a nature trail with native plants now rare on Key Biscayne.

④① Also in the park is the oldest structure in south Florida, the **Cape Florida Lighthouse,** erected in 1825 to help ships avoid the shallows and reefs offshore. In 1836 a band of Seminole Indians attacked the lighthouse and killed the keeper's helper. You can climb the 122 steps to the top of the 95-foot-tall lighthouse and visit a keeper's dwelling reconstructed and furnished as it might have appeared in the early 1900s, when Key Biscayne was a coconut plantation with just a handful of residents. *1200 S. Crandon Blvd., Key Biscayne, tel. 305/361-5811. Park open all year 8-sunset. Lighthouse tours daily except Tues. at 10:30, 1, 2:30, and 3:30. Admission to park: $1 per vehicle with*

*driver, 50 cents per passenger, children under 6 free; to light-
house and keeper's residence: $1 per person.*

When you leave Cape Florida, follow Crandon Boulevard back
to Crandon Park through Key Biscayne's commercial center, a
mixture of posh shops and stores catering to the needs of the
neighborhood. On your way back to the mainland, pause as you
approach the Powell Bridge to admire the downtown Miami
skyline. At night, the brightly lit Centrust Building looks from
this angle like a clipper ship running under full sail before the
breeze.

Exploring Little Haiti

Of the nearly 150,000 Haitians who have settled in Greater Miami, some 60,000 live in Little Haiti, a 200-block area on
Miami's northeast side. More than 350 small Haitian businesses
operate in Little Haiti.

For many Haitians, English is a third language. French is
Haiti's official language, but much day-to-day conversation
takes place in Creole, a French-based patois. Smiling and
pointing will bridge any language barriers you may encounter.

This tour takes you through the Miami Design District on the
margin of Little Haiti, then along two main thoroughfares
which form the spine of the Haitian community. The tour
begins in downtown Miami. Take Biscayne Boulevard north to
N.E. 36th Street, turn left, go about four-tenths of a mile west
to North Miami Avenue. Turn right, and go north through the
Miami Design District, where about 225 wholesale stores,
showrooms, and galleries feature interior furnishings and decorative arts.

Little Haiti begins immediately north of the Design District in
an area with some of Miami's oldest dwellings, dating from the
dawn of the 20th Century through the 1920s land-boom era.
Drive the side streets to see elegant Mediterranean-style
homes, and bungalows with distinctive coral rock trim.

Return to North Miami Avenue and go north. A half-block east
on 54th Street is the tiny storefront office of the **Haitian Refugee Center,** a focal point of political activity in the Haitian
community. *32 N.E. 54th St., tel. 305/757-8538.*

Continue north on North Miami Avenue past the former Cuban
consulate, a pretentious Caribbean-Colonial mansion that is
now a Haitian physician's clinic.

North of 85th Street, cross the Little River Canal into **El Por-
tal,** a tiny suburban village of modest homes where more than a
quarter of the property is now Haitian-owned. Turn right on
N.E. 87th Street and right again on N.E. 2nd Avenue. You are
now southbound on Little Haiti's main commercial thoroughfare.

Time Out Stop for Haitian breads and cakes made with coconut and other
tropical ingredients at **Baptiste Bakery.** *7488 N.E. 2nd Ave.,
tel. 756-1119. Open 8-8.*

Along N.E. 2nd Avenue between 79th Street and 45th Street, a
riot of color assails your eyes. Merchants have painted their

buildings in vivid yellows, greens, reds, pinks, purples, and blues that Haitians find congenial and mellow.

❷ Look for the **Caribbean Marketplace,** which the Haitian Task Force (an economic development organization) expects to open by early 1990. Its 32 merchants will sell tropical fruits and vegetables, handmade baskets, and Haitian art and craft items. *5927 N.E. 2nd Ave., Miami, tel. Haitian Task Force, 305/751–9783, for marketplace phone number.*

This concludes the Little Haiti tour. To return to downtown Miami, take N.E. 2nd Avenue south to N.E. 35th Street, turn left, go east one block to Biscayne Boulevard, and turn right to go south.

Exploring South Dade

This tour directs you to major attractions in the suburbs southwest of Dade County's urban core. A Junior League book, *Historic South Dade,* locates and describes 40 historic structures and attractions in a South Dade County driving tour.

From downtown Miami, take the Dolphin Expressway (Rte. 836) west to the Palmetto Expressway (Rte. 826) southbound. Bear left south of Bird Road (S.W. 40th St.) onto the Don Shula Expressway (Rte. 874). Exit westbound onto Killian Drive (S.W. 104th St.) and go west to Lindgren Road (S.W. 137th Ave.). Turn left and go south to S.W. 128th Street, the entrance to the Tamiami Airport and **Weeks Air Museum,** where aircraft on display include a World War I-vintage Sopwith Camel (of Snoopy fame), and a B–17 Flying Fortress bomber and P–51 Mustang from World War II. *14710 S.W. 128th St., tel. 305/233–5197. Open: Wed.–Sun. 10–5. Admission: $4 adults, $2 children 12 and under and seniors.*

❸ Continue south on Lindgren Road to Coral Reef Drive (S.W. 152nd St.). Turn left and go east to **Metro Zoo** and the **Gold Coast Railroad Museum.**

Metro Zoo covers 290 acres and is cageless; animals roam free on islands surrounded by moats. In "Wings of Asia," a 1.5-acre aviary, hundreds of exotic birds from southeast Asia fly through a rain forest beneath a protective net enclosure. The zoo has 3 miles of walkways, a monorail with 4 stations, and an open-air amphitheater for concerts. Paws, a petting zoo for children, opened in 1989. *12400 Coral Reef Dr. (S.W. 152nd St.), tel. 305/251–0400 for recorded information. Gates open daily 10–4. Park closes at 5:30. Admission: $6 adults, $3 children 3–12, under 3 free. Monorail tickets (unlimited use on day of purchase) $3 adults, $2 children. AE, MC; no credit cards at monorail and snack bar.*

The railroad museum's collection includes a 1949 Silver Crescent dome car; and the *Ferdinand Magellan,* the only Pullman car ever constructed specifically for U.S. presidents, used by Roosevelt, Truman, Eisenhower, and Reagan. *12450 Coral Reef Dr. (S.W. 152nd St.), tel. 305/253–0063. Open weekdays 10–3, weekends 10–5. Train rides weekends, holidays. Phone for details.*

Return to Coral Reef Drive, turn right (east) to the Homestead Extension of Florida's Turnpike, take the turnpike south, exit at Hainlin Mill Drive (S.W. 216th St.), and turn right. Cross

South Dixie Hwy. (U.S. 1), go three miles west, and turn right
into **Monkey Jungle,** home to more than 4,000 monkeys representing 50 species—including orangutans from Borneo and
Sumatra, golden lion tamarins from Brazil, and brown lemurs
from Madagascar. Performing monkey shows begin at 10 AM
and run continuously at 45-minute intervals. The walkways of
this 30-acre attraction are caged; the monkeys roam free. *14805
Hainlin Mill Dr. (S.W. 216 St.), tel. 305/235–1611. Open daily
9:30–5. Admission: $7.50 adults, $6.50 seniors, $4 children 5–
12. AE, MC.*

Continue west on Hainlin Mill Drive to Newton Road (S.W.
157th Ave.), turn left and go south to **Orchid Jungle,** where you
can stroll under live-oak trees to see orchids, ferns, bromeliads,
and anthuriums, and peer through the windows of an orchid-
cloning laboratory. *26715 SW 157th Ave., Homestead, tel. 305/
247–4824, FL 800/344–2457, or US 800/327–2832. Open daily
8:30–5:30. Admission: $5 adults, $4 seniors, $4 children
13–17, $1.50 children 6–12.*

Continue south on Newton Road to South Dixie Hwy. (U.S. 1),
and turn left. Almost immediately, you'll find **Coral Castel of
Florida** on your right. It was built by Edward Leedskalnin, a
Latvian immigrant, between 1920 and 1940. The 3-acre castle
has a 9-ton gate a child can open, an accurate working sundial,
and a telescope of coral rock aimed at the north star, Polaris.
*28655 South Dixie Hwy., Homestead, tel. 305/248–6344. Open
daily 9–9. Admission: $7.25 adults, $4.50 children 6–12. MC,
V.*

Leaving Coral Castle, take South Dixie Highway to Biscayne
Drive (S.W. 288th St.) and go east to the turnpike. Take the
turnpike back to the Don Shula Expressway (Rte. 874), which
leads to the Palmetto Expressway (Rte. 826), which leads in
turn to the Dolphin Expressway (Rte. 836).

Miami for Free

Concerts **PACE** (Performing Arts for Community and Education, tel.
305/681–1470) supports free concerts in parks and cultural and
religious institutions throughout the Greater Miami Area.

University of Miami School of Music (tel. 305/284–6477) offers
many free concerts on the Coral Gables campus.

Museums Some museums are free all the time. Others have donation
days, when you may pay as much or as little as you wish. *(See*
Exploring and Historical Buildings and Sites for free-
admission policies at major museums.)

Views Ride an elevator to the 18th floor of the new Metro-Dade Center to enjoy spectacular views east to Miami Beach and
Biscayne Bay and west to the Orange Bowl and Miami International Airport. Open Mon.–Fri. 8–5 *(see* Exploring Downtown
Miami).

What to See and Do with Children

Greater Miami is a family-oriented vacation destination. Most
of the major hotels can provide access to baby-sitting for young
children. Although the area lacks major theme parks, families
stay occupied with visits to the beach, zoo, and museums. Ac-

tivities for teenagers are most prevalent on the beaches during spring break but occur throughout the year.

Family Activities **Dade County Youth Fair.** For 18 days at the end of March each year, Greater Miami's only amusement park comes to life at the Dade County Youth Fair in 260-acre Tamiami Park. The fairgrounds features a mile-long midway with over 80 amusement and thrill rides. The world's largest youth fair displays 50,000 student exhibits in 30 categories, including science projects and farm animals and equipment. Professional entertainers perform daily on seven stages. If you buy something at a local Publix supermarket, you'll get a gate pass good for free admission on Thursdays. *10901 Coral Way, Miami, tel. 305/223–7060. Open weekdays 4–11, weekends, 10 AM–11 PM. Admission: $4 adults, $3 children 6–12.*

Shopping

Except in the heart of the Everglades, visitors to the Greater Miami area are never more than 15 minutes away from a major shopping area. Downtown Miami long ago ceased to be the community's central shopping hub. Today Dade County has more than a dozen major malls, an international free zone, and hundreds of miles of commercial streets lined with storefronts and small neighborhood shopping centers. Many of these local shopping areas have an ethnic flavor, catering primarily to one of Greater Miami's immigrant cultures.

In the Latin neighborhoods, children's stores sell *vestidos* (party dresses) made of organza and lace. Men's stores sell the *guayabera*, a pleated, embroidered shirt that replaces the tie and jacket in much of the tropics. Traditional bridal shops display formal dresses that Latin families buy or rent for a daughter's *quince*, a lavish 15th-birthday celebration.

No standard store hours exist in Greater Miami. Phone ahead. When you shop, expect to pay Florida's 6% sales tax unless you have the store ship your goods out of Florida.

Shopping Districts Greater Miami is the fashion marketplace for the southeastern
Fashion District United States, the Caribbean, and Latin America. Many of the 500 garment manufacturers in Miami and Hialeah sell their clothing locally, in more than 30 factory outlets and discount fashion stores in the Miami Fashion District, east of I-95 along 5th Avenue from 29th Street to 25th Street. Most stores in the district are open 9–5 Monday–Saturday and accept credit cards.

Miami Free Zone The Miami Free Zone (MFZ) is an international wholesale trade center where the U.S. Customs Service supervises the exhibition and sales space. You can buy goods duty-free for export or pay duty on goods released for domestic use. More than 140 companies sell products from 75 countries, including aviation equipment, chemicals, clothing, computers, cosmetics, electronics, liquor, and perfumes. The 54-acre MFZ is five minutes west of Miami International Airport off the Dolphin Expressway (Rte. 836), and about 20 minutes from the Port of Miami. *Miami Free Zone, 2305 N.W. 107th Ave., tel. 305/591–4300. Open weekdays 9–5.*

Cauley Square A tearoom and craft, antiques, and clothing shops now occupy this complex of clapboard, coral-rock, and stucco buildings erected 1907–20 for railroad workers who built and maintained the line to Key West. Turn right off U.S. 1 at S.W. 224th Street. *22400 Old Dixie Hwy., Goulds, tel. 305/258–3543. Open Mon.–Sat. 10–4:30.*

Books Greater Miami's best English-language bookstore, **Books & Books, Inc.,** specializes in books on the arts, architecture, Floridiana, and contemporary and classical literature. Collectors enjoy browsing through the rare book room upstairs, which doubles as a photography gallery. Frequent poetry readings and book signings. *296 Aragon Ave., Coral Gables, tel. 305/442–4408, and 933 Lincoln Rd. (Sterling Bldg.), Miami Beach, tel. 305/532–3222. Open weekdays 10–8, Sat. 10–7, Sun. noon–5. AE, MC, V.*

Children's Books and Toys The friendly staff at **A Likely Story** will help you choose books and educational toys that are appropriate to your child's interests and stage of development. *5740 Sunset Dr., South Miami, tel. 305/667–3730. Open Mon.–Sat. 10–5. MC, V.*

Wine The largest retail collection of fine wines in Florida is at *Foremost Sunset Corners,* home of the Miami chapter of *Les Amis du Vin.* Catalog available. *8701 Sunset Dr., Miami 33173, tel. 305/271–8492. Open Mon.–Sat. 8 AM–9:45 PM. MC, V.*

Beaches

Miami Beach From Haulover Cut to Government Cut, a broad sandy beach extends for 10 continuous miles. Amazingly, it's a man-made beach—a marvel of modern engineering to repair the ravages of nature.

Along this stretch, erosion had all but eliminated the beach by the mid-1970s. Waves threatened to undermine the seawalls of hotels and apartment towers. From 1977 to 1981, the U.S. Army Corps of Engineers spent $51.5 million to pump tons of sand from offshore, restoring the beach to a 300-foot width. Between 21st and 46th streets, Miami Beach built boardwalks and protective walk-overs atop a sand dune landscaped with sea oats, sea grape, and other native plants whose roots keep the sand from blowing away.

The new beach lures residents and visitors alike to swim and stroll. More than 7 million people visit the 7.1 miles of beaches within the Miami Beach city limits annually. The other 2.9 miles are in Surfside and Bal Harbour. Here's a guide to where kindred spirits gather:

The best windsurfing on Miami Beach occurs at First Street, just north of the Government Cut jetty, and at 21st Street. You can also windsurf at Penrod's windsurfing area in Lummus Park at 10th Street and in the vicinity of 3rd, 14th, and 21st streets. Lifeguards discourage windsurfing from 79th Street to 87th Street.

From 1st Street to 14th Street, senior citizens predominate early in the day. Later, a younger crowd appears, including family groups who flock to the new children's play areas in Lummus Park, between Ocean Drive and the beach at 5th and 14th streets.

The beaches opposite the Art Deco District, between 6th Street and 21st Street, attract a diverse clientele of locals and tourists from Europe and Asia. In this area, in an effort to satisfy foreign visitors, city officials don't enforce the law against female bathers going topless as long as everyone on the beach behaves with decorum. Topless bathing also occurs from 35th to 42nd streets. Gays tend to gather at 21st Street.

University of Miami students like the stretch of beach along Millionaires' Row, around 46th Street, where the big hotels have outdoor concession stands on the beach.

If you like a quiet beach experience, go to 35th, 53rd, or 64th streets. Tired young professionals there seek solitude to read a book. Paradoxically, young mothers like to bring their children to these beaches. The two groups coexist nicely.

French-Canadians frequent the 72nd Street beach.

High-schools groups gather at 1st, 10th, 14th, and 85th streets for pickup games of volleyball and football.

During the winter, the wealthy condominium crowd clusters on the beach from 96th Street to 103rd Street in Bal Harbour.

City of Miami Beach beaches open daily with lifeguards, winter 8–5, summer 9–6. Bal Harbour and Surfside have no lifeguards, beaches open daily 24 hours. Beaches free in all three communities; metered parking nearby.

County Park Beaches Metropolitan Dade County operates beaches at several of its major parks. Each county park operates on its own schedule that varies from day to day and season to season. Phone the park you want to visit for current hours and information on special events.

Crandon Park. Atlantic Ocean beach, popular with young Hispanics and with family groups of all ethnic backgrounds. *4000 Crandon Park Blvd., Key Biscayne, tel. 305/361–5421. Open daily winter 8–5, summer 8–7. Admission: $2 per car.*
Haulover Beach Park. Atlantic Ocean beach. A good place to be alone. Lightly used compared to other public beaches, except on weekends and in the peak tourist season, when it attracts a diverse crowd. *10800 Collins Ave., Miami, tel. 305/947–3525. Open daily winter 9–5, summer 9–7. Admission: $2 per car.*

Cape Florida **Bill Baggs Cape Florida State Recreation Area** (*see* Exploring Virginia Key and Key Biscayne).

Sports and Fitness

Miami's subtropical climate is paradise for active people, a place where refugees from the frozen north can enjoy warm-weather outdoor sports, such as boating, swimming, and golf, all year long. During Miami's hot, humid summers, people avoid the sun's strongest rays by playing early or late in the day. We've listed below some of the most popular individual and group sports activities.

Spa The **Doral Saturnia International Spa Resort** opened in 1988 on the grounds of the Doral Resort and Country Club. Formal Italian gardens contain the spa pool and a special waterfall under which guests can enjoy natural hydromassage from the gentle pounding of falling water. The spa's 100-foot-high atrium accommodates a 5,000-pound bronze staircase railing created in 1920 by French architect Alexandre Gustave Eiffel and fabricated by artist Edgar Brandt for Paris's Bon Marché department store. The spa combines mud baths and other European pampering techniques with state-of-the-art American fitness and exercise programs. A one-day sampler is available. *8755 N.W. 36th St., Miami 33178, tel. 305/593–6030. 48 suites. Facilities: 4 exercise studios (2 with spring-loaded floors), 3 outdoor heated swimming pools, David fitness equipment, beauty salon, 2 restaurants. AE, CB, DC, MC, V.*

Water Sports
Marinas Listed below are the major marinas in Greater Miami. The dock masters at these marinas can provide information on other marine services you may need. Also ask the dockmasters for *Teall's Tides and Guides, Miami-Dade County,* and other local nautical publications.

The U.S. Customs Service requires boats of less than five tons that enter the country along Florida's Atlantic Coast south of Sebastian Inlet to report to designated marinas and call U.S. Customs on a direct phone line. The phones, located outside marina buildings, are accessible 24 hours a day. U.S. Customs phones in Greater Miami are at Haulover Marina and Watson Island Marina (both listed below).

Dinner Key Marina. Operated by City of Miami. Facilities include dockage with space for transients and a boat ramp. *3400 Pan American Dr., Coconut Grove, tel. 305/579–6980. Open daily 7 AM–11 PM.*
Haulover Park Marina. Operated by county lessee. Facilities include a bait-and-tackle shop, marine gas station, and boat launch. *10800 Collins Ave., Miami Beach, tel. 305/944–9647. Open daily 7 AM–5 PM.*
Watson Island Marina. City of Miami marina. Facilities include bait and tackle, boat ramp, and fuel. When the marina is busy, it stays open until all boaters are helped. *1050 MacArthur Causeway, Miami, tel. 305/371–2378. Open Mon.–Thurs. 7 AM–7:30 PM, Fri.–Sun. 7 AM–11 PM.*

Sailing Dinner Key and the Coconut Grove waterfront remain the center of sailing in Greater Miami, although sailboat moorings and rentals are located along other parts of the bay and up the Miami River.

Windsurfing and Jet Skis **Penrod's.** Plans to rent jet skis, Hobie Cats, Windsurfers, and surfboards. *1001 Ocean Dr., Miami Beach, tel. 305/534–0687 or 305/538–1111. Open daily 10–sunset.*
Sailboards Miami. *(See* Exploring Virginia Key and Key Biscayne.)

Diving Summer diving conditions in greater Miami equal or exceed the best of those in the Caribbean. Winter diving can be adversely affected when cold fronts come through. Dive-boat schedules vary with the season and with local weather conditions.

Fowey, Triumph, Long, and Emerald Reefs all are shallow 10–15-foot dives that are good for snorkelers and beginning divers. These reefs are on the edge of the continental shelf, a quarter of a mile from depths greater than 100 feet. You can also paddle around the tangled prop roots of the mangrove trees that line Florida's coastline, peering at the fish, crabs, and other onshore creatures that hide there.

Dive Boats and Instruction. Look for instructors who are affiliated with PADI (Professional Association of Dive Instructors) or NAUI (National Association of Underwater Instructors).

Divers Paradise Corp (4000 Crandon Blvd., Key Biscayne, tel. 305/361–DIVE). Complete dive shop and diving charter service, including equipment rental and scuba instruction. PADI affiliation.

Omega Diving International. Private instruction throughout Greater Miami. Equipment consultation and specialty courses, including instructor training and underwater photography. PADI affiliation. *8420 S.W. 133 Ave., Miami, tel. 305/385–0779 or 800/255–1966. Open daily 8–6.*

Diver's Dream. This all-purpose dive shop is located right on the Miami Beach marina. *1290 5th St., Miami Beach 33139, tel. 305/534–7710. Open Mon.–Sat. 10 AM–7 PM. Beach store open weekdays 9 AM–7 PM, weekends 7 AM–6 PM.*

Tennis Greater Miami has more than 60 private and public tennis centers, of which 11 are open to the public. All public tennis courts charge nonresidents an hourly fee.

Florida Tennis Association (801 N.E. 167th St., Suite 301, North Miami Beach 33162, tel. 305/652–2866). Contact for amateur tournament information.

Coral Gables **Biltmore Tennis Center.** Ten well-maintained hard courts. Site of annual Orange Bowl Junior International Tennis Tournament for children 18 and under in December. *1210 Anastasia Ave., tel. 305/442–6565. Open weekdays 8 AM–10 PM, weekends 8–8. Nonresident day rate $3.04, night rate $4.33 per person per hour.*

Miami Beach **Flamingo Tennis Center.** Has 20 well-maintained clay courts. Site of the Rolex-Orange Bowl Junior International Tennis Tournament for teenagers 18 and under. *1000 12th St., tel. 305/673–7761. Open weekdays 8 AM–9 PM, weekends 8–6. Cost: day $2.12, night $2.65 per person per hour.*

Metropolitan Dade County **International Tennis Center.** Has 17 Laykold Cushion Plus hard courts, four lighted. Reservations necessary for night play. Closed to public play for about two weeks before and after the annual Lipton International Players Championships in March. *7300 Crandon Blvd., Key Biscayne, tel. 305/361–8633. Open daily 9 AM–9 PM. Cost: weekdays $3, weeknights $4, weekend days $4, weekend nights $5 per person per hour.*

Spectator Sports

Greater Miami offers a broad variety of spectator sports events, including such popular pastimes as football and baseball, and more specialized events, such as boat racing and rugby. However, the community lacks a central clearinghouse for sports information and ticket sales.

You can find daily listings of local sports events on page 3 of *The Miami Herald* sports section. The weekend section on Friday carries detailed schedules and coverage of spectator sports. The *Herald* provides a recorded "sports line" message with a brief selection of major sports scores (tel. 305/376–3505).

Orange Bowl Festival. The activities of the annual Orange Bowl and Junior Orange Festival take place early November-late February. Best-known for its *King Orange Jamboree Parade* and the *Federal Express/Orange Bowl Football Classic*, the festival also includes two tennis tournaments: the *Rolex/Orange Bowl International Tennis Championships* for top amateur national and international tennis players 16 and under, and an international tennis tournament for players 14 and under.

Other Orange Bowl sports events include a regatta series for university and professional sailors, a 5-km run in Coral Gables, the *Orange Bowl 10-km Race* on the 6.2-mile Grand Prix course, the annual *American Savings/Orange Bowl Marathon*, which draws over 2,500 runners, soccer games, bowling events, and a sports competition for physically disabled athletes. For tickets and a calendar of events: **Tickets, Orange Bowl Committee** (Box 350748, Miami 33135, tel. 305/642–5211).

Auto Racing **Hialeah Speedway.** The Greater Miami area's only independent raceway holds stock-car races on a ⅓-mile asphalt speedway in a 5,000-seat stadium. Four divisions of stock cars run weekly. The Marion Edwards, Jr., Memorial Race for late-model stock cars is in November. Located on U.S. 27, ¼ mile east of Palmetto Expressway (Rte. 826). *3300 W. Okeechobee Rd., Hialeah, tel. 305/821–6644. Open every Sat. late Jan.–early Dec. Gates open 6 PM, racing 7:45–11. Admission: $7 adults, $1 children 6–12.*

Grand Prix of Miami. Held in February for the Camel GT Championship on a 1.9-mile, E-shape track in downtown Miami, south of MacArthur Causeway and east of Biscayne Boulevard. Drivers race three hours; the winner completes the most laps. Sanctioned by International Motor Sports Association (IMSA). *Miami Motor Sports, Inc., 7254 S.W. 48th St., Miami 33155, tel. 305/662–5660. Tickets available from Miami Motor Sports, Inc., tel. 305/665–RACE or 800/233–RACE or Ticketmaster* (see *Important Addresses and Numbers*).

Baseball **University of Miami Hurricanes.** The baseball Hurricanes play home games in the 5,000-seat Mark Light Stadium, at 1 Hurricane Drive on UM's Coral Gables campus. The Hurricanes were the 1982 and 1985 NCAA baseball champions. *University of Miami Athletic Department, Box 248167, Coral Gables 33124, tel. 305/284–2655 or 800/GO-CANES. Open weekdays 8–6, Sat. 10–2. Season: 48 home games Feb.–May, day games 2 PM, night games 7:30. AE, CB, DC, MC, V.*

Basketball **Miami Heat.** Second 41 home game season November–May for Miami's National Basketball Association Team. *Tickets: Miami Arena, Miami 33136–4102, tel. 305/577–HEAT or Ticketmaster* (see *Important Addresses and Numbers*). **University of Miami Hurricanes.** Games are held in the Miami arena. *University of Miami Athletic Department, Box 248167, Coral Gables 33124, tel. 305/284–2655, 800/GO-CANES. Open weekdays 8–6, Sat. 10–2. Game time 7:30. AE, CB, DC, MC, V.*

Dog Racing The Biscayne Kennel Club, the Flagler Dog Track in Greater Miami, and Hollywood Greyhound Park in Ft. Lauderdale divide the annual racing calendar. Check with the individual tracks for dates. **Biscayne Kennel Club.** Greyhounds chase a mechanical rabbit around illuminated fountains in the track's infield. Near I-95 at N.W. 115th Street. *320 N.W. 115th St., Miami Shores, tel. 305/754–3484. Season: Nov.–Dec. and May–June. Admission: reserved seats $1, grandstand $1, clubhouse $2. Parking 50 cents–$2.*

Flagler Dog Track. Inner-city track in the middle of Little Havana, five minutes east of Miami International Airport off Dolphin Expressway (Rte. 836) and Douglas Road (N.W. 37th Ave.). *401 N.W. 38th Ct., Miami, tel. 305/649–3000. Open Sept.*

5–Oct. 30. General admission $1, clubhouse $2, parking 50 cents–$2.

Football **Miami Dolphins.** Owner Joe Robbie enjoys a reputation for doing things his own way. In 1987, he moved the Dolphins from the Orange Bowl near downtown Miami into his own privately financed $100-million Joe Robbie Stadium. Robbie also intends to use the stadium for baseball.

The new 74,914-seat stadium has a grass playing-field surface, with built-in drainage under the sod to carry off rainwater quickly. Stadium tours include the field, team locker rooms, sky boxes, executive suites, and football press boxes. *Tel. 305/ 623–6471. Tours daily, except event days, 11 AM, 1, 3, and 5 PM. Admission: $4.*

Joe Robbie Stadium is on a 160-acre site, 16 miles northwest of downtown Miami, one mile south of the Dade-Broward County line, accessible from I-95 and Florida's Turnpike. On game days, the Metro-Dade Transit Authority runs buses to the stadium. Bus information, tel. 305/638–6700.

Dolphins tickets: *Miami Dolphins, Joe Robbie Stadium, 2269 N.W. 199th St., Miami 33056, tel. 305/620–2578. Open weekdays 10–6. Also available through Ticketmaster (see Important Addresses and Numbers).*

University of Miami Hurricanes. The Hurricanes, winners of the 1987 national college football championship, play home games in the Orange Bowl, near the Dolphin Expressway (Rte. 836) just west of downtown Miami. *1400 N.W. 4th St., tel. 305/ 579–6971. Game time 7:30 PM (unless changed for the convenience of the TV networks). Schedule and tickets: University of Miami Athletic Department, Box 248167, Coral Gables 33124, tel. 305/284–2655 or 800/GO-CANES. Open weekdays 8–6.*

Horse Racing **Calder Race Course.** Opened in 1971, Calder is Florida's largest glass-enclosed, air-conditioned sports facility. This means that Calder actually has two racing seasons, one in fall or winter, another in spring or summer. Contact the track for this year's dates. In April, Calder holds the Tropical Park Derby for three-year-olds, the last major race in Florida before the Kentucky Derby. On the Dade-Broward County line near I-95 and the Hallandale Beach Boulevard exit., ¾ mile from Joe Robbie Stadium. *21001 N.W. 27th Ave., Miami, tel. 305/625–1311. Gates open 11 AM, post time 1 PM, races end about 5 PM. General admission $2, clubhouse $4, programs 50 cents, parking $1–$3.*

Hialeah Park. A superb setting for Thoroughbred racing, Hialeah's 228 acres of meticulously landscaped grounds surround paddocks and a clubhouse built in a classic French Mediterranean style. Since it opened in 1925, Hialeah Park has survived hurricanes, economic reverses, and changing trends in racing without losing its air of elegant informality.

During the racing season, the gates open early Sunday mornings for breakfast at Hialeah Park. Admission is free. You can watch the horses work out, explore Hialeah's gardens, munch on breakfast fare of tolerable palatability, and admire the park's breeding flock of 600 Cuban flamingos.

When racing is not in session, Hialeah Park opens daily for free tours 10–4:30. Metrorail's Hialeah Station is on the grounds of

Hialeah Park. *2200 E. 4th Ave., Hialeah, tel. 305/885–8000. Admission: grandstand $2, clubhouse $4, parking $1.50–$4 during racing season.*

Jai Alai **Miami Jai-Alai Fronton.** This game, invented in the Basque region of northern Spain, is the world's fastest. Jai-alai balls, called *pelotas,* have been clocked at speeds exceeding 170 mph. The game is played in a 176-foot-long court called a *fronton.* Players climb the walls to catch the ball in a *cesta*—a woven basket—with an attached glove. You bet on a team to win or on the order in which teams will finish. Built in 1926, Miami Jai-Alai is the oldest fronton in America. Each evening, it presents 13 games—some singles, some doubles. Located a mile east of Miami International Airport. *3500 N.W. 37th Ave., Miami, tel. 305/633–6400. Open nightly late Nov.–early Sept. except Sun., 7:15–midnight. Matinees Mon., Wed., and Sat. noon–5. Admission: $1, clubhouse $5. Dinner available.*

Rugby Without a large corporate organization, a regular office staff, or even a permanent home field, local rugby players have organized themselves into two regular teams. Although one team is called the *University of Miami Rugby Team,* it is not part of the university. The other is the *Miami Tridents.* Weekly throughout the year, a local rugby team plays a visiting team from a 16-team Florida league, from the Caribbean, or from a foreign ship in port. Both local teams participate each August in an annual tournament. Games Saturday 2 PM. *Holy Rosary Church, 9500 S.W. 184th St., Perrine. Spectators welcome. Free. For game information, call Bruce Swidarski, 8550 S.W. 126th Terr., Miami 33156, tel. 305/251–3305 (nights).*

Soccer **Miami Sharks.** This American Soccer League team played its first season in spring 1988. The Sharks' 1990 season includes at least 10 regular-season home games and five international exhibition games, all in the stadium at Milander Park (4800 Palm Ave., Hialeah). *Tickets: 240 E. 1st Ave., Suite 208, Hialeah 33010, tel. 305/888–0838 or Ticketmaster (see Important Addresses and Numbers).*

Tennis **Lipton International Players Championship (LIPC).** Shearson Lehman Brothers sponsors this two-week spring tournament at the 64-acre International Tennis Center of Key Biscayne. The tournament follows the Grand Slam format of the Australian, United States and French Opens and Wimbledon. The two main professional tennis organizations—Association of Tennis Professionals and Women's International Tennis Association—helped create this tournament and own part of it. *7300 Crandon Blvd., Key Biscayne, tel. for tickets 305/361–5252 or Ticketmaster (see Important Addresses and Numbers).*

Triathlon **Bud Light U.S. Triathlon Series.** Opens the triathlon season in May in Miami, with 1,500 participants in a 1.5-km swim, a 40-km bicycle ride, and a 10-km run. Swimmers swim .9 miles in 75-degree water in Biscayne Bay near Bicentennial Park. The 24.8-mile bike course goes from the Grand Prix course in downtown Miami to Key Biscayne and back. The 6.2-mile run loops around the Japanese Garden on Watson Island along the MacArthur Causeway. Contact CAT Sports, Inc. (5966 La Place Court, Suite 100, Carlsbad, CA 92008, tel. 619/438–8080), producer of the event.

Dining

by Rosalie Leposky You can eat your way around the world in Greater Miami, enjoying just about any kind of cuisine imaginable in every price category. The rich mix of nationalities here encourages individual restaurateurs and chefs to retain their culinary roots. Thus, Miami offers not just Latin fare but dishes distinctive to Spain, Cuba, Nicaragua, and other Hispanic countries; not just Oriental fare but specialties of China, India, Thailand, Vietnam, and other Asian cultures.

And don't neglect American fare just because it's not "foreign." Miami today is a center for innovation in regional cuisine and in combinations reflecting the diversity of domestic climates and cultures.

The most highly recommended restaurants in each price category are indicated by a star ★.

Category	Cost*
Very Expensive	over $55
Expensive	$35–$55
Moderate	$15–$35
Inexpensive	under $15

per person, excluding drinks, service, and 6% sales tax.

The following credit card abbreviations are used: AE, American Express; CB, Carte Blanche; DC, Diners Club; MC, MasterCard; V, Visa.

American
Coral Gables

Aragon Cafe. If George Merrick, the founder of Coral Gables, entered the bar of Aragon Cafe, he would see on display some of his mother's hand-painted china and silver and portraits of his sisters and wife on the dining room walls. In this new restaurant designed to look old and classy, subdued lighting emanates from gaslight-style chandeliers and etched-glass wall lights. The menu emphasizes fresh fish and reflects Merrick's desire to recreate the best of the Mediterranean in a Florida setting. Specialties include seafood minestrone made with shrimp, scallops, clams, new potatoes, carrots, and kidney and green beans; grilled goat cheese in banana leaves; grilled Florida dolphin with native starfruit sauce; and tuna steak au poivre in a mushroom-based sauce of peppercorns and cream. Dessert offerings include a white chocolate terrine with pistachio sauce. *180 Aragon Ave. in the Colonnade Hotel, Coral Gables 33134, tel. 305/448–9966. Reservations advised. Jacket required. No lunch Sat., no dinner Sun. Free valet parking. AE, DC, MC, V. Expensive.*

Downtown Miami
★

The Pavillon Grill. By day a private club, the Pavillon Grill becomes a gourmet restaurant at night. The mahogany, jade marble, and leather appointments of its salon and dining room exude the conservative classiness of an English private club. A harpist plays. The attentive staff serves regional American fare, including items that are low in calories, cholesterol, and sodium for diners who are on restricted diets. Specialties include marinated confit of duck and red Hawaiian papaya, grilled wild mushrooms, Pacific salmon pillows, cherry smoked lamb chops. The menu changes often. *100 Chopin Plaza, tel. 305/577–1000, ext. 4494 or 4462. Jacket and tie. Reservations required. AE, CB, DC, MC, V. Closed Sun. Very Expensive.*

Kendall
(S.W. Suburb)

Savannah Moon. Though you drive up to a typical shopping center, Savannah Moon's door leads to the foyer of a Southern mansion, complete with formal staircase. In the second-floor dining room, bentwood chairs, hanging plants, shuttered windows, sheer curtains, and original Audubon engravings suggest a tidewater inn. Evening and late-night entertainment —mellow blues, conservative jazz—makes the place popular with suburban professionals. This restaurant gives a nouvelle-cuisine twist to traditional Low Country coastal fare. Specialties include jambalaya (red rice with Creole sauce, chicken, shrimp, escargot, and Texas sausage); lamb with Southern Comfort sauce; and a dessert cart groaning with delights such as Kirsch-toasted almond cake, and southern bread pudding with nuts and raisins. *13505 South Dixie Hwy., tel. 305/238–8868. Jacket and tie. Reservations required on weekends, advised other times. AE, CB, DC, MC, V. No lunch on weekends. Expensive.*

Shorty's Bar-B-Q. Shorty Allen opened his barbecue restaurant in 1951 in a log cabin. Parents bring their teenage children to show them where mom and dad ate on their honeymoon. Huge fans circulate fresh air through the single screened dining room, where you dine family style at long picnic tables. The walls display an assortment of cowboy hats, horns, saddles, an ox yoke, and heads of boar and caribou. Specialties include barbecued pork ribs, chicken, and pork steak slow cooked over hickory logs and drenched in Shorty's own warm, spicy sauce, and side orders of tangy baked beans with big chunks of pork, corn on the cob, and coleslaw. *9200 South Dixie Hwy., tel. 305/665–5732. A second location opened in 1989 at 5989 South University Dr., Davie, tel. 305/680–9900. Dress: informal. Reservations not accepted. No credit cards. Closed Thanksgiving and Christmas. Inexpensive.*

North Miami Beach
★

Chef Allen's. In an art-deco world of glass block, neon trim, and fresh flowers, your gaze nonetheless remains riveted on the kitchen. Chef Allen Susser designed it with a picture window, 25 feet wide, so you can watch him create new American masterpieces almost too pretty to eat. Specialties include mesquite-grilled rare tuna with glazed onions and cranberry chutney; and lamb medallions with pine nuts and wilted spinach garnished with goat cheese. Desserts include white-chocolate macadamia nut torte, chocolate pizza, and a sugar junkie's delight—scoops of chocolate, raspberry, caramel, and pistachio ice cream floating in caramel sauce. Fine wines by the glass from a wine bar. *19088 N.E. 29th Ave., tel. 305/935–2900. Dress: informal weekdays, tie and jacket weekends. Reservations accepted. AE, MC, V. Closed for lunch weekends. Expensive.*

★

Max's Place. Owner/chef Mark Militello cooks *nouvelle* American regional fare in a special oak-burning oven imported from Genoa, behind a display case where you can admire the evening's selections of fish and meat awaiting preparation. The menu changes nightly, based on the availability of fresh ingredients. Typical selections include sea scallops and asparagus sautéed in butter and chardonnay with fresh basil, oregano, and thyme; wild mushrooms (shittake, tree oyster, chanterelles, angel trumpets, and brown hedgehog) roasted in the oak oven and served with grilled olive and walnut bread; whole yellowtail snapper with oriental ginger, black bean sauce, and a garnish of edible pansies; and cobia filet sautéed in brown butter mixed with orange segments, fresh mint, and bourbon. Desserts include chocolate espresso torte with a hazelnut crust and a warm apple tart with homemade vanilla and caramel sauce. *2286 N.E. 123rd St., North Miami 33181, tel. 305/893–6888. Reservations advised. Jacket and tie required. Closed Christmas. No lunch weekends. AE, DC, MC, V. Very Expensive.*

Chinese
Key Biscayne

Two Dragons. Robert Chow and his staff run this place like a small family restaurant, serving a Chinese cuisine with all ingredients fresh and prepared to order. Specialties include a Cantonese seafood nest (shrimp, scallops, and crabmeat with Chinese vegetables in a nest of crisp noodles), an orange beef Mandarin, and Szechuan eggplant with a spicy garlic-mustard sauce guaranteed to clear the sinuses. Dine in an intimate pagodalike booth behind hanging curtains of wooden beads or at an open table overlooking an outdoor Oriental garden. A Japanese steak house—the "second dragon"—serves Teppanyaki-style cuisine at six cooking tables in a separate room. *Sonesta Beach Hotel, 350 Ocean Dr., tel. 305/361–2021. Dress: semiformal. Dinner only. Reservations advised. AE, CB, DC, MC, V. Closed 2 weeks in Aug. or Sept. Moderate.*

South Miami

Tiger Tiger Teahouse. Design awards have been bestowed on Tiger Tiger's contemporary Chinese decor, with its embroidered silk panels depicting fierce tigers and its elegant rosewood chairs with jade cushions. Specialties include Peking duck (available without advance notice), lean and succulent beneath crisp orange-glazed skin, wrapped with plum sauce in wheat pancakes; hot, spicy Szechuan beef, marinated in sherry and spices, then stir-fried with Chinese vegetables; honey-garlic chicken; and creamy-smooth litchi ice cream. *The Bakery Center, 5785 Sunset Dr., tel. 305/665–5660. Dress: casual. Closed for lunch Sun. Reservations accepted. AE, CB, DC, MC, V. Closed Thanksgiving. Moderate.*

Continental
Coconut Grove
★

Grand Cafe. Understated elegance at all hours is the Grand Cafe's hallmark—a bilevel room with pink tablecloths and floral bouquets, sunbathed by day, dim and intimate after dark. Japanese-born, French-trained executive chef Katsuo Sugiura creates "international" cuisine, combining ingredients from all over the world in pleasing presentations that intrigue the palate. Specialties include black linguini (colored with squid ink); fresh smoked salmon; a superbly rich she-crab soup with roe, sherry, and cayenne pepper; "boned" Maine lobster presented in the shape of a lobster, with artichokes and a cream sauce of vermouth and saffron. Dessert specialties include a white-chocolate and pistachio mousse, with blackberry sauce and Beaujolais essence. The menu changes frequently. *2669 S. Bayshore Dr., tel. 305/858–9600. Jacket preferred. Reservations advised. AE, CB, DC, MC, V. Very Expensive.*

Kaleidoscope Restaurant. The tropical ambience here extends to a choice of indoor or outdoor seating—all in air-conditioned comfort, because fans blow cold air around a glass-roofed terrace overlooking a landscaped courtyard. Specialties include veal Oscar, and the chef's own fresh apple strudel. *3112 Com-*

Miami Area Dining

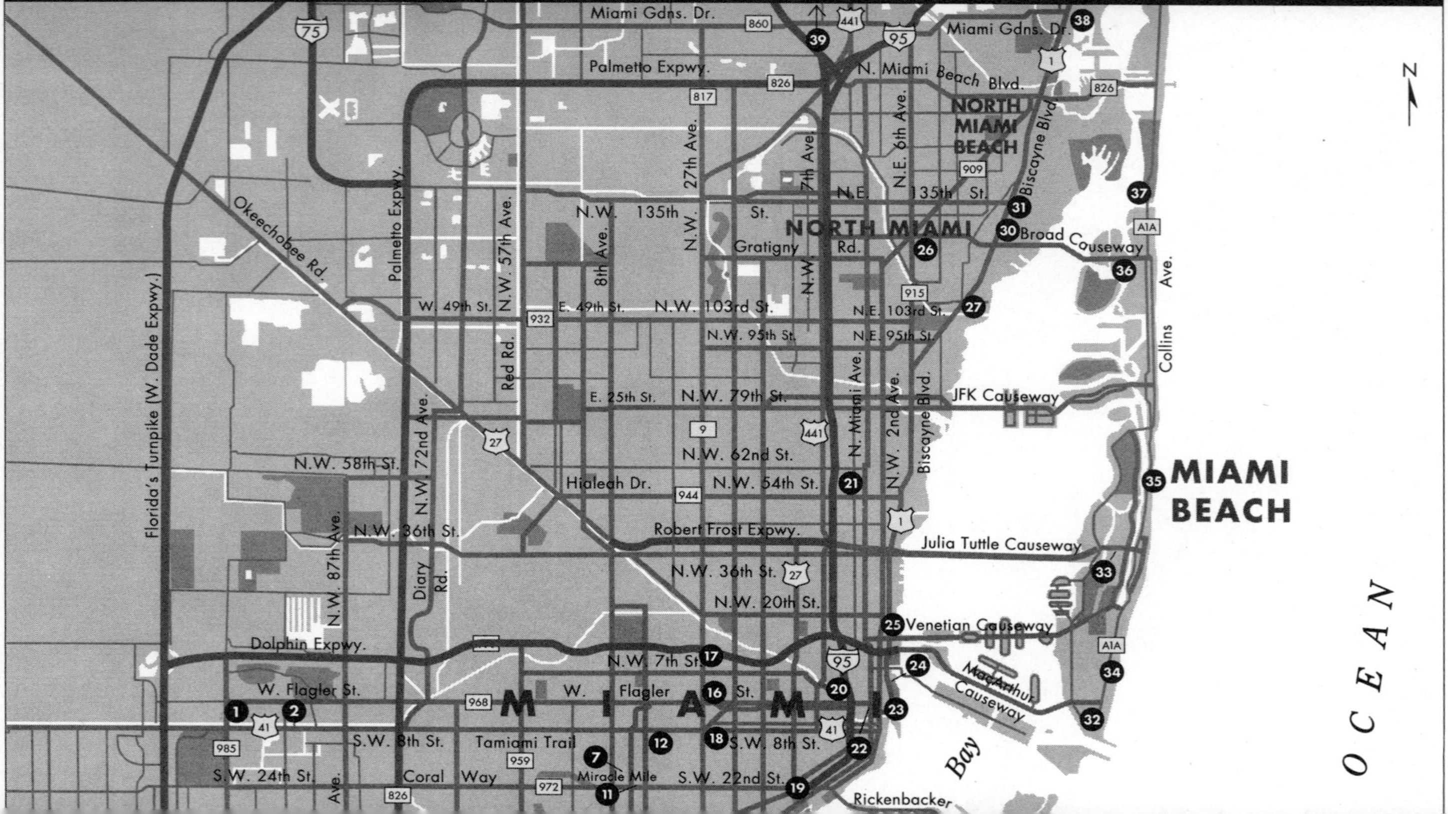

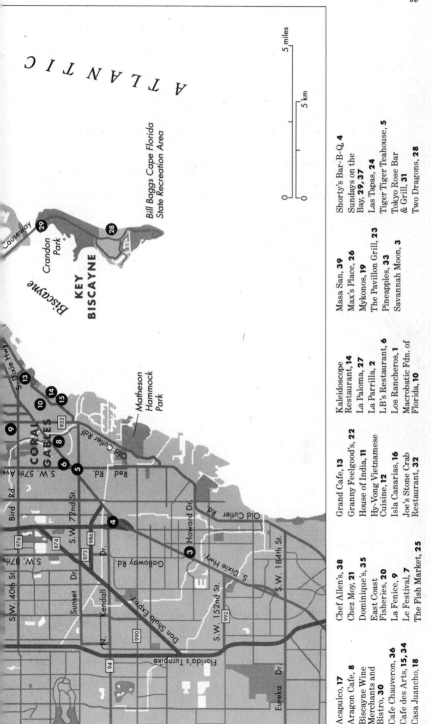

ATLANTIC

Biscayne Bay

KEY BISCAYNE

Crandon Park

Causeway **29**

28

Bill Baggs Cape Florida
State Recreation Area

5 miles

5 km

0

Matheson Hammock Park

S. Dixie Hwy.

13

10
14
15

9

8

953

CORAL GABLES

S.W. 57th Ave.

Old Cutler Rd.

Red Rd.

6
5

Bird Rd.

S.W. 72nd St.

976

874

986

973

4

Howard Dr.

Old Cutler Rd.

S.W. 184th St.

S.W. 40th St.

S.W. 87th

Sunset Dr.

Kendall Dr.

Galloway Rd.

3

S. Dixie Hwy.

S.W. 152nd St.

992

Don Shula Expwy.

N. Kendall Dr.

990

Florida's Turnpike

94

Eureka Dr.

Acapulco, **17**
Aragon Cafe, **8**
Biscayne Wine
Merchants and
Bistro, **30**
Cafe Chauveron, **36**
Cafe des Arts, **15, 34**
Casa Juancho, **18**

Chef Allen's, **38**
Chez Moy, **21**
Dominique's, **35**
East Coast
Fisheries, **20**
La Fenice, **9**
Le Festival, **7**
The Fish Market, **25**

Grand Cafe, **13**
Granny Feelgood's, **22**
House of India, **11**
Hy-Vong Vietnamese
Cuisine, **12**
Isla Canarias, **16**
Joe's Stone Crab
Restaurant, **32**

Kaleidoscope
Restaurant, **14**
La Paloma, **27**
La Parrilla, **2**
LB's Restaurant, **6**
Los Rancheros, **1**
Macrobatic Fdn. of
Florida, **10**

Masa San, **39**
Max's Place, **26**
Mykonos, **19**
The Pavillon Grill, **23**
Pineapples, **33**
Savannah Moon, **3**

Shorty's Bar-B-Q, **4**
Sundays on the
Bay, **29, 37**
Las Tapas, **24**
Tiger Tiger Teahouse, **5**
Tokyo Rose Bar
& Grill, **31**
Two Dragons, **28**

modore Plaza, tel. 305/446–5010. Dress: casual. Reservations advised. AE, CB, DC, MC, V. Moderate.

North Miami   **Biscayne Wine Merchants and Bistro.** In this 35-seat retail beer and wine store with a deli counter, strangers often become friends while sharing tables and sampling the merchandise. Owners Jan Sitko and Esther Flores stock over 300 wines (sold by the glass or bottle) and over 60 brands of beer. The menu changes daily but always includes bean and cream soups. Typical fare may include chicken Crustaces (a chicken breast stuffed with leeks, dill, and crab with a light dill sauce) and daily fresh fish specials such as amberjack, dolphin, shark, snapper, swordtail, and wahoo. Sitko and Flores like to create new dishes with fresh herbs, spices, fruits, and vegetables. One favorite is a tangy-sweet sauce with jalapeno and citrus. *12953 Biscayne Blvd., North Miami, tel. 305/899–1997. No Reservations. Dress: informal. Closed Thanksgiving, Christmas, and New Year's Day. No lunch weekends. AE, MC, V. Moderate.*

La Paloma. This fine Swiss Continental restaurant offers a total sensory experience: fine food, impeccable service, and the ambience of an art museum. In sideboards and cases throughout, owners Werner and Maria Staub display ornate European antiques that they have spent decades collecting. The treasures include Bacarrat crystal, Limoges china, Meissen porcelains, and Sevres clocks. The staff speak Spanish, French, German, Portuguese, or Arabic. Specialties include fresh local fish and seafood; Norwegian salmon Caroline (poached, served on a bed of spinach with hollandaise sauce); Wiener schnitzel; lamb chops à la *diable* (coated with bread crumbs, mustard, garlic, and herbs) passion-fruit sorbet; and kiwi soufflé with raspberry sauce. *10999 Biscayne Blvd., tel. 305/891–0505. Jackets requested. Reservations advised. AE, MC, V. Closed Mon. and July and part of Aug. Expensive.*

Cuban   **Islas Canarias.** A gathering place for Cuban poets, pop music
Little Havana   stars, and media personalities. Wall murals depict a Canary Islands street scene and an indigenous dragon tree *(Dracaena draco)*. The menu includes such Canary Islands dishes as baked lamb, ham hocks with boiled potatoes, and *tortilla Española* (a Spanish omelet with onions and chorizo sausage), as well as Cuban standards, including palomilla steak, and fried kingfish. Don't miss the three superb varieties of homemade chips— potato, malanga, and plantain. Islas Canarias has another location in Westchester. *285 N.W. Unity Blvd. (N.W. 27th Ave.), tel. 305/649–0440. Dress: informal. Reservations not accepted. No credit cards. Inexpensive.*

Family Style   **LB's Restaurant.** Town and gown meet at this sprout-laden ha-
Coral Gables   ven a half-block from the University of Miami's baseball stadium. Kitschy food-related posters plaster the walls. Relaxed atmosphere, low prices, no waiters. You order at the counter and pick up your food when called. Vegetarians thrive on LB's salads and daily meatless entrees, such as lasagna and moussaka. Famous for Saturday night lobster. (If you plan to come after 8, call ahead to reserve a lobster.) Other specialties include barbecued baby-back ribs, lime chicken, croissant sandwiches, and carrot cake. *5813 Ponce de León Blvd., tel. 305/661–7091. Dress: informal. Reservations not accepted. No credit cards. Closed Sun. Inexpensive.*

French
Coral Gables

Le Festival. The modest canopied entrance to this classical French restaurant understates the elegance within. Decor includes etched-glass filigree mirrors and light pink walls. Specialties include appetizers of salmon mousse, baked oysters with garlic butter, and lobster in champagne sauce en croute; rack of lamb (for two), and medallions of veal with two sauces—a pungent, creamy lime sauce and a dark port-wine sauce with mushrooms. Entrées come with real french-fried potatoes. Don't pass up dessert here; the mousses and soufflés are positively decadent. *2120 Salzedo St., tel. 305/442–8545. Jacket and tie. Reservations required for dinner, and for lunch parties of 5 or more. AE, MC, V. Closed Sat. noon, all day Sun., and Sept.–Oct. Expensive.*

Miami Beach
★

Cafe Chauveron. André Chauveron traces his cafe's roots to Cafe Chambord, which his father began in New York in 1935 on the block where the Citicorp Building now stands. A Florida institution since 1972, Cafe Chauveron serves classical French cuisine in rooms decorated with original paintings and wood paneling. The atmosphere is hushed, the service superb. Mounted pheasants guard the wine cabinet. Specialties include wild duck and pheasant pâté, filet of sole *bonne femme*, frogs' legs Provençale, sautéed veal chop Bercy (white wine and shallots) with braised endive, and dessert soufflés flambéed at tableside. *9561 E. Bay Harbor Dr., tel. 305/866–8779. Jacket and tie. Reservations required. AE, CB, DC, MC, V. Closed Aug.–Sept. Very Expensive.*

Cafe des Arts. Enjoy French-provincial cuisine in an art-deco setting amid tropical plants, antiques, and an art gallery that changes every six to eight weeks. Indoor and outdoor seating. Specialties include smoked-salmon pasta with artichokes, mushrooms, and brie sauce; roast duck in grape sauce; and quail salad. *918 Ocean Dr., tel. 305/534–6267. In 1989, a second location was opened at 3138 Commodore Plaza, Coconut Grove, tel. 305/446–3634. Dress: casual. Reservations advised. AE, MC, V. Closed 2 weeks in Aug. Moderate.*

★ **Dominique's.** Woodwork and mirrors from a Vanderbilt home and other demolished New York mansions create an intimate setting for a unique nouvelle-cuisine dining experience. Specialties include exotic appetizers, such as buffalo sausage, sautéed alligator tail, and rattlesnake-meat salad; rack of lamb (which accounts for 35% of the restaurant's total sales) and fresh seafood; and an extensive wine list. The restaurant also serves brunch on Sunday. *Alexander Hotel, 5225 Collins Ave., tel. 305/865–6500. Jacket required. Reservations advised. AE, CB, DC, MC, V. Very Expensive.*

Greek
Southwest Miami

Mykonos. A family restaurant serving typical Greek fare in a Spartan setting—a single 74-seat room adorned with Greek travel posters. Specialties include gyro; moussaka; marinated lamb and chicken; kalamari (squid) and octopus sautéed in wine and onions; and sumptuous Greek salads thick with feta cheese and briny olives. *1201 Coral Way, tel. 305/856–3140. Dress: informal. Reservations accepted for dinner. AE. Closed Sun. at noon, Christmas, and New Year's Day. Inexpensive.*

Haitian
Little Haiti

Chez Moy. Seating is outside on a shaded patio or in a pleasant room with oak tables and high-backed chairs. Specialties include *grillot* (pork boiled, then fried with spices); fried or boiled fish; stewed goat; and conch with garlic and hot pepper. Try a tropical fruit drink, such as sweet sop (also called *anon or* *cachiman)* or sour sop (also called *guanabana* or *corrosol)* blended with milk and sugar, and sweet potato pie for dessert. *1 N.W. 54th St., tel. 305/756-7540. Dress: informal. No reservations. No smoking allowed inside. MC, V. Moderate.*

Indian
Coral Gables
★

House of India. The haunting strains of sitar music lull diners at this popular spot in Coral Gables. Specialties include hot coconut soup with cardamon, milk, rose water, and sugar; curried goat; and authentic chicken tandoori, cooked in a clay oven. The weekday luncheon buffet is a good bargain. *22 Merrick Way, tel. 305/444-2348. Dress: casual. Weekend reservations accepted. AE, MC, V. Closed for Sun. lunch, Labor Day, Christmas. Moderate.*

Italian
Coral Gables

La Fenice. The restaurant is named for the Venice opera house that rose, phoenixlike, from the ashes of an earlier structure after an 1831 fire; and it is decorated with paintings of St. Mark's Square in Venice, ornate mahogany chairs from Padua, a four-tier fountain, and stained-glass windows. Specialties include rigatoni in creamy vodka sauce topped with caviar; veal scallopini sautéed with Gorgonzola cheese, cream sauce, and mushrooms; and poached salmon with a sauce of sweet red peppers pureed with lemon juice. *2728 Ponce de León Blvd., tel. 305/445-6603. Jacket and tie. Reservations advised. AE, MC, V. Closed Sat.-Sun. noon. Moderate.*

Japanese
North Miami

Tokyo Rose Bar & Grill. Starkly modern decor—neon lights against a minimalist black-and-white backdrop—complements the menu concept of contemporary Japanese fare. While nibbling on a bowl of boiled soybeans, you choose from an extensive à la carte menu or a selection of daily Japanese- and American-style specials. Typical offerings include California Naki, a nori roll with crab, avocado, and cucumber served with *wasabi* (horseradish) and ginger; Kamikaza salad, a conch salad with cucumber and a spicy Korean-style hot pepper dressing; Ginza strip, rare sirloin marinated in vinegar and sesame; Kaizoku, a pasta dish with calamari, scallops, and shrimp in white wine sauce; Tokyo's salmon, prepared with Japanese mayo, flying fish eggs *(masago)*, onions, and lemon butter; and fresh Japanese desserts with coconut-flour crust. Owner Masa Yamazaki plans to open a Japanese bakery next door to Tokyo Rose in late 1989. *13400 Biscayne Blvd., North Miami 33181, tel. 305/945-7782. Dress: neat but casual. Reservations advised. No lunch. Live jazz by Kenny Millions Tues.-Sat. AE, DC, MC, V. Moderate.*

Masa-San. Owner Masa Yamazaki, a Tokyo native who came to the University of Miami in 1971 to study marketing, opened this traditional Japanese restaurant in 1980. It's in a Japanese-style building with a high wood ceiling, rice-paper windows, a tropical fish aquarium, and an 18-seat sushi bar. All sushi is made to order, depending on what Japanese and local fish are available. Try cobia (a species of sea catfish) in sashimi and sushi. Specialties include smoked freshwater eel sushi; *wakame* (Japanese seaweed) with dried squid, herring eggs, ginger, and cucumber; *koba* (seaweed) with ponzu sauce (soy sauce, vinegar, sweet cooking wine, anon juice, sesame seeds, and scallions); Chinese shark's-fin soup garnished with whole hard-boiled quail eggs; *harumaki*, a Japanese-style eggroll containing bean sprouts, broccoli, cabbage, carrots, celery, and onions; *komochi-age*, deep fried mushroom with seafood stuffing; tempura with a light, crisp batter; and teriyaki. *19355 N.W. 2nd*

Ave. (US 441), Miami 33169, tel. 305/651–7782. Dress: neat but casual. Reservations advised. No lunch weekends. Closed July 4 and Thanksgiving. AE, DC, MC, V. Moderate.

Mexican
Little Havana

Acapulco. Authentic Mexican cuisine in an intimate 70-seat room with adobe walls, wooden beams, tabletops of Mexican tiles, and sombreros and serapes on the walls. As soon as you sit down, a waiter descends on you with a free, ample supply of *totopos*, homemade corn chips served hot and crunchy, salt free, with a fiery *pico de gallo* sauce. Specialties include a rich, chunky guacamole; *carnitas asadas* (marinated pork chunks in lemon and butter sauce); *mole poblano* (chicken in chocolate sauce); shrimp and rice in a cherry wine sauce; and combination platters of tacos, burritos, and enchiladas. 727 N.W. Unity Blvd. (N.W. 27th Ave.), tel. 305/642–6961. Dress: informal. Weekend reservations required. AE, CB, DC, MC, V. Inexpensive.

Natural
Coconut Grove

Macrobiotic Foundation of Florida. All-natural meals are prepared fresh daily with organic vegetables, seeds, grains, and fruits to balance acid and alkaline, Yin and Yang. Even if you don't share this philosophy, the people are nice and the food is tasty. Meals are served boardinghouse style at long tables in a former church parish house. Specialties include miso soup, whole grains, pasta primavera and *arame* (an edible seaweed). International Night, on Friday, features cuisine of a different country each week. 3291 Franklin Ave., tel. 305/448–6625. Dress: informal. Reservations required. No smoking allowed. Sunday brunch. MC, V. Closed for lunch Sat. and dinner Mon., Wed., and Sun. Moderate.

Downtown Miami

Granny Feelgood's. "Granny" is a shrewd gentleman named Irving Field, who caters to health-conscious lawyers, office workers, and cruise-ship crews at five locations. Specialties include chicken salad with raisins, apples, and cinnamon; spinach fettuccine with pine nuts; grilled tofu; apple crumb cake; and carrot cake. 190 S.E. 1st Ave., tel. 305/358–6233. Dress: casual. No reservations. No smoking in restaurant. AE, MC, V. Closed Sun. Inexpensive.

Miami Beach

Pineapples. Art-deco pink pervades this health-food store and restaurant. Specialties include Chinese egg rolls; lasagna filled with tofu and mushrooms; spinach fettuccine with feta cheese, fresh garlic, walnuts, and cream sauce; and salads with a full-flavored Italian-style dressing. 530 Arthur Godfrey Rd., tel. 305/538–0350. Dress: casual. No reservations. No smoking in restaurant. AE, MC, V. Moderate.

Nicaraguan
Little Managua

La Parrilla. Ten miles west of downtown Miami, about 50,000 Nicaraguans have moved into the Fontainebleau Park subdivision and the tiny suburban town of Sweetwater. Typical of their fare are the beef and fish at La Parilla (Spanish for "the grille"), where hanging plants and sloping barrel-tile roofs above the booths create a rural ambience. An adjoining bar is popular with Nicaraguan *contras*. Specialties include *gallos pintos* (red beans and rice); *chicharron* (fried pork with yucca); and *pargo a la Tipitapa*, baby red snapper fried and served whole in Creole sauce with onions and peppers. 9611 W. Flagler St., tel. 305/553–4419. Dress: informal. Reservations accepted. AE, CB, DC, MC, V. Moderate.

Los Ranchos. Julio Somoza, owner of Los Ranchos and nephew of Nicaragua's late president, Anastasio Somoza, fled to south

Florida in 1979. Somoza sustains a tradition begun 30 years ago in Managua, when the original Los Ranchos instilled in Nicaraguan palates a love of Argentine-style beef—lean, grass-fed tenderloin with *chimichurri*, a green sauce of chopped parsley, garlic, oil, vinegar, and other spices. Nicaragua's own sauces are a tomato-based marinara and the fiery *cebollitas encurtidas*, with slices of jalapeño pepper and onion pickled in vinegar. Specialties include *chorizo* (sausage); *cuajada con maduro* (skim cheese with fried bananas); and shrimp sautéed in butter and topped with a creamy jalapeño sauce. *125 S.W. 107th Ave., tel. 305/221–9367. Also at Bayside Marketplace. Dress: informal. Reservations advised, especially on weekends. AE, CB, DC, MC, V. Closed Good Friday, Christmas, New Year's Day. Moderate.*

Seafood
Downtown Miami

East Coast Fisheries. This family-owned restaurant and retail fish market on the Miami River features fresh Florida seafood from its own 38-boat fleet in the Keys. From tables along the second-floor balcony railing, watch the cooks prepare your dinner in the open kitchen below. Specialties include a complimentary fish-pâté appetizer, blackened pompano with owner David Swartz's personal herb-and-spice recipe, lightly breaded fried grouper, and a homemade Key-lime pie so rich it tastes like ice cream. *360 W. Flagler St., tel. 305/373–5515. Dress: informal. Beer and wine only. AE, MC, V. Inexpensive.*

The Fish Market. Tucked away in a corner of the Omni International Hotel's lobby, this fine restaurant boasts waiters fluent in French, German, and Spanish and a kitchen staff fluent in seafood's complexities. The menu changes with availability of fresh fish, fruits, and vegetables. Typical menu items include smoked salmon and dolphin mousse; seafood ravioli filled with shrimp, lobster, and scallop puree in a sauce made with ginger, white wine, and cream; and seafood sausage made from ground grouper, scallops gelatin, and cream served with brandied lobster sauce over Julienne carrots and celery. Daily seafood specials may include bluefish, dolphin, lemon sole, marlin, pompano, puppy shark, redfish, sea bass, sea trout, and tuna. Desserts include chocolate Key lime pie with a Graham-cracker crust and pistachio chocolate terrine with orange cream sauce. *Biscayne Blvd. at 16th St., Miami 33132, tel. 305/374–0000. Reservations accepted. Jacket required. Closed Sun. Free valet parking. AE, DC, MC, V. Expensive.*

Key Biscayne

Sundays on the Bay. Two locations overlook the water—the Crandon Park Marina at Key Biscayne and the Intracoastal Waterway at Haulover. Both have inside dining and outdoor decks, bars, live bands nightly playing reggae and top 40 hits, and an energetic young serving staff. Specialties from an extensive seafood menu include conch fritters, conch chowder (tomato-based, served with sherry and Tabasco sauce), and baked grouper topped with crabmeat and shrimp scampi. *Key Biscayne: 5420 Crandon Blvd., tel. 305/361–6777; Haulover Beach Park: 10880 Collins Ave., tel. 305/945–5115. Dress: informal. Reservations accepted; advised for Sun. brunch. AE, CB, DC, MC, V. Moderate.*

Miami Beach
★

Joe's Stone Crab Restaurant. A south Florida tradition since 1913, Joe's is a family restaurant in its fourth generation. You go to wait, people watch, and finally settle down to an ample à la carte menu. Joe's serves about a ton of stone crab claws a day, with drawn butter, lemon wedges, and a piquant mustard sauce (recipe available). Popular side orders include a vinegary coleslaw, salad with a brisk house vinaigrette dressing, creamed garlic spinach, french-fried onion rings and eggplant, and hash brown potatoes. Save room for dessert—a slice of Key-lime pie with graham cracker crust and real whipped cream or apple pie with a crumb-pecan topping. *227 Biscayne St., tel. 305/673-0365. Dress: informal, but no T-shirts, tank tops, or shorts. No reservations; to minimize the wait, come for lunch before 11:30, for dinner before 5 or after 9. AE, CB, DC, MC, V. Closed May 15–Oct. 15. Moderate.*

Spanish
Downtown Miami

Las Tapas. *Tapas*—"little dishes"—come in appetizer-size portions to give you a variety of tastes during a single meal. Specialties include *la tostada* (smoked salmon on melba toast, topped with a dollop of sour cream, across which are laid baby eels, black caviar, capers, and chopped onion) and *samfaina con lomo* (eggplant, zucchini, green pepper, onions, tomato, and garlic sautéed with two thin, delicately flavored slices of fresh boneless pork loin). Also available are soups, salads, sandwiches, and standard dinners. *Bayside Marketplace, 401 Biscayne Blvd., tel. 305/372-2737. Dress: casual. Reservations for large parties only. AE, CB, DC, MC, V. Moderate.*

Little Havana
★

Casa Juancho. A meeting place for the movers and shakers of Miami's Cuban community, Casa Juancho serves a cross section of Spanish regional cuisines. The interior recalls old Castile: brown brick, rough-hewn dark timbers, and walls adorned with colorful Talavera platters. Strolling Spanish balladeers will serenade you. Specialties include *cochinillo Segoviano* (roast suckling pig), and *parrillada de mariscos* (fish, shrimps, squid, and scallops grilled in a light garlic sauce) from the Pontevedra region of northwest Spain. For dessert, the *crema Catalana* has a delectable crust of burnt caramel atop a rich pastry custard. The wine list includes fine labels from Spain's Rioja region. *2436 S.W. 8th St., tel. 305/642-2452. Dress: semiformal. Reservations advised; not accepted after 8 PM Fri. and Sat. AE, CB, DC, MC, V. Closed Christmas Eve. Expensive.*

Vietnamese
Little Havana
★

Hy-Vong Vietnamese Cuisine. Chef and part owner Tung Nguyen's magic has poured forth from the tiny kitchen of this 36-seat restaurant since 1980. Now the word is out, so come before 7 PM to avoid a long wait. Specialties include spring rolls, a Vietnamese version of an egg roll, with ground pork, cellophane noodles, and black mushrooms wrapped in homemade rice paper; a whole fish panfried with *nuoc man* (a garlic-lime fish sauce); and thinly sliced pork, barbecued with sesame seeds and fish sauce, served with bean sprouts, rice noodles, and slivers of carrots, almonds, and peanuts. *3458 S.W. 8th St., tel. 305/446-3674. Dress casual. Reservations accepted for 5 or more. No smoking. No credit cards. Closed Mon., American and Vietnamese/Chinese New Years, and 2 weeks in Aug. Moderate.*

Lodging

Few urban areas can match Greater Miami's diversity of hotel accommodations. The area has hundreds of hotels and motels with lodgings in all price categories, from $8 for a night in a dormitory-style hostel bed to $2,000 for a night in the luxurious presidential suite atop a posh downtown hotel.

As recently as the 1960s, many hotels in Greater Miami opened only in the winter to accommodate Yankee "snowbirds." Now most stay open all year. In summer, they cater to business travelers and to vacationers from the American South and Latin America who find Miami quite congenial despite the heat, humidity, and intense thunderstorms almost every afternoon.

Although some hotels (especially on the mainland) have adopted year-round rates, many still adjust their rates to reflect the ebb and flow of seasonal demand. The peak occurs in winter, with only a slight dip in summer when families with schoolchildren take vacations. You'll find the best values between Easter and Memorial Day (a delightful time in Miami but a difficult time for many people to travel), and in September and October (the height of hurricane season).

The list that follows is a representative selection of the best hotels and motels, organized geographically.

The rate categories in the list are based on the all-year or peak-season price; off-peak rates may be a category or two lower.

The most highly recommended places in each price category are indicated by a star ★.

Category	Cost*
Very Expensive	over $120
Expensive	$90–$120
Moderate	$50–$90
Inexpensive	under $50

All prices are for a standard double room, excluding 6% state sales tax and nominal tourist tax.

The following credit card abbreviations are used: AE, American Express; CB, Carte Blanche; DC, Diners Club; MC, MasterCard; V, Visa.

Coconut Grove   **Doubletree Hotel at Coconut Grove.** This high rise with a bay view was built in 1970 and renovated in 1988. Rooms are large, most with balcony, comfortable chairs, armoires, original artwork. Choice of a mauve or turquoise color scheme. Best rooms are on upper floors with bay views. Homemade chocolate-chip cookies are offered to arriving guests. *2649 S. Bayshore Dr., Coconut Grove, 33133, tel. 305/858–2500 or 800/528–0444. 190 rooms with bath, including 32 nonsmoker rooms, and 3 rooms for handicapped guests. Facilities: outdoor freshwater pool, 2 tennis courts, restaurant, bar. Guests have access to Casablanca, a private club on the top floor. AE, CB, DC, MC, V. Expensive.*

★   **Grand Bay Hotel.** This modern high rise overlooks Biscayne

Bay; rooms have traditional furnishings and original art. The building's stairstep facade, like a Mayan pyramid, gives each room facing the bay a private terrace. Best views, at the northeast corner, include downtown Miami. The staff pays meticulous attention to guests' desires. Only slightly more special than most rooms is 814, Luciano Pavarotti's two-level suite with a baby-grand piano, circular staircase, and canopied king-size bed. You can rent it when he's not there. *2669 S. Bayshore Dr., Coconut Grove 33133, tel. 305/858-9600. 181 rooms with bath, including 48 suites, 20 nonsmoker rooms. Facilities: outdoor pool, hot tub, health club, saunas, masseur, afternoon tea in lobby, gourmet restaurant and lounge, poolside bar. AE, CB, DC, MC, V. Very Expensive.*

★ **Grove Isle.** This luxurious mid-rise urban resort sits on a 26-acre island and adjoins the equally posh condominium apartment towers and private club. Developer Martin Margulies displays selections from his extensive private art collection on the premises *(see* Exploring). The oversized rooms have patios, bay views, ceiling fans, and tropical decor with area rugs and Spanish tiles. The rooms with the most light and best bay view are 201–205. *4 Grove Isle Dr., Coconut Grove 33133, tel. 305/858-8300 or 800/858-8300. 49 rooms with bath, including 9 suites. Facilities: outdoor freshwater swimming pool and whirlpool; 12 tennis courts; 85-slip marina; 40-ft. sailboat that guests can charter; health spa with saunas and steam rooms, Nautilus equipment, masseur and masseuse, running track around the island; in-room refreshment bar and coffee maker; free cable TV; free movies in room; complimentary Continental breakfast; restaurant with indoor and outdoor seating. AE, CB, DC, MC, V. Very Expensive.*

Mayfair House. This European-style luxury hotel sits within an exclusive open-air shopping mall *(see* Exploring). Public areas have Tiffany windows, polished mahogany, marble walls and floors, and imported ceramics and crystal. A glassed-in elevator whisks you to the corridor on your floor—a balcony overlooking the mall's central fountains and walkways. In all suites, outdoor terraces face the street, screened from view by vegetation and wood latticework. Each has a Japanese hot tub on the balcony or a Roman tub in the bathroom. Otherwise, each suite is unique in size and furnishings. Sunset (Room 505) is one of 48 suites with antique pianos. Some aspects of the building's design are quirky; you can get lost looking for the ballroom or restaurant, and, in many rooms, you must stand in the bathtub to turn on the water. The worst suite for sleeping is Featherfern (Room 356), from which you can hear the band one floor below in the club. *3000 Florida Ave., Coconut Grove 33133, tel. 305/441-0000 or 800/433-4555. 181 suites, including 22 nonsmoker suites. Facilities: rooftop recreation area with sauna in a barrel, small outdoor freshwater swimming pool, and snack bar; preferred shopper card for discounts in mall shops; complimentary airport limousine service. AE, CB, DC, MC, V. Very Expensive.*

Coral Gables **The Biltmore Hotel.** A historic high rise built in 1926, the Biltmore was restored and renovated in 1986 and reopened as a luxury hotel, but the luxury exists primarily in the historic, restored public spaces *(see* Exploring). The rooms have high-quality furnishings befitting their price tag, but they are nondescript, lacking the boom-time ambience you might expect from such a legendary property. The service can be uneven.

Miami Area Lodging

OCEAN

MIAMI BEACH

NORTH MIAMI BEACH

NORTH MIAMI

Miami Gdns. Dr.

Miami Gdns. Dr.

N. Miami Beach Blvd.

Biscayne Blvd.

Broad Causeway

Collins Ave.

Collins

JFK Causeway

Julia Tuttle Causeway

Biscayne Blvd.

N. Miami Ave.

N.W. 2nd Ave

N.E. 2nd Ave.

N.E. 6th Ave.

N.E. 135th St.

N.E. 103rd St.

N.E. 95th St.

Gratigny Rd.

N.W. 7th Ave.

N.W. 27th Ave.

N.W. 8th Ave.

N.W. 135th St.

N.W. 103rd St.

N.W. 95th St.

N.W. 79th St.

N.W. 62nd St.

N.W. 54th St.

Robert Frost Expwy.

N.W. 36th St.

N.W. 20th St

E. 25th St.

E. 49th St.

Hialeah Dr.

W. 4th Ave.

W. 49th St.

Red Rd.

Palmetto Expwy.

Palmetto Expwy.

Okeechobee Rd.

Diary Rd.

N.W. 36th St.

N.W. 72nd Ave.

N.W. 58th St.

W. 87th Ave.

Miami River

Palmetto Expwy.

Beach Blvd.

N

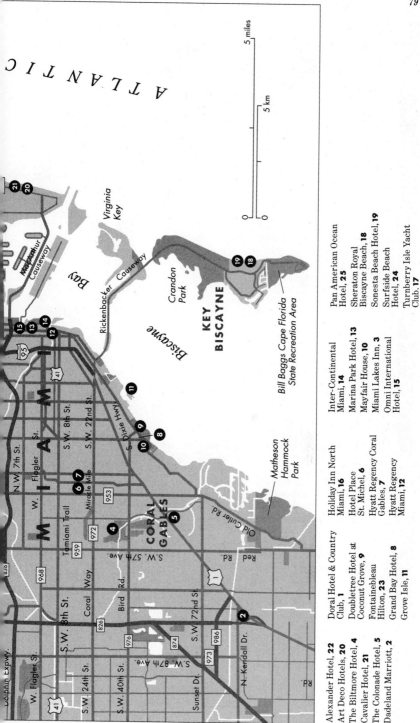

ATLANTIC

MIAMI

Virginia
Key

MacArthur Causeway

Biscayne
Bay

Rickenbacker Causeway

Crandon
Park

KEY
BISCAYNE

Biscayne

Bill Baggs Cape Florida
State Recreation Area

Matheson
Hammock
Park

CORAL
GABLES

Miracle Mile

Tamiami Trail

Coral Way

Bird Rd.

Sunset Dr.

Dolphin Expwy.

W. Flagler St.

S.W. 24th St.

S.W. 40th St.

S.W. 8th St.

S.W. 87th Ave.

S.W. 72nd St.

N. Kendall Dr.

Rd.

N.W. 7th St.

W. Flagler St.

S.W. 8th St.

S.W. 22nd St.

S. Dixie Hwy.

S.W. 57th Ave.

Red Rd.

Old Cutler Rd.

5 miles

5 km

Alexander Hotel, **22**
Art Deco Hotels, **20**
The Biltmore Hotel, **4**
Cavalier Hotel, **21**
The Colonade Hotel, **5**
Dadeland Marriott, **2**

Doral Hotel & Country
Club, **1**
Doubletree Hotel at
Coconut Grove, **9**
Fontainebleau
Hilton, **23**
Grand Bay Hotel, **8**
Grove Isle, **11**

Holiday Inn North
Miami, **16**
Hotel Place
St. Michel, **6**
Hyatt Regency Coral
Gables, **7**
Hyatt Regency
Miami, **12**

Inter-Continental
Miami, **14**
Marina Park Hotel, **13**
Mayfair House, **10**
Miami Lakes Inn, **3**
Omni International
Hotel, **15**

Pan American Ocean
Hotel, **25**
Sheraton Royal
Biscayne Beach, **18**
Sonesta Beach Hotel, **19**
Surfside Beach
Hotel, **24**
Turnberry Isle Yacht
Club. **17**

Without telling guests in the tower suites, the management often turns off the tower elevators to discourage sightseers from going up there. Upper-floor rooms facing north and east toward the airport, downtown Miami, and Biscayne Bay have the most spectacular views but more airplane noise. *1200 Anastasia Ave., Coral Gables 33134, tel. 305/445–1926 or 800/445–2586. 275 rooms with bath, including 45 suites. Facilities: 18-hole championship golf course, 10 lighted tennis courts, health spa with sauna, swimming pool, restaurant, coffee shop, and lounge. AE, CB, DC, MC, V. Very Expensive.*

★ **The Colonnade Hotel.** The twin 13-story towers of this $65-million hotel, office, and shopping complex dominate the heart of Coral Gables, echoing architecturally the adjoining two-story Corinthian-style rotunda on Miracle Mile from which 1920s developer George Merrick sold lots in his fledgling city. Merrick's family provided old photos, paintings, and other heirlooms that are on display throughout the hotel. The oversize rooms come in 26 different floor plans, each with a sitting area, built-in armoires, and traditional furnishings of mahogany. The hospitality bars have marble counters and gold-plated faucets with 1920s-style ceramic handles. The pool is on a 10th-floor terrace, which offers a magnificent view south toward Biscayne Bay. *180 Aragon Ave., Coral Gables 33134, tel. 305/441–2600 or 800/533–1337. 157 rooms, including 17 suites, 18 nonsmoker rooms, and 4 rooms for handicapped guests. Facilities: outdoor heated pool with 2 saunas, Nautilus exercise equipment, 24-hr room service, 2 restaurants. AE, DC, MC, V. Very Expensive.*

★ **Hotel Place St. Michel.** Historic low-rise urban hotel built in 1926 and restored 1981–86. Art-nouveau chandeliers suspended from vaulted ceilings grace the public areas of this intimate jewel in the heart of downtown Coral Gables. Paddle fans circulate the air, filled with the scent of fresh flowers. Each room has its own dimension, personality, and imported antiques from England, Scotland, and France. *162 Alcazar Ave., Coral Gables 33134, tel. 305/444–1666. 28 rooms with bath, including 3 suites. Facilities: welcome basket of fruit and cheese in every room, Continental breakfast, restaurant, lounge, French snack shop. AE, CB, DC, MC, V. Moderate.*

★ **Hyatt Regency Coral Gables.** This urban high rise caters to business travelers. Opened in 1987, the hotel is part of a megastructure that includes two office towers. The entire structure follows the area tradition of Spanish Mediterranean architecture, with tile roofs, white-frame casement windows, and pink-stucco exterior. The hotel's interior decor of pastel hues and antique-style furnishings gives a comfortable, residential feel to the rooms and public areas. The best rooms face the pool; the worst face north toward the airport. *500 Alhambra Plaza, Coral Gables 33134, tel. 305/441–1234. 242 rooms with bath, including 50 suites, 45 nonsmoker rooms. Facilities: 2,900-sq.-ft. ballroom, restaurant, lounge, rooftop swimming pool, outdoor whirlpool, health club with Nautilus equipment and Life Cycles, and sauna and steam rooms. AE, CB, DC, MC, V. Very Expensive.*

Downtown Miami
★ **Hotel Inter-Continental Miami.** Stand on the fifth-floor recreation plaza and gaze up at this granite 34-story monolith that appears to be arching over you. This optical illusion aside, the Inter-Continental deals in congenial realities. The grain in the lobby's marble floor matches that in *The Spindle,* a massive

centerpiece sculpture by Henry Moore. With all that marble, the lobby could easily look like a mausoleum—and did before the addition of palm trees, colorful umbrellas, and wicker chairs and tables. Atop a five-story atrium, a skylight lets the afternoon sun pour in. The triangular hotel tower offers bay, port, and city views that improve with height. *100 Chopin Plaza, Miami 33131, tel. 305/577–1000 or 800/327–0200. 645 rooms with bath, including 34 suites, 48 nonsmoker rooms; corner rooms have extra-wide doors for handicapped guests. Facilities: out-door heated freshwater swimming pool beside the bay, 2 lighted clay tennis courts, 2 indoor racquetball courts, ¼-mile jogging track with rubber surface, in-room minibar, restaurants, nightclub, and lounge. AE, CB, DC, MC, V. Very Expensive.*

Hyatt Regency Miami. This centrally located, 24-story convention hotel adjoins the James L. Knight International Center (*see* Exploring). It nestles beside the Brickell Avenue Bridge on the north bank of the Miami River. From its lower lobby, you can watch tugboats, freighters, and pleasure craft ply the river. The best rooms are on the upper floors, facing east toward Biscayne Bay. A $7-million renovation of the hotel's public area has continued into 1989. Room renovations began in late 1988. *400 S.E. 2nd Ave., Miami 33131, tel. 305/358–1234 or 800/228–9000. 615 rooms with bath, 25 suites, 43 nonsmoker rooms, 19 rooms for handicapped guests. Facilities: outdoor freshwater swimming pool; health club with sauna; in-room safe; in-house pay-TV movies, 2 restaurants, and a lounge. AE, CB, DC, MC, V. Very Expensive.*

Marina Park Hotel. Centrally located mid rise owned by a French chain. A stark exterior hides the hotel's warm Gallic personality. Rooms have an attractive pastel color scheme with rattan and wicker furnishings, soft mattresses, and trilingual TV. The best views are from east rooms that overlook Bayside and the Port of Miami. *340 Biscayne Blvd., Miami 33132, tel. 305/371–4400 or 800/327–6565. 200 rooms with bath, including 25 suites, 100 newly remodeled. Facilities: pool, restaurant, bar. AE, CB, DC, MC, V. Moderate.*

Omni International Hotel. A 20-story hotel built in 1977, the Omni stands atop a 10.5-acre shopping and entertainment complex that includes Jordan Marsh and J. C. Penney department stores, 120 specialty shops, the Children's Workshop child-care center, and a hand-made Italian wood carousel. The lowest hotel floor is five stories up; rooms on upper floors have spectacular views of downtown Miami and Biscayne Bay. A $1.25 million room renovation in 1987 eschewed tropical-chic in favor of more traditional decor, with a blue-and-tan color scheme and mahogany furniture in many rooms. *1601 Biscayne Blvd., Miami 33132, tel. 305/374–0000 or 800/THE-OMNI. 535 rooms, including 50 suites, 25 nonsmokers rooms, and 1 room for handicapped guests. Facilities: outdoor heated pool on a terrace 5 stories above the street, lobby bar, terrace café, restaurant (The Fish Market), access to nearby health club and spa. AE, DC, MC, V. Very Expensive.*

Kendall **Dadeland Marriott.** Catering to business travelers, this 24-story hotel is part of a megastructure that includes the Datran Center office building and the southernmost Metrorail station, Dadeland South. Within walking distance of Dadeland Mall, the hotel has a four-story atrium overlooking the Datran Center's lobby and its extensive sculpture collection. The hotel's contemporary decor, in corals and light greens, incorporates Asian accents. All rooms have desks and good reading lights. The best rooms face the city on the upper floors; 717 and 719 have glass doors opening to the pool. The worst room, 805, overlooks the roof of the exercise room. *9090 Dadeland Blvd., Miami 33156, tel. 305/663–1035 or 800/228–9290. 303 rooms with bath, including 2 suites, nonsmoker floor with 15 rooms, 4 rooms for handicapped guests. Facilities: outdoor heated freshwater swimming pool, Jacuzzi, whirlpool, sauna, exercise room, restaurant, lounge, complimentary airport transportation. AE, MC, V. Expensive.*

Key Biscayne **Sheraton Royal Biscayne Beach Resort and Racquet Club.** Art-deco pinks, wicker furniture, and chattering macaws and cockatoos in the lobby set the tone for this three-story beachfront resort set amid the waving fronds of coconut palms. Built in 1952 and restored in 1985, this laid-back place has managed to keep its casual demeanor even after starring as a "Miami Vice" set. All rooms have garden and bay views; most have terraces. *555 Ocean Dr., Key Biscayne 33149, tel. 305/361–5775. 192 rooms with bath, including 4 suites with ocean view, 15 suites with kitchenette, 15 nonsmoker rooms. Facilities: a ¼-mile of ocean beachfront; 2 outdoor freshwater heated swimming pools; children's wading pool and playground; 10 tennis courts (4 lighted); sailboats, Windsurfers, Hobie Cats, aquabikes, snorkeling kits, and bicycles for rent; pay-TV movies, unisex beauty salon; restaurants and lounge. AE, CB, DC, MC, V. Expensive.*

★ **Sonesta Beach Hotel & Tennis Club.** Built in 1969, this eight-story beachfront resort underwent a $5-million renovation in 1985. Tropical hues focus attention on museum-quality modern art by prominent painters and sculptors. Don't miss Andy Warhol's five drawings of rock star Mick Jagger in the hotel's disco bar, Desires. The best rooms face the ocean on the eighth floor, a "club floor" with a small lobby and bar where breakfast is served. *350 Ocean Dr., Key Biscayne 33149, tel. 305/361–2021 or 800/343–7170. 315 rooms with bath, including 12 suites and 15 villas (3-, 4-, and 5-bedroom homes with full kitchens and screened-in swimming pools). Facilities: 750 feet of oceanfront beach; outdoor freshwater heated Olympic-size swimming pool and whirlpool; 10 tennis courts (3 lighted); health center with Jacuzzi, dry and hot steam rooms, aerobic dance floor, weight room, massage room, and tanning room; gift shops; restaurants, snack bar, deli, disco lounge. AE, CB, DC, MC, V. Very Expensive.*

Miami Beach **Alexander Hotel.** Newly remodeled throughout, with antique
★ furnishings and original art in every suite, this 16-story hotel offers ocean and bay views from every room. Rooms facing south have the best views. A computer keeps track of the mattresses, so you can request the degree of firmness you prefer. *5225 Collins Ave., Miami Beach 33140, tel. 305/865–6500. 212 suites, each with two baths. Facilities: ocean beach, 2 outdoor heated freshwater pools, 4 poolside Jacuzzis, cabanas, Sunfishes and catamarans for rent, Dominique's gourmet restaurant, and coffee shop. AE, DC, MC, V. Expensive.*

Art Deco Hotels. A trio of restored three-story hotels facing the beach are under common ownership and management. The **Hotel Cardozo** dates from 1939, the **Hotel Carlyle** from 1941, and the **Hotel Leslie** from 1937. All three are attractively decorated in art-deco pinks, whites, and grays. Many contain original walnut furniture, restored and refinished. Rooms are comfortable but small; inspect your room before registering to assure that it meets your needs. Air-conditioning has been installed, but most of the time you won't need it—especially in rooms facing the water, where a sea breeze usually blows. *1244 Ocean Dr., Miami Beach 33139, tel. 305/534–2135 or 800/338–9076. 168 rooms with bath, including 15 suites. Facilities: restaurants and bars with live entertainment in the Carlyle and Cardozo. AE, CB, DC, MC, V. Moderate.*

Fontainebleau Hilton Resort and Spa. The Miami area's foremost convention hotel boasts an opulent lobby with massive chandeliers, a sweeping staircase, and new meeting rooms in art-deco hues. However, many guest rooms need refurbishing. Upper-floor rooms in the Chateau Building have the best views. *4441 Collins Ave., Miami Beach 33140, tel. 305/538–2000. 1,206 rooms with bath, including 60 suites, 55 nonsmoker rooms. Facilities: ocean beach with 30 cabanas, windsurfing, parasailing, Hobie Cats, volleyball, basketball, 2 outdoor pools (one fresh, one salt), 3 whirlpool baths, 7 lighted tennis courts, health club with exercise classes, saunas, marina, free children's activities, 12 restaurants and lounges, Tropigala night club. AE, CB, DC, MC, V. Expensive.*

★ **Hotel Cavalier.** Rooms in this three-story beachfront hotel have period maple furnishings, new baths, and air-conditioning. The Cavalier is popular with the film and fashion industry; many guests are artists, models, photographers, and writers. The best rooms face the ocean; the worst are on the ground floor, rear south, where the garbage truck goes by in the morning. *1320 Ocean Dr., Miami Beach 33139, tel. 305/531–6424 or 800/ 338–9076. 44 rooms with bath, including 2 suites. Facilities: bottled water and flowers in all rooms, Continental breakfast in lobby each morning, airport pickup available. AE, CB, MC, V. Expensive.*

★ **Pan American Ocean Hotel, A Radisson Resort.** This beach hotel sits back from Collins Avenue behind a refreshing garden of coconut palms and seasonal flowers. It first opened in 1954, but a complete renovation took place in 1988–89. The best view faces the ocean from rooms 330, 332, and 333 on the third floor of the north wing. Street noise makes west-facing rooms the least desirable. *17875 Collins Ave., Miami Beach 33160, tel. 305/932– 1100. 146 rooms, including 4 suites, 5 nonsmokers rooms; 3 rooms for handicapped guests available part of the year. Facilities: 400 ft of Atlantic Ocean beach, outdoor heated pool, 4 hard-surface tennis courts, tennis pro and pro shop, 2 shuffleboard courts, 9-hole putting green, beauty salon, coffee shop, pool gazebo bar, terrace lounge and restaurant, ping-pong room, video game room, card room, free shuttle service to Bal Harbor and Aventura shopping malls, coin-operated laundry room, refrigerators in all rooms. AE, CB, DC, MC, V. Very Expensive.*

Surfside Beach Hotel. If you like classic American cars of the 1950s, you'll love this 10-story Quality Inn franchise. Built in 1951, it was restored in 1986 and transformed into a museum for owner Michael Dezer's collection of cars and automotive memorabilia. The lobby display includes a turquoise 1955 Ford Thunderbird hardtop, a 1957 Studebaker Golden Hawk, a red 1950 Willys Jeepster, and their ancestor—a 1931 Ford Model A roadster. Every room is named after a car. *8701 Collins Ave., Miami Beach 33154, tel. 305/865–6661 or 800/228–5151. 220 rooms with bath, including 36 nonsmoker rooms. Facilities:*

300 feet of ocean beach frontage, outdoor freshwater swimming pool with mosaic of pink 1959 Cadillac El Dorado convertible on the bottom, American Classics restaurant, Chevy's dance club, lobby bar, gift shop. AE, CB, DC, MC, V. Moderate.

North Dade **Holiday Inn North Miami—Golden Glades.** Mid-rise suburban hotel at major highway interchange; two miles from the beach, from Calder Race Course, and from Joe Robbie Stadium (where the Miami Dolphins football team plays home games). A 1987 renovation gave public areas modern furnishings and mauve, peach, and purple wallpaper. Rooms have a green-and-white color scheme with oak furniture. Local police patrol the premises nightly. Restaurant offers Weight Watchers menu. *148 N.W. 167th St., Miami 33169, tel. 305/949–1441 or 800/HOLIDAY. 163 rooms with bath, including 18 nonsmoker rooms, 12 lady executive rooms, 1 room for handicapped guests. Facilities: outdoor freshwater swimming pool, children's pool, outdoor exercise area for aerobics, in-room refreshment center, restaurant, and lounge. AE, CB, DC, MC, V. Moderate.*

Miami Lakes Inn, Athletic Club, Golf Resort. This low-rise suburban resort is part of a planned town being developed by Florida Senator Bob Graham's family about 14 miles northwest of downtown Miami. The golf resort opened in 1962 and added two wings in 1978. Its decor is English-traditional throughout, rich in leather and wood. All rooms have balconies. The inn opened in 1983 with a typically Florida-tropic look—light pastel hues and furniture of wicker and light wood. In both locations, the best rooms are near the lobby for convenient access; the worst are near the elevators. *Main St., Miami Lakes 33014, tel. 305/821–1150. 310 rooms with bath, including 32 suites. Facilities: 2 outdoor freshwater swimming pools; 9 lighted tennis courts; golf (18-hole par-72 course, lighted 18-hole par-54 executive course, golf school); saunas, steamrooms, and whirlpool baths; 8 indoor racquetball courts; Nautilus fitness center; full-size gym for volleyball and basketball; aerobics classes; restaurants and lounges; shopping discount at Main St. shops. AE, CB, DC, MC, V. Very Expensive.*

★ **Turnberry Isle Yacht and Country Club.** Part of an upscale condominium community on a 300-acre bayfront site 12 miles north of downtown Miami. Celebrities who live here include tennis stars Jimmy Connors, Vitas Gerulitis, and John McEnroe. Choose from the European-style Marina Hotel or the Country Club Inn beside the golf course. Rooms are oversize, with light woods and earth-tone colors at the inn, a nautical-blue motif at the hotel, large curving terraces, Jacuzzis, honor bar, and in-room safes. *19735 Turnberry Way, North Miami Beach 33163, tel. 305/932–6200. 250 rooms with bath, including 47 suites. (By spring 1990, 2 new 5-story minitowers and 24 tennis villas will be open, bringing the total room count to 370.) Facilities: Ocean Club with 250 feet of private beach frontage, diving gear, Windsurfers and Hobie Cats for rent, and complimentary shuttle service to the hotel; 2 outdoor freshwater swimming pools; 24 tennis courts, 18 with lights; 2 18-hole golf courses; helipad; marina with moorings for 125 boats up to 150 ft.; full-service spa with physician, nutritionist, saunas, steamrooms, whirlpools, facials, herbal wraps, Nautilus exercise equipment, indoor racquetball courts, and jogging course; 5 private restaurants, lounge, nightly entertainment. AE, CB, DC, MC, V. Very Expensive.*

West Dade **Doral Resort & Country Club.** Millions of airline passengers annually peer down upon this 2,400-acre jewel of an inland golf and tennis resort while fastening their seat belts. It's seven miles west of Miami International Airport and consists of eight separate three- and four-story lodges nestled beside the golf links. A renovation completed in 1988 gave the resort a tropical theme, with light pastels, wicker, and teak furniture. All guest rooms have minibars; most have private balconies or terraces with views of the golf courses or tennis courts. This is the site of the Doral Ryder Open Tournament, played on the Doral "Blue Monster" golf course. *4400 N.W. 87th Ave., Miami 33178, tel. 305/592–2000. 650 rooms with bath, including 56 suites. Facilities: 5 18-hole golf courses, and a 9-hole, par-3 executive course; pro shop and boutique; 15 tennis courts; Olympic-size heated outdoor freshwater swimming pool; 24-stall equestrian center, offers riding instruction; 3-mi jogging and bike path; bicycle rentals; lake fishing; restaurant and lounge; transportation to beach. AE, CB, DC, MC, V. Very Expensive.*

The Arts

Performing arts aficionados in Greater Miami will tell you they survive quite nicely despite the area's historic inability to support a professional symphony orchestra. In recent years, this community has begun to write a new chapter in its performing arts history.

The New World Symphony, a unique advanced-training orchestra, marks its third season in 1990. The fledgling Miami City Ballet has risen rapidly to international prominence in its four-year existence. The opera company ranks with the nation's best, and a venerable chamber music series brings renowned ensembles to perform here. Several churches and synagogues also run classical music series with international performers.

In theater, Miami offers English-speaking audiences an assortment of professional, collegiate, and amateur productions of musicals, comedy, and drama. Spanish theater also is active.

In the cinema world, the Miami Film Festival attracts more than 45,000 people annually to screenings of new films from all over the world—including some made here.

Arts Information. Greater Miami's English-language daily newspaper, *The Miami Herald*, publishes information on the performing arts in its Weekend Section on Friday and the Lively Arts Section on Sunday. The *Herald* is notorious for its inaccurate listings of the location and time of arts events. Phone ahead to confirm details before you go.

If you read Spanish, check *El Nuevo Herald* (a Spanish version of *The Miami Herald*) or *Diario Las Americas* (the area's largest independent Spanish-language paper) for information on the Spanish theater and a smattering of general performing arts news.

Other good sources of information on the performing arts are the calendar in *Miami Today*, a free weekly newspaper available each Thursday in downtown Miami, Coconut Grove, and Coral Gables; and *New Times*, a free weekly distributed throughout Dade County each Wednesday.

Arts. Miami's official guide to the arts is a pocket»size monthly
publication covering music of all kinds, from the classics to rock
and art gallery openings, theater, and major cultural events in
Greater Miami, Broward, and Palm Beach. Editor Margo Morrison tries to be encylopedic and does a good job. Sold at
newsstands all over Greater Miami. *Tel. 305/854-1790. 9-5.
Annual subscription $15, individual copy $2. No credit cards.*

WTMI (93.1 FM) provides concert information on its Cultural
Arts Line (tel. 305/550-9393).

Ballet   **Miami City Ballet.** Florida's first major fully professional resident ballet company. Edward Villella, the artistic director,
was principal dancer of the New York City Ballet under George
Balanchine. Now the Miami City Ballet re-creates the Balanchine repertoire and has begun to introduce new works of its
own. Miami City Ballet performances are at Gusman Center for
the Performing Arts. Demonstrations of works in progress are
at the 450-seat Colony Theater on Miami Beach. Villella nar-
rates the children's and works-in-progress programs. *905
Lincoln Rd., Miami Beach 33139, tel. 305/532-7713. Season:
Oct.–May. AE, MC, V. Ticketmaster (see Important Addresses and Numbers).*

Cinema   **The Miami Film Festival.** During eight days in February, new
films from all over the world are screened in the Gusman Center
for the Performing Arts. Tickets and schedule: *444 Brickell
Ave., Miami 33131, tel. 305/377-3456. AE, MC, V. Ticketmaster (see Important Addresses and Numbers).*

Concerts   **Concert Association of Greater Miami.** A not-for-profit organization, directed by Judith Drucker, this is the South's largest
presenter of classical artists. Ticket and program information:
*555 Hank Meyer Blvd. (17th St.), Miami Beach 33139, tel. 305/
532-3491. AE, CB, DC, MC, V.*
Friends of Chamber Music (44 W. Flagler St., Miami 33130, tel.
305/372-2975) presents an annual series of chamber concerts
by internationally known guest ensembles, such as the Beaux
Arts Trio, I Musici, and the Julliard String Quartet.

Drama   **Check** *Miami's Guide to the Arts* for a complete English-
language theater schedule. Traveling companies come and go;
amateur groups form, perform, and disband. Listed below are
the more enduring groups of Greater Miami's drama scene.
Coconut Grove Playhouse. Arnold Mittelman, artistic director,
stages Broadway-bound plays and musical reviews and experimental productions. *3500 Main Hwy., Coconut Grove 33133,
tel. 305/442-4000. AE, MC, V.*
Ruth Forman Theater. Six Actors Equity productions are
staged here throughout the year. Each production lasts five
weeks. *At Barry University, 11300 N.E. 2nd Ave., Miami
Shores 33161. Oct.–May. MC, V. Write for details.*
Ring Theater. The University of Miami's Department of Theatre Arts presents four complete plays a year in this 311-seat
hall. *University of Miami, 1312 Miller Dr., Coral Gables
33124, tel. 305/284-3355. No credit cards.*

Opera   **Greater Miami Opera.** Miami's resident opera company has the
seventh-largest operating budget of any American opera organization. It presents two complete casts for five operas in the
Dade County Auditorium. The International Series brings
such luminaries as Placido Domingo and Luciano Pavarotti; the
National Series features rising young singers in the principal

roles, with the same sets and chorus, but with more modest ticket prices. All operas are sung in their original language, with titles in English projected onto a screen above the stage. *1200 Coral Way, Miami 33145, tel. 305/854-7890. AE, MC, V. Ticketmaster (see Important Addresses and Numbers).*

Symphony **New World Symphony.** Although Greater Miami still has no resident symphony orchestra, the New World Symphony, conducted by Michael Tilson Thomas, helps to fill the void. It's a unique phenomenon, a national advanced training orchestra for musicians aged 21–30 who have finished their academic studies and need performing experience in a professional setting before moving on to a permanent job. *541 Lincoln Rd., Miami Beach 33139, box office tel. 305/673-3331, main office 305/673-3330. AE, CB, DC, MC, V. Season: Oct.–Apr. Ticketmaster (see Important Addresses and Numbers).*

Theaters Greater Miami lacks a modern performing arts center. Every auditorium and theater in town suffers from a shortage of space on and off the stage, and some have acoustical problems.

Dade County Auditorium (2901 W. Flagler St., Miami 33135, tel. 305/545-3395) satisfies patrons with 2,497 comfortable seats, good sight lines, and acceptable acoustics. Performers grumble at its shortcomings. The lack of a proper orchestra pit frustrates the Greater Miami Opera Association, and storage space is so minimal that the opera company must keep its paraphernalia outside the hall in trailers between performances.

Jackie Gleason Theater of the Performing Arts (1700 Washington Ave., Miami Beach 33119, tel. 305/673-8300), with 3,000 seats, has visibility and acoustics problems. Many top performers reportedly won't play there; many patrons are outspoken about not attending.

Gusman Center for the Performing Arts (174 E. Flagler St., Miami 33131, (tel. 305/372-0925). In downtown Miami, the center has 1,700 seats made for sardines—and the best acoustics in town. An ornate former movie palace, the hall resembles a Moorish courtyard. Lights twinkle, starlike, from the ceiling. Musicians dread Gusman because they must carry everything they need in and out for each performance.

Gusman Concert Hall (1314 Miller Dr., Coral Gables 33124, tel. 305/284-2438). This 600-seat hall on the University of Miami's Coral Gables campus has good acoustics, an orange and purple color scheme, and plenty of room for UM's basketball players to stretch their legs. Parking is a problem when school is in session.

Hirschfeld Theatre. Situated in the Castle Hotel and Resort, this 840-seat restored former cabaret once hosted Jackie Gleason and Rowan and Martin. Nine musicals are produced annually. *5445 Collins Ave., Miami Beach 33140, tel. 305/865-PLAY. AE, DC, MC, V.*

Spanish Theater Spanish theater prospers, although many companies have short lives. About 20 Spanish companies perform light comedy, puppetry, vaudeville, and political satire. To locate them, read the Spanish newspapers. When you phone, be prepared for a conversation in Spanish. Most of the box-office personnel don't speak English.

Teatro Avanite (232 Minorca Ave). Three to six productions are staged annually in the 220-seat Minorca Playhouse. A Hispanic theater festival is held each May. *Box 453005, Miami, 33245, tel. 305/858-4155.*

Prometo. Has produced three to four bilingual Spanish-English plays a year for 15 years. *Miami-Dade Community College, New World Center Campus, 300 N.E. 2nd Ave., Miami, tel. 305/347–3263.*

Teatro de Bellas Artes. A 255-seat theater on Calle Ocho, Little Havana's main commercial street, presents eight Spanish plays and musicals a year. *Dramas Fri.–Sat. 9 PM and Sun. 3 PM. Musical comedy Sat. midnight and Sun. 9 PM. Recitals Sun. 6 PM. 2173 S.W. 8th St., Miami, tel. 305/325–0515. No credit cards.*

Nightlife

Greater Miami has no concentration of night spots like Bourbon Street in New Orleans or Rush Street in Chicago, but nightlife thrives throughout the Miami area in scattered locations, including Miami Beach, Little Haiti, Little Havana, Coconut Grove, the fringes of downtown Miami, and south-suburban Kendall. Individual clubs offer jazz, various forms of rock-and-roll, and top 40 sounds on different nights of the week. Some clubs refuse entrance to anyone under 21; others set the age limit at 25.

For current information, see the Weekend Section in the Friday edition of *The Miami Herald;* the calendar in *Miami Today*, a free weekly newspaper available each Thursday in downtown Miami, Coconut Grove, and Coral Gables; and *New Times*, a free weekly distributed throughout Dade County each Wednesday.

Love 94 (WLVE, 93.9 FM) sponsors a concert line with information on touring groups of all kinds, except classical (tel. 305/654–9436). Blues Hot Line lists local blues clubs and bars (tel. 305/666–6656). Jazz Hot Line lists local jazz programs (tel. 305/382–3938).

On Miami Beach, where the sounds of jazz and reggae spill into the streets, fashion models and photographers frequent the lobby bars of small art-deco hotels.

Throughout the Greater Miami area, bars and cocktail lounges in larger hotels operate discos nightly, with live entertainment on weekends. Many hotels extend their bars into open-air courtyards, where patrons dine and dance under the stars throughout the year.

Bars   **Churchill's Hideaway.** This enclave of Anglicism in Little Haiti is popular with cruise-line employees and international sports fans. Its satellite dish picks up BBC news programs, and a Sharp Six System VHS plays foreign-format tapes of international soccer and rugby games. Four English beers on tap, 40 kinds of imported bottled beers. Four dart boards. The outdoor bar in back came from an old Playboy Club on Biscayne Boulevard. Entertainment on weekends. *5501 N.E. 2nd Ave., Miami, tel. 305/757–1807. Open 10 AM–2 AM Mon.–Thurs. and Sun., to 3 AM Fri.–Sat. No credit cards.*

Hungry Sailor. This small English-style pub is decorated with nautical charts, marine flags, and flotsam and jetsam. Five English ales and beers are on tap. There's traditional English food, and live entertainment nightly: folk, jazz, or reggae. *3064½ Grand Ave., Coconut Grove, tel. 305/444–9359. Open 11:30 AM–2:30 AM. AE, CB, DC, MC, V.*

Stuart's Bar-Lounge. Named for its owner and located in the Hotel Place St. Michel, Stuart's is an original Coral Gables hostelry built in 1926. *Esquire* called Stuart's one of the best new bars of 1987. It is decorated with beveled mirrors, mahogany paneling, French posters, pictures of old Coral Gables, and art-nouveau lighting. Live jazz on weekends. *162 Alcazar Ave., Coral Gables, tel. 305/444–1666. Open 5 PM–12:30 AM Mon.–Sat., 6 PM–12:30 AM Sun. AE, CB, DC, MC, V.*

Taurus Steak House. The bar, built in 1922 of native cypress, nightly draws an over-30 singles crowd that drifts outside to a patio. A band plays on weekends. Lunch and dinner. *3540 Main Hwy., Coconut Grove, tel. 305/448–0633. Open daily 5 PM–midnight. AE, CB, DC, MC, V.*

Tobacco Road. This bar, opened in 1912, holds Miami's oldest liquor license. Upstairs, in space occupied by a speakeasy during Prohibition, local and national blues bands perform Friday and Saturday and in scheduled weeknight concerts. The bar draws a diverse clientele from all over south Florida. *626 S. Miami Ave., Miami, tel. 305/374–1198. Open weekdays 11:30 AM–5 AM, weekends 1 PM–5 AM. Lunch served Mon.–Fri. Dinner served Sun.–Thurs. AE, DC.*

Tropics International Restaurant. Reggae is featured in art deco surroundings in the lobby of the Edison Hotel, built in 1936. Dinner. *960 Ocean Dr., Miami Beach, tel. 305/531–5335. Open daily 5 PM–3 AM. AE, MC, V.*

Comedy Clubs   **Coconuts Comedy Clubs.** This 1980s version of vaudeville comedy thrives with humor that's adult, but not obscene. Two acts per show; new performers each week. *Dadeland Marriott Hotel, 9090 S. Dadeland Blvd., Kendall, tel. 305/670–2022. Shows Wed., Thurs., and Sun. 9 PM; Fri. 9 and 11 PM; Sat. 8 PM, 10 PM, and midnight. Also at Howard Johnson, 16500 N.W. 2nd Ave., North Miami Beach, tel. 305/948–6887. Thurs. and Sun. 9 PM, Fri. 9 and 11 PM, Sat. 9 and 11 PM. Both suggest reservations. Cover and drink minimum. AE, MC, V.*

Disco/Rock Clubs   **Stringfellows.** Opened in May 1989, Peter Stringfellow's Coconut Grove club has been attracting guests from international artistic, business, and social circles, many of whom are already familiar with Stringfellow's other clubs in London and New York. Guests enter through green glass doors decorated with an etched-glass butterfly crest and ascend to the club's second-floor restaurant and nightclub. The restaurant, decorated with art-deco furnishings, pink tablecloths, and fresh orchids, features well-prepared international cuisine. A dinner-hour trio plays jazz. The nightclub, which opens at 11:30, features rock music pumped through a state-of-the-art sound system and a sophisticated light system capable of producing hundreds of variations. *3390 Mary St., Miami 33143, tel. 305/446–7555. Reservations advised. Club cover charge: $10 Sun.–Thurs., $15 Fri., $20 Sat. Closed Christmas. A-la-carte menu served 8 PM–2:30 AM, late-night supper from 2:30–4 AM. Club open 11:30 PM–5 AM. AE, DC, MC, V.*

Club Oz. This is a haven for south-suburban yuppies. The theme changes nightly, with many special events. Wood dance floor. *19995 S. Dixie Hwy., Miami, tel. 305/238–3700. Open Wed.–Sat. 9 PM–5 AM. AE, MC, V.*

Stefano's of Key Biscayne. Live band performs nightly, 7–11 PM. Then this northern Italian restaurant becomes a disco. Wood dance floor. *24 Crandon Blvd., Key Biscayne, tel. 305/361–7007. Open 5 PM–5 AM nightly. AE, CB, DC, MC, V.*

Club Nu. The decor at this club changes every three–four months. A large New York–style nightclub with separate champagne room and dining area, this spot attracts a fashion-conscious under-30 crowd, many in bizarre garb. Large terrazzo dance floor. *245 22nd St., Miami Beach 33139, tel. 305/672–0068. Open Wed.–Sun. 9 PM–5 AM.*

Folk Music **Our Place Natural Foods Eatery.** On weekends, this small South Beach vegetarian restaurant becomes Greater Miami's only smoke-free live folk music club. Features local and national artists. Last Saturday of each month is "open mike" night. Full menu all night. *830 Washington Ave., Miami Beach, tel. 305/674–1322. Open 8 PM Fri.–Sat. till the musicians quit. No credit cards.*

Nightclubs **Les Violins Supper Club.** This standby has been owned for 25 years by the Cachaidora-Currais family, who ran a club and restaurant in Havana. The club's ceiling rises 10 feet during two nightly Las Vegas–style reviews, reminiscent of old Busby Berkeley movies. Live dance band. Wood dance floor. Dinner. *1751 Biscayne Blvd., Miami, tel. 305/371–8668. Open 7 PM. Closes Tues.–Thurs. and Sun. 1 AM, Fri. 2 AM, Sat. 3 AM. Closed Mon. Reservations suggested. AE, CB, DC, MC, V.*

Club Tropigala at La Ronde in the Fontainebleau Hilton Hotel. A seven-level round room decorated with orchids, banana leaves, and philodendrons to resemble a tropical jungle, this club is operated by owners of Les Violins. Two bands play Latin music for dancing on wood floor. Two live costumed shows nightly. Dinner. Long wait for valet parking. *4441 Collins Ave., Miami Beach, tel. 305/672–7469. Open Weds.–Sun. 7 PM–4 AM. Reservations advised. AE, CB, DC, MC, V.*

3 The Everglades

Introduction

*by George and
Rosalie Leposky*

Greater Miami is the only metropolitan area in the United States with two national parks in its backyard: Everglades and Biscayne. Both have image problems.

Because Everglades is famous, people come expecting a spectacle like the mountainous western parks. What they see is a wide expanse of saw grass that at first glance looks frustratingly like a midwestern wheat field. In sea-girded Biscayne, you need a boat and snorkel or scuba gear.

At least these parks are easy to reach. You can drive to either one from downtown Miami in an hour, and their main entrances are just 21 miles apart. Between them sits Homestead, a bustling agricultural city of 25,000.

The creation of Everglades National Park in 1947 made many people in Homestead unhappy. The farmers wanted to plow much of the land that came under the park service's protection.

Today, Homestead is beginning to view the park with a less-jaundiced eye and transforming itself into a tourist center. New motels, shopping centers, and restaurants have opened; old ones are sprucing up. City officials have created a historic district downtown to promote restoration of Homestead's commercial heart. It's all an effort to house, feed, and amuse many of the million visitors who will explore the Everglades in 1990—and the 30,000 hardy souls who will discover Biscayne.

If you intend to spend just one day at Everglades National Park, take the 38-mile main park road from the Main Visitor Center to Flamingo to see a cross section of the park's ecosystems: hardwood hammock (tree islands), freshwater prairie, pineland, freshwater slough, cypress, coastal prairie, mangrove, and marine/estuarine.

At Shark Valley, on the park's northern edge, a 14-mile tram ride takes you to an observation tower overlooking the "river of grass" (*see* Guided Tours).

The Gulf Coast and Key Largo ranger stations and the Flamingo Visitor Center offer access to the mangroves and marine habitats—Gulf Coast in the Ten Thousand Islands region along the Gulf of Mexico near Everglades City; Flamingo and Key Largo in Florida Bay. You can take tour boat rides from Everglades City and Flamingo through this ecosystem (*see* Guided Tours) and hire a fishing guide to show you where the big ones bite (*see* Participant Sports).

Biscayne National Park encompasses almost 274 square miles, of which 96% are under water. Biscayne includes 18 miles of inhospitable mangrove shoreline on the mainland and 45 mangrove-fringed barrier islands seven miles to the east across Biscayne Bay. The bay is a lobster sanctuary and a nursery for fish, sponges, and crabs. Manatees and sea turtles also frequent its warm, shallow waters.

The islands (called keys) are fossilized coral reefs that emerged from the sea when glaciers trapped much of the world's water supply during the Ice Age. Today, a tropical hardwood forest grows in the crevices of these rocky keys.

East of the keys, coral reefs three miles seaward attract divers and snorkelers (*see* Participant Sports). Biscayne is the only national park in the continental United States with living coral reefs and is the nation's largest marine park.

The park boundary encompasses the continental shelf to a depth of 60 feet. East of that boundary, the shelf falls rapidly away to a depth of 400 feet at the edge of the Gulf Stream.

Getting Around

By Plane *Commercial Flights.* **Miami International Airport** (MIA) is the closest commercial airport to Everglades National Park and Biscayne National Park. It's 34 miles from Homestead and 83 miles from the Flamingo resort in Everglades National Park.

By Car From the north, the main highways to Homestead-Florida City are U.S. 1, the Homestead Extension of the Florida Turnpike, and Krome Avenue (Rte. 997).

From Miami to Biscayne National Park, take the turnpike extension to the Tallahassee Road (S.W. 137th Ave.) exit, turn left, and go south. Turn left at North Canal Drive (S.W. 328th St.), go east, and follow signs to park headquarters at Convoy Point. The park is about 30 miles from downtown Miami.

From Homestead to Biscayne National Park, take U.S. 1 or Krome Avenue (Rte. 997) to Lucy Street (S.E. 8th St.). Turn east. Lucy Street becomes North Canal Drive (S.W. 328th St.). Follow signs about eight miles to the park headquarters.

From Homestead to Everglades National Park's Main Visitor Center and Flamingo, take U.S. 1 or Krome Avenue (Rte. 997) south to Florida City. Turn right (west) onto Rte. 9336. Follow signs to the park entrance. The Main Visitor Center is 11 miles from Homestead; Flamingo is 49 miles from Homestead.

To reach the north end of Everglades National Park, take U.S. 41 (the Tamiami Trail) west from Miami. It's 40 miles to the Shark Valley Information Center and 83 miles to the Gulf Coast Ranger Station at Everglades City.

To reach the south end of Everglades National Park in the Florida Keys, take U.S. 1 south from Homestead. It's 27 miles to the Key Largo Ranger Station (between Mile Markers 98 and 99 on the Overseas Hwy.).

Rental Cars **Homestead Freedom Rent-a-Car** (tel. 305/248–8352 or 305/257–2525). Rental cars also available at MIA (*see* Miami Arriving and Departing).

By Bus **Metrobus** Route 1A runs from Homestead to MIA only during peak weekday hours: 6:30–9 AM and 4–6:30 PM.
Greyhound/Trailways operates two trips daily north and south from MIA (*see* Miami Arriving and Departing).

By Taxi **Homestead Cab Company.** Service in Homestead-Florida City area. Full service to and from Flamingo and the tour boats in Biscayne National Park. Service from Homestead to MIA; *416 N.E. 1st Rd., Homestead, tel. 305/247–7777. Open 24 hours daily except 6 AM Sun.–5 AM Mon. No credit cards.*

By Boat **U.S. Customs.** The nearest U.S. Customs phones to the two national parks are at **Watson Island Marina** (1050 MacArthur Causeway, Miami, tel. 305/371–2378), about 25 nautical miles to Biscayne National Park headquarters, 50 nautical miles to Flamingo; and **Tavernier Creek Marina** (Mile Marker 90–½,

U.S. 1, Tavernier, tel. 305/252–0194 from Miami, 305/852–5854 from the Keys), about 48 nautical miles to Biscayne National Park headquarters, 25 nautical miles to Flamingo.

Scenic Drives **Main road to Flamingo in Everglades National Park.** It's 38 road miles from the Main Visitor Center to Flamingo, across six distinct ecosystems (with access from the road to two others). Highlights of the trip include a dwarf cypress forest, the ecotone (transition zone) between sawgrass and mangrove forest, and a wealth of wading birds at Mrazek and Coot Bay Ponds. Boardwalks and trails along the main road and several short spurs allow you to see the Everglades without getting your feet wet. Well-written interpretive signs en route will help you understand this diverse wilderness.

Tamiami Trail. U.S. 41 from Miami to the Gulf Coast crosses the Everglades and the Big Cypress National Preserve. Highlights of the trip include sweeping views across the sawgrass to the Shark River Slough, a visit to the Miccosukee Indian Reservation, and the Big Cypress National Preserve's variegated pattern of wet prairies, ponds, marshes, sloughs, and strands. It's 83 miles to the Gulf Coast Ranger Station at Everglades City.

Guided Tours

Tours of Everglades National Park and Biscayne National Park typically focus on native wildlife, plants, and park history. Concessionaires operate the Everglades tram tours and the boat cruises in both parks.

In addition, the National Park Service organizes a variety of free programs at Everglades National Park. Ask a ranger for the daily schedule.

Orientation Tours **All Florida Adventure Tours.** All-day narrated 250-mile tour of south Florida wetlands, through the Big Cypress National Preserve to Everglades City and Chokoloskee Island, and Corkscrew. *11137 North Kendall Dr., D105, Miami 33176, tel. 305/270–0219. Tours Tues. and Sat. Cost: $69.50 adults, $49.50 children. No credit cards.*

Miami Vision. Miccosukee Indian Village, lunch, and airboat ride. Minivan and private car tours. Well-informed, congenial guides speak English, Spanish, French, German, Italian, and Portuguese. *2699 Collins Ave., Suite 113, Miami Beach, tel. 305/532–0040. Cost: $49 adults, $39 children. MC, V.*

Safari Sightseeing Tours. Everglades tour includes airboat ride, Indian village, Shark Valley, and lunch. *6547 S.W. 116th Pl., Miami, tel. 305/226–6923 (day) or 305/223–3804 (night). Tours Wed., Sat., Sun. 8:30–5. Cost: $29.50 adults, $14.75 children under 12, includes transportation and admissions (but not lunch). No credit cards.*

Special-Interest Tours **Buffalo Tiger's Florida Everglades Airboat Ride.** The former chairman of the Miccosukee tribe will take you on a 30-minute *Airboat Rides* airboat ride through the Everglades, with a stop at an old Indian camp. Opportunities to watch birds, turtles, and alligators. *Tour location: 29701 S.W. 8th St., 12 mi west of Krome Ave., 20 mi west of the Miami city limits (Rte. 997), tel. 305/559–5250. Open daily 9–6. Cost: $6 adults, $4 children under 10. No credit cards.*

Coopertown Airboat Ride. Chuck Norris filmed *Invasion U.S.A.* here. A 30-minute airboat ride through the Everglades sawgrass to visit two hammocks (subtropical hardwood forests) and alligator holes. Bird-watching opportunities. *Tour location: S.W. 8th St., 5 mi west of Krome Ave., 15 mi west of Miami city limits, tel. 305/226–6048. Open daily 8 AM–dusk. Cost: $7 per person. No credit cards.*

Everglades Air Boat Tours. A four-mile, 30-minute tour of the River of Grass leaves every half hour. *Tour location: 40351 S.W. 192nd Ave., tel. 305/AIRBOAT. Open daily 9–5. Cost: $7.50 adults, $6.50 senior citizens, $3.50 children 4–12, under 4 free. No credit cards.*

Boat Tours **Biscayne National Park Tour Boats.** You'll ride to Biscayne National Park's living coral reefs 10 miles offshore on a 53-foot glass-bottom boat. A separate tour to Elliott Key visitor center, on a barrier island seven miles offshore across Biscayne Bay, is conducted only in winter when mosquitoes are less active. *Tour location: East end of North Canal Dr. (S.W. 328th St.), Homestead, tel. 305/247–2400. Office open daily 8:30– 5:30. Phone for daily schedule. Reservations required. AE, MC, V.*

Back Country Tour. A two-hour cruise from Flamingo Lodge Marina & Outpost Resort aboard a 40-passenger pontoon boat covers 12–15 miles through tropical estuaries fringed with impenetrable mangrove forests. You may see manatees, dolphins, sharks, alligators, and many species of bird life, including bald eagles. *Tour location: Flamingo Marina, Flamingo, tel. 305/ 253–2241 or 813/695–3101. Cruises daily. Phone for schedule. Reservations accepted. AE, DC, MC, V.*

Everglades National Park Boat Tours. Sammy Hamilton operates three separate 14-mile tours through the Ten Thousand Islands region along the Gulf of Mexico on the western margin of the park. *Tour location: At Everglades National Park's Gulf Coast Ranger Station on Rte. 29, about 3 mi south of U.S. 41 (Tamiami Trail), tel. 813/695–2591 or in FL 800/445–7724. Office open daily 8:30–4:30. Phone for schedule. No credit cards.*

Florida Bay Cruise. A 90-minute tour of Florida Bay from Flamingo Lodge Marina & Outpost Resort aboard *Pelican*, a 42-passenger pontoon boat. The tour offers a close look at bird life on rookery islands in the bay and on sandbars during low tide. In winter, you're likely to see white pelicans; in summer, magnificent frigatebirds. Also offers Backcountry and Sunset tours. *Tour location: Flamingo Marina, Flamingo, tel. 305/ 253–2241 or 813/695–3101. Cruises daily. Phone for schedule. Reservations accepted. AE, DC, MC, V.*

Florida Boat Tours. Back-country tours outside Everglades National Park in Everglades City area. Runs three 24-passenger airboats for 30-minute rides, 48-passenger pontoon boat for one-hour cruise. Boats are Coast Guard approved. *Tel. 813/ 695–4400 or in FL 800/282–9194. Phone for schedule. MC, V.*

Tram Tours **Wilderness Tram Tour.** Snake Bight is an indentation in the Florida Bay shoreline near Flamingo. You can go there aboard a 48-passenger screened tram on this two-hour tour through a mangrove forest and a coastal prairie to a 100-yard boardwalk over the mud flats at the edge of the bight. It's a good birding spot. Tram operates subject to mosquito, weather, and trail conditions. Driver has insect repellent on board. *Departs from Flamingo Lodge, tel. 305/253–2241 or 813/695–3101. Phone for schedule. Reservations accepted. AE, CB, DC, MC, V.*

Shark Valley Tram Tours. The trams take a new 15-mile loop road, which is two feet higher, has 200 culverts, and is considerably less flood prone when the summer rains come. Propane-powered trams travel into the interior, stopping at a 50-foot observation tower on the site of an oil well drilled in the 1940s. From atop the tower, you'll view the Everglades' vast "river of grass" sweeping south toward the Gulf of Mexico. The trams are covered but have open sides, so carry rain gear. *Tour location: Shark Valley entrance to Everglades National Park, 40 mi west of Miami off U.S. 41 (Tamiami Trail), tel. 305/221–8455. Open daily all year 9–4. Cost: $5 adults, $2.50 children, $4.50 senior citizens. Reservations recommended Dec.–Mar. No credit cards.*

Personal Guides **Flamingo Lodge Marina & Outpost Resort.** Captains of charter fishing boats are available to give individual tours out of Flamingo. Make reservations several weeks in advance through the marina store. *TW Services Inc., Everglades National Park, Box 428, Flamingo 33030, tel. 305/253–2241 or 813/695–3101. Nov. 1–Apr. 30 (except Christmas week). Cost: $215 a day, $140 a half day per person. AE, CB, DC, MC, V (see Miami Guided Tours).*

Important Addresses and Numbers

Tourist **South Dade Visitors Information Center.** *100 U.S. 1, Florida*
Information *City 33034, tel. 305/245–9180. Open daily 8–5:30.*

Greater Homestead-Florida City Chamber of Commerce (650 U.S. 1, Homestead 33030, tel. 305/247–2332).

Emergencies Homestead, Florida City, and unincorporated Dade County use the same emergency number, 911. You can dial free from pay phones.

In the national parks, the rangers perform police, fire, and medical-emergency functions. Look for the rangers at park visitor centers and information stations, or phone the park switchboards: *Biscayne* (tel. 305/247–2044); *Everglades* (tel. 305/247–6211).

Hospitals **James Archer Smith Hospital.** 24-hour emergency room. *160 N.W. 13th St., Homestead, tel. 305/248–3232. Physician referral service, tel. 305/248–DOCS.*

Marine Phone **Biscayne National Park** (tel. 305/247–2044). Rangers staff
Numbers Elliott Key Visitor Center and Adams Key Information Center around the clock and can call the mainland on ship-to-shore radio. Park headquarters on Convoy Point open daily 8–5.

Florida Marine Patrol. Law-enforcement arm of the Florida Department of Natural Resources. Boating emergencies: *24-hour tel. 305/325–3346.* Natural resource violations, including marine fishery laws, mangrove cuttings, manatee reports, filling of wetlands. 24-hour Resource Alert Hot Line: *tel. 800/342–1821, nonemergencies 305/325–3346.*

National Weather Service. National Hurricane Center office in Coral Gables supplies local forecasts. *Open Mon.–Fri. 7:30–5,* *tel. 305/665–0429. For 24-hr phone weather recording, tel. 305/661–5065.*

U.S. Coast Guard **Miami Beach Coast Guard Base** (tel. 305/535–4314 or 305/535–4315, VHF-FM Channel 16). Local marine emergencies, search-and-rescue, and reporting of navigation hazards.

Exploring Biscayne National Park

Numbers in the margin correspond with points of interest on the Everglades and Biscayne National Parks map.

Because 96% of Biscayne National Park's acreage is under water, you must take a boat ride to visit most of it and snorkel or scuba dive to appreciate it fully. If you don't have your own boat, a concessionaire will take you to the coral reefs 10 miles offshore. These dome-shape patch reefs—some the size of a student's desk, others as broad as a large parking lot—rely on the delicate balance of temperature, depth, light, and water quality that the park was created to maintain.

A diverse population of colorful fish flits through the reefs: angelfish, gobies, grunts, parrot fish, pork fish, wrasses, and many more.

From December through April, when the mosquito population is relatively quiescent, you can comfortably explore several of the mangrove-fringed barri r islands seven miles offshore. Tropical hardwood forests cloak the upper reaches of these fossilized coral reefs.

The list below describes the facilities at each of Biscayne National Park's visitor service areas, and also at the Metro-Dade County parks within the national park's boundaries.

❶ **Adams Key Information Station.** Boat dock, picnic area, rest rooms, short nature trail. Ranger station has ship-to-shore radio contact with mainland. Day use only.

❷ **Boca Chita Key.** Mark C. Honeywell, former president of Minneapolis' Honeywell Co., bought this island in 1937 and built the ornamental lighthouse, rainwater catchment cisterns, a wall, and other buildings of coral rock. There is a boat dock, picnic area, and rest rooms. Lighthouse open on occasion; ask rangers.

❸ **Convoy Point Information Station.** Park headquarters. Small visitor center and outdoor kiosk with bulletin boards. Launching ramp for canoes and small boats. Boardwalk over shallow water near shore to jetty and path along jetty. Picnic area. Dock where you board tour boats to reefs and Elliott Key. *At east end of North Canal Dr. (S.W. 328th St.), Homestead, tel. 305/247–2044. Open Dec.–Apr. weekdays 8–5, weekends 9–5:30; May–Nov. weekdays 10–4, weekends 10–6. Admission free.*

❹ **Elliott Key Visitor Center.** Indoor exhibit area on second floor displays coral, sponges, and sea-turtle shells on a "touching table" that children especially enjoy. A screened enclosure under the exhibit area houses picnic tables, bulletin boards, and a slide show. *Open Sat.–Sun. and holidays only 10–4.*

Sands Key. Back-country camping allowed; no facilities.

The Everglades and Biscayne National Parks

Exploring the Everglades

Winter is the best time to visit Everglades National Park. Temperatures and mosquito activity are moderate. Low water levels concentrate the resident wildlife around sloughs that retain water all year. Migratory birds swell the avian population.

Winter is also the busiest time in the park. Make reservations and expect crowds at Flamingo, the Main Visitor Center, and Royal Palm—the most popular visitor service areas.

In spring the weather turns increasingly hot and dry. After Easter, fewer visitors come, and tours and facilities are less crowded. Migratory birds depart, and you must look harder to see wildlife. Be especially careful with campfires and matches; this is when the wildfire-prone saw-grass prairies and pinelands are most vulnerable.

Summer brings intense sun and billowing clouds that unleash torrents of rain on the Everglades. Thunderstorms roll in almost every afternoon, bringing the park 90% of its annual 60-inch rainfall from June through October. Water levels rise. Wildlife disperses. Mosquitoes hatch, swarm, and descend on you in voracious clouds. It's a good time to stay away, although some brave souls do come to explore. Europeans constitute 80% of the summer visitors.

Summer in south Florida lingers until mid-October, when the first cold front sweeps through. The rains cease, water levels start to fall, and the ground begins to dry out. Wildlife moves toward the sloughs. Flocks of migratory birds and tourists swoop in, as the cycle of seasons builds once more to the winter peak activity.

Whenever you come, we urge you to experience the real Everglades by getting your feet wet—but most people who visit the park won't do that. Boat tours at Everglades City and Flamingo, a tram ride at Shark Valley, and boardwalks at several locations along the main park road allow you to see the Everglades with dry feet.

The list below describes the facilities at each of the park's visitor service areas.

❺ Flamingo. Museum, lodge, restaurant, lounge, gift shop, marina, and campground. *Mailing address: Box 279, Homestead 33030, tel. 305/247–6211 (Park Service), tel. 305/253–2241 (Everglades Lodge). Visitor center open daily 8–5.*

❻ Gulf Coast Ranger Station. Visitor center, where back-country campers pick up required free permits; exhibits; gift shop. *Follow Everglades National Park signs from Tamiami Trail (U.S. 41) south on Rte. 29, tel. 813/695–3311. Open daily winter 8–5, reduced hours in summer. Admission free.*

❼ Key Largo Ranger Station. No exhibits. *98710 Overseas Hwy., Key Largo, tel. 305/852–5119. Not always staffed; phone ahead. Admission free.*

❽ Main Visitor Center. Exhibits, film, bookstore, park headquarters. *11 mi west of Homestead on Rte. 9336, tel. 305/247–6211.*

Visitor Center open 8–5. Park open 24 hrs. Admission: $5 per car (good for 7 days); $3 per person on foot, bicycle, or motorcycle; senior citizens over 62 free.

9 Royal Palm Visitor Center. Anhinga Trail boardwalk, Gumbo Limbo Trail through hammock, museum, bookstore, vending machines. *Tel. 305/247–6211. Open 8–4:30, with a half hour off for lunch.*

10 Shark Valley. Tram tour, ¼-mile boardwalk, hiking trails, rotating exhibits, bookstore. *Box 42, Ochopee 33943, tel. 305/221–8776. Open daily 8:30–6. Admission: $3 per car, $1 per person on foot, bicycle, or motorcycle (good for 7 days); senior citizens over 62 free. Show Shark Valley admission receipt at Main Visitor Center and pay only the difference there.*

11 Miccosukee Indian Village. Near the Shark Valley entrance to Everglades National Park, the Miccosukee tribe operates an Indian village as a tourist attraction. You can watch Indian families cooking and making clothes, dolls, beadwork, and baskets. You'll also see an alligator-wrestling demonstration. The village has a boardwalk and a museum. *On Tamiami Trail (U.S. 41) 40 mi west of Miami. Mailing address: Box 440021, Miami 33144, tel. 305/223–8380. Open daily 9–5. Admission: $5 adults, $3.50 children. Airboat rides: $6 for 30-min trip to another Indian camp on an island in the heart of the Everglades.*

Shopping

Biscayne National Park **Biscayne National Park Tour Boats.** T-shirts, snorkeling and diving gear, snacks, and information on Biscayne National Park are available at park headquarters north of the canal. A dive shop van with air compressor is parked south of the canal at Homestead Bayfront Park. *Tel. 305/247–2400. Open daily. Office open 8:30–5:30. AE, MC, V.*

Everglades National Park **Flamingo Lodge Marina & Outpost Resort.** The gift shop sells mosquito repellent, Everglades guides, popular novels, T-shirts, souvenirs, and artwork (*see* Participant Sports). *Tel. 305/253–2241 or 813/695–3101. Open daily Nov.–Apr. 8–5. AE, CB, DC, MC, V.*

Florida City **Robert is Here.** A remarkable fruit stand. Robert grows and sells (in season) any tropical fruit that will grow near Everglades National Park. *19200 Palm Dr. (S.W. 344th St.), tel. 305/246–1592. Open daily 8–7. No credit cards.*

Homestead Homestead's main shopping streets are Homestead Boulevard (U.S. 1), Krome Avenue (Rte. 997), and Campbell Drive (S.W. 312th St., N.E. 8th St.). Shopping centers with major department stores are 10–20 miles north of Homestead along South Dixie Highway (U.S. 1).

Participant Sports

Most of the sports and recreational opportunities in Everglades National Park and Biscayne National Park are related in some way to water or nature study, or both. Even on land, be prepared to get your feet wet on the region's marshy hiking trails. In summer, save your outdoor activities for early or late in the day to avoid the sun's strongest rays and use a sunscreen. Carry mosquito repellent at any time of year.

Water Sports
Boating Carry aboard the proper *NOAA Nautical Charts* before you cast off to explore the waters of the parks. The charts cost $12.50 each. They are sold at many marine stores in south Florida, at the Convoy Point Visitor Center in Biscayne National Park, and in Flamingo Marina.

Waterway Guide (southern regional edition) is an annual publication of *Boating Industry Magazine*, which many boaters use as a guide to these waters. Bookstores all over south Florida sell it, or you can order it directly from the publisher. *Circulation Department,* Waterway Guide, *850 Third Ave., New York, NY 10022, tel. 800/233–3359 or 212/715–2600 in NY. Cost: $18.95 plus $3 shipping and handling.*

Canoeing The subtropical wilderness of southern Florida is a mecca for flat-water paddlers. In winter, you'll find the best canoeing that the two parks can offer. Temperatures are moderate, rainfall is minimal, and the mosquitoes are tolerable.

Before you paddle into the back country and camp overnight, get a required free permit from the rangers in the park where you plan to canoe (at Convoy Point, Elliott Key, and Adams Key for Biscayne; at Everglades City or Flamingo for Everglades. The Biscayne permit isn't valid for Everglades, and vice versa).

You don't need a permit for day-trips, but tell someone where you're going and when you expect to return. Getting lost out there is easy, and spending the night without proper gear can be unpleasant, if not dangerous.

At Biscayne, you can explore five creeks through the mangrove wilderness within 1½ miles of park headquarters at Convoy Point.

Everglades has six well-marked canoe trails in the Flamingo area, including the southern end of the 100-mile Wilderness Waterway from Flamingo to Everglades City. North American Canoe Tours in Everglades City runs a seven-hour shuttle service to haul people, cars, and canoes 151 road-miles between Everglades City and Flamingo.

The vendors listed below all rent aluminum canoes. Most have 17-foot Grummans. Bring your own cushions.

Biscayne National Park Tour Boats. At Convoy Point in Biscayne National Park. *Tel. 305/247–2400. Office open daily 8:30–5:30. Cost: $5 per hr, $17.50 for 4 hrs, $22.50 per day. No launch fee. AE, MC, V.*

Everglades National Park Boat Tours. Gulf Coast Ranger Station in Everglades City. *Tel. 813/695–2591, in FL 800/445–7724. Open daily 8:30–4:30. Cost: $10 per half day, $15 per day; Flamingo-Everglades City shuttle: $100. No credit cards.*

North America Canoe Tours at Glades Haven. This outfitter rents canoes and runs guided Everglades trips approved by the National Park Service. *800 S.E. Copeland Ave., Box 443, Everglades City 33929, tel. 813/695–2746. Open daily 7 AM–9 PM; guided trips Nov. 1–Mar. 31. Canoes $18 the first day, $15 per day thereafter. No children under age 8 on guided tours. No pets in park campsites. Reservations required. MC, V.*

Marinas Listed below are the major marinas serving the two parks. The dock masters at these marinas can provide information on other marine services you may need.

Black Point Marina. A new 155-acre Metro-Dade County Park with a hurricane-safe harbor basin, five miles north of Homestead Bayfront Park. Facilities include storage racks for 300 boats, 178 wet slips, 10 ramps, fuel, a bait-and-tackle shop, canoe-launching ramp, power-boat rentals, and police station. Shrimp fleet docks at the park. At east end of Coconut Palm Drive (S.W. 248th St.). From Florida's Turnpike, exit at S.W. 112th Avenue, go two blocks north, and turn east on Coconut Palm Drive. *24775 S.W. 87th Ave., Naranja, tel. 305/258–4092. Open daily 6 AM–9 PM. AE, MC, V.*

Marine Management. At Black Point Marina. Rents 18–25-foot Well Craft. *Tel. 305/258–3500. Open daily Oct.–Mar. 8–5, Apr.–Sept. daily except Christmas. MC, V.*

Pirate's Spa Marina. Just west of Black Point Park entrance. Shrimp boats dock along canal. Facilities include boat hoist, wet and dry storage, fuel, bait and tackle, and boat rental. *8701 Coconut Palm Dr. (S.W. 248th St.), Naranja, tel. 305/257–5100. Open weekdays 7 AM–sundown, weekends open 6 AM. No credit cards.*

Flamingo Lodge Marina & Outpost Resort. Fifty-slip marina rents 40 canoes, 10 power skiffs, 5 houseboats, and several private boats available for charter. There are two ramps, one for Florida Bay, the other for Whitewater Bay and the back country. The hoist across the plug dam separating Florida Bay from the Buttonwood Canal can take boats up to 26 feet long. A small marina store sells food, camping supplies, bait and tackle, and automobile and boat fuel. *Tel. 305/253–2241 from Miami, 813/695–3101 from Gulf Coast. Open winter 6 AM–7 PM, summer 7–6. AE, DC, MC, V.*

Homestead Bait and Tackle. Facilities include dock and wet slips, fuel, bait and tackle, ice, boat hoist, and ramp. The marina is near Homestead Bayfront Park's tidal swimming area and concessions. *North Canal Dr., Homestead, tel. 305/245–2273. Open daily weekdays 7–5, weekends 7–6. MC, V.*

Diving
Dive Boats and Instruction

Biscayne National Park Tour Boats. This is the official concessionaire for Biscayne National Park. The center provides equipment for dive trips and sells equipment. Snorkeling and scuba trips include about 2½ hours on the reefs. *Reef Rover V*, an aluminum dive boat, carries up to 49 passengers. The resort course and private instruction lead to full certification. *Office and dive boat at Convoy Point. Mailing address: Box 1270, Homestead 33030, tel. 305/247–2400. Open daily 8:30–5:30. Snorkeling and scuba trips Tues. and Sat. 1–5; group charters any day. Cost: $19.52 snorkeling, $24.50 scuba. Reservations required. Children welcome. AE, MC, V.*

Pirate's Cove Dive Center. This is the last dive store north of the Keys, and it rents, sells, and repairs diving equipment. Staff teaches all sport-diving classes, including resort course, deep diver, and underwater photography. The center does not have a boat; instead they use dive boats at Homestead Bayfront Park. PADI affiliation. *116 N. Homestead Blvd., Homestead 33030, tel. 305/248–1808. Open all year weekdays 9–6:30, Sat. 8–6, Sun. 8–4. Open to 7:30 May–Sept., around the clock during annual 4-day sport divers' lobster season (in July or Aug.). AE, DC, MC, V.*

Fishing

The rangers in the two parks enforce all state fishing laws and a few of their own. Ask at each park's visitor centers for that park's specific regulations.

Swimming **Homestead Bayfront Park.** This saltwater atoll pool, adjacent to Biscayne Bay, which is flushed by tidal action, is popular with local family groups and teenagers. *N. Canal Dr., Homestead, tel. 305/247–1543. Open daily, 7 AM to sundown. Admission: $2 per car.*

Elliott Key. Boaters like to anchor off Elliott Key's 30-foot-wide sandy beach, the only beach in Biscayne National Park. It's about a mile north of the harbor on the west (bay) side of the key.

Bicycling and **Biscayne National Park.** Elliott Key's resident rangers lead in-
Hiking formal nature walks on a 1½-mile nature trail.

You can also walk the length of the seven-mile key along a rough path that developers bulldozed before the park was created.

Everglades National Park. Shark Valley's concessionaire has rental bicycles. You may ride or hike along the Loop Road, a 14-mile round-trip. Yield right of way to trams. *Shark Valley Tram Tours, Miami 33144, tel. 305/221–8455. Rentals daily 8:30–3, return bicycles by 4. Cost: $1.50 per hr. No reservations. No credit cards.*

Ask the rangers for *Foot and Canoe Trails of the Flamingo Area,* a leaflet that also lists bike trails. Inquire about water levels and insect conditions before you go. Get a free back-country permit if you plan to camp overnight.

Dining

Although the two parks are wilderness areas, there are restaurants within a short drive of all park entrances: between Miami and Shark Valley along the Tamiami Trail (U.S. 41), in the Homestead-Florida City area, in Everglades City, and in the Keys along the Overseas Highway (U.S. 1). The only food service in either park is at Flamingo in the Everglades.

The list below is a selection of independent restaurants on the Tamiami Trail, in the Homestead-Florida City area, and at Flamingo. Many of these establishments will pack picnic fare that you can take to the parks. (You can also find fast-food establishments with carryout service on the Tamiami Trail and in Homestead-Florida City.) The most highly recommended restaurants are indicated with a star ★.

Category	Cost*
Very Expensive	over $60
Expensive	$40–$60
Moderate	$20–$40
Inexpensive	under $20

per person without sales tax (6% in Florida), service, or drinks

The following credit card abbreviations are used: AE, American Express; CB, Carte Blanche; DC, Diners Club; MC, MasterCard; V, Visa.

Flamingo
American

Flamingo Restaurant. The view from this three-tier dining room on the second floor of the Flamingo Visitor Center will knock your socks off. Picture windows overlook Florida Bay, giving you a bird's-eye view (almost) of soaring eagles, gulls, pelicans, terns, and vultures. Try to dine at low tide when flocks of birds gather on a sandbar just offshore. Specialties include a flavorful, mildly spiced conch chowder; teriyaki chicken breast; and pork loin roasted Cuban-style with garlic and lime. The tastiest choices, however, are the seafood. If marlin is on the dinner menu, order it fried so that the moisture and flavor of the dark, chewy meat are retained. *Picnic baskets available. Will cook fish you catch if you clean it at the marina. At Flamingo Visitor Center in Everglades National Park, Flamingo, tel. 305/253–2241 from Miami, 813/695–3101 from Gulf Coast. Dress: informal. Reservations required for dinner. AE, MC, V. Closed early May–mid-Oct. (The snack bar at the marina store stays open all year.) Moderate.*

Florida City
Mixed Menu
★

Richard Accursio's Capri Restaurant and **King Richard's Room.** This is where locals dine out—business groups at lunch, the Rotary Club each Wednesday at noon, and families at night. Specialties include pizza with light, crunchy crusts and ample toppings; mild, meaty conch chowder; mussels in garlic-cream or marinara sauce; Caesar salad with lots of cheese and anchovies; antipasto with a homemade, vinegary Italian dressing; pasta shells stuffed with rigatoni cheese, in tomato sauce; yellowtail snapper Française; and Key-lime pie with plenty of real Key lime juice. *935 N. Krome Ave., Florida City, tel. 305/247–1542. Dress: Capri informal, jacket and tie in King Richard's. Reservations advised. AE, MC, V. Closed Sun. except Mother's Day and Christmas. Inexpensive.*

Seafood
★

Captain Bob's. The Greek family who owns this restaurant has a list of more than 800 ways to prepare seafood. Specialties include snapper wrapped in phyllo dough in dill volute sauce; sea trout senator, with sliced almonds, mushrooms, scallions, and sherry-lemon butter sauce; and blackened wahoo. Save room for the Key-lime pie. *326 S.E. 1st Ave., Florida City, tel. 305/247–8988. Dress: informal. Reservations accepted. AE, CB, DC, MC, V. Inexpensive.*

Homestead
American

Downtown Bar and Outdoor Cafe. A south Florida interpretation of a New Orleans courtyard restaurant, complete with a wrought-iron gate and live entertainment. Specialties include Buffalo chicken wings (hot or mild) with celery and bleu-cheese dip; blackened or grilled dolphin or grouper from the Keys; raspberry nut cake; and refreshingly tart lemonade. *28 S. Krome Ave., Homestead, tel. 305/245–8266. Dress: informal. Reservations accepted. AE, MC, V. Closed Easter, Thanksgiving, Christmas. Inexpensive.*

Potlikker's. This southern country-style restaurant takes its name from the broth—*pot liquor*—left over from the boiling of greens. Live plants dangle from open rafters in the lofty pine-lined dining room. Specialties include fried Okeechobee catfish (all you can eat on Mondays), with Cajun spicing in a cornmeal-matzo-meal breading; roast turkey with homemade dressing, and at least 11 different vegetables to serve with lunch and dinner entrées. For dessert, try sweet potato pie. The Key-lime pie here is four inches tall and frozen; it tastes great if you dawdle over dessert while it thaws. *591 Washington Ave.,*

Homestead, tel. 305/248–0835. Dress: informal. No reservations. MC, V. Inexpensive.

Mexican **El Toro Taco.** The Hernandez family came to the United States from San Luis Potosí, Mexico, to pick crops. They opened this Homestead-area institution in 1971. They make salt-free tortillas and nacho chips with corn from Texas that they cook and grind themselves. The cilantro-dominated salsa is mild for American tastes; if you like more fire on your tongue, ask for a side dish of minced jalapeño peppers to mix in. Specialties include chile rellenos (green peppers stuffed with meaty chunks of ground beef and topped with three kinds of cheese), and chicken *fajitas* (chunks of chicken marinated in vinegar and spices, charbroiled with onions and peppers, and served with tortillas and salsa). Bring your own beer and wine; the staff will keep it cold for you and supply lemon for your Corona beer. *1 S. Krome Ave., Homestead, tel. 305/245–5576. Dress: informal. No reservations. No credit cards. Closed Christmas Day and Dec. 26. Inexpensive.*

Seafood **The Seafood Feast Restaurant.** Bob and Julie Cisco gave up a steak-house franchise to open this all-you-can-eat seafood buffet. It features shrimp, crabs' legs, frogs' legs, several choices of fish, salads, breads, and desserts. Specialties include Cajun-style crawfish from Louisiana, garlic crabs, steamed mussels, and oysters on the half shell (on request). *27835 S. Dixie Hwy., Naranja (3½ mi northeast of downtown Homestead), tel. 305/246–1445. Dress: informal. Reservations not accepted. No alcohol on premises. AE, MC, V. Moderate.*

Tamiami Trail **The Pit Bar-B-Q.** This place will overwork your salivary glands
American with its intense aroma of barbecue and blackjack oak smoke. You order at the counter, then come when called to pick up your food. Specialties include barbecued chicken and ribs with a tangy sauce, french fries, coleslaw, and fried biscuit, and catfish, frogs' legs, and shrimp breaded and deep-fried in vegetable oil. *16400 S.W. 8th St., Miami, tel. 305/226–2272. Dress: informal. No reservations. MC, V. Closed Christmas Day. Inexpensive.*

American Indian **Miccosukee Restaurant.** Murals with Indian themes depict women cooking and men engaged in a powwow. Specialties include catfish and frogs' legs breaded and deep-fried in peanut oil, Indian fry bread (a flour-and-water dough deep-fried in peanut oil), pumpkin bread, Indian burger (ground beef browned, rolled in fry bread dough, and deep-fried), and Indian taco (fry bread with chili, lettuce, tomato, and shredded cheddar cheese on top). *On Tamiami Trail, near the Shark Valley entrance to Everglades National Park, tel. 305/223–8380, ext. 332. Dress: informal. No reservations. AE, CB, DC, MC, V. Inexpensive.*

Floridian **Coopertown Restaurant.** A rustic 30-seat restaurant full of Floridiana, including alligator skulls, stuffed alligator heads, alligator accessories (belts, key chains, and the like). Specialties include alligator and frogs' legs, breaded and deep-fried in vegetable oil, available for breakfast, lunch, or dinner. *22700 S.W. 8th St., Miami, tel. 305/226–6048. Dress: informal. No reservations. No credit cards. Inexpensive.*

Lodging

Many visitors to the two parks stay in the big-city portion of Greater Miami and spend a day visiting one or both of the parks. For serious outdoors people, such a schedule consumes too much time in traffic and leaves too little time for nature-study and recreation.

At Shark Valley, due west of Miami, you have no choice. Only the Miccosukee Indians live there; there is no motel.

Southwest of Miami, Homestead has become a bedroom community for both parks. You'll find well-kept older properties and shiny new ones, chain motels, and independents. Prices tend to be somewhat lower than in the Miami area.

Hotel and motel accommodations are available on the Gulf coast at Everglades City and Naples.

The list below is a representative selection of hotels and motels in the Homestead area. Also included are the only lodgings inside either park. The rate categories in the list are based on the all-year or peak-season price; off-peak rates may be a category or two lower.

Category	Cost*
Very Expensive	over $120
Expensive	$90–$120
Moderate	$50–$90
Inexpensive	under $50

per room, double occupancy, without 6% state sales tax and modest resort tax

The following credit card abbreviations are used. AE, American Express; CB, Carte Blanche; DC, Diners Club; MC, MasterCard; V, Visa.

Flamingo Lodge Marina & Outpost Resort. This rustic low-rise wilderness resort, the only lodging inside Everglades National Park, is a strip of tentative civilization 300 yards wide and 1½ miles long. Accommodations are basic but attractive and well kept. An amiable staff with a sense of humor helps you become accustomed to alligators bellowing in the sewage-treatment pond down the road, raccoons roaming the pool enclosure at night, and the flock of ibis grazing on the lawn. The rooms have wood-paneled walls, contemporary furniture, floral bedspreads, and art prints of flamingos and egrets on the walls. Most bathrooms are near the door, so you won't track mud all over the room. Television reception varies with wind conditions and vultures perching on the antenna, but you don't come here to watch TV. All motel rooms overlook Florida Bay. The cottages are in a wooded area on the margin of a coastal prairie. Ask about reserving tours, skiffs, and canoes when you make reservations. *Box 428, Flamingo 33030, tel. 305/253–2241 from Miami, 813/695–3101 from Gulf Coast. 121 units with bath, including 102 motel rooms, 2 2-bath suites for up to 8 people, 17 kitchenette cottages (2 for handicapped guests). Facilities: screened outdoor freshwater swimming pool, restaurant,* *lounge, marina, marina store with snack bar, gift shop, coin laundry. AE, CB, DC, MC, V. Lodge, marina, and marina store open all year; restaurant, lounge, and gift shop closed May 1–Oct. 31. Moderate.*

Greenstone Motel. Centrally located low-rise motel, in downtown Homestead's Historic District, this place was built in 1960 and remodeled in 1987. Rooms decorated in earth tones, with photos of waves and seagulls over the beds, which are medium firm. The best rooms face south, overlooking a vestpocket park with benches and shrubbery. The second floor balcony in front is a good vantage point to see the magnolia design in the pavement on the street below. *304 N. Krome Ave., Homestead 33030, tel. 305/247–8334. 24 rooms. Facilities: free HBO, coffee bar in lobby. AE, CB, DC, MC, V. Moderate.*

Holiday Inn. Low-rise motel on a commercial strip. The best rooms look out on the landscaped pool and adjoining Banana Bar. Rooms have contemporary walnut furnishings and firm, bouncy mattresses. *990 N. Homestead Blvd., Homestead 33030, tel. 305/247–7020 or 800/HOLIDAY. 139 rooms with bath. Facilities: outdoor freshwater swimming pool, restaurant and lounge with entertainment Wed.–Sat., poolside bar, radio and cable TV, massage shower heads. AE, CB, DC, MC, V. Moderate.*

Knights Inn. This low-rise motel opened in 1987 on a commercial strip next door to a McDonald's. Beds are a foot longer than normal, and the mattresses are firm. The inn is decorated in English half-timber style, inside and out. *401 U.S. 1, Florida City 33034, tel. 305/245–2800. 100 rooms, 11 fully equipped kitchenettes, 27 for handicapped guests. Facilities: outdoor freshwater swimming pool, free HBO and TV movies, free ice, free local phone calls, coffee bar in lobby, security at night. AE, CB, DC, MC, V. Moderate.*

Park Royal Inn. This low-rise motel on a commercial strip has rooms with rough wood walls, flower bedspreads, blue or gray carpet, gray chairs and dressers, and lamps with a shell or pelican design. No closet, very small clothes rack. *100 U.S. 1, Florida City 33034, tel. 305/247–3200 or 800/521–6004. 163-unit motel, including 1 efficiency apartment, 7 rooms for handicapped guests. Facilities: outdoor freshwater swimming pool, minirefrigerator in each room, color TV, phone. AE, CB, DC, MC, V. Moderate.*

Camping
Biscayne
National Park
You can camp on designated keys seven miles offshore at primitive sites or in the back country. Carry all your food, water, and supplies onto the keys, and carry all trash off when you leave. Bring plenty of insect repellent. *Free. No reservations. No ferry or marina services. For back-country camping, obtain a required free permit from rangers at Adams Key, Convoy Point, or Elliott Key.*

Everglades
National Park
All campgrounds are primitive, with no water or electricity. Come early to get a good site, especially in winter. Bring plenty of insect repellent. *Open all year. Check-out time 10 AM. Admission: $7 per site in winter, free in summer. Stay limited to 14 days Nov. 1–Apr. 30. Register at campground.*

Long Pine Key. 108 campsites, drinking water, sewage dump station.

Flamingo. 235 drive-in sites, 60 walk-in sites, drinking water, cold-water showers, and sewage dump station.

Back country. 34 designated sites, most with chickees (raised wood platforms with thatch roofs). All have chemical toilets. Carry all your food, water, and supplies in; carry out all trash. Get free permit from rangers at Everglades City or Flamingo. Permits issued for a specific site. Capacity and length of stay limited.

4 Fort Lauderdale

Introduction

If you think of Fort Lauderdale only as a spring-break mecca for collegians seeking sun, suds, and surf, your knowledge is both fragmentary and out of date. The 1960 film, *Where the Boys Are*, attracted hordes of young people to the city's beaches for more than two decades, but now the center of spring-break activity has shifted north to Daytona Beach.

Fort Lauderdale today emphasizes year-round family tourism focused on a wide assortment of sports and recreational activities, an extensive cultural calendar, artistic and historic attractions, and fine shopping and dining opportunities.

Sandwiched between Miami to the south and Palm Beach to the north along southeast Florida's Gold Coast, Fort Lauderdale is the county seat of Broward County. The county encompasses 1,197 square miles—17 square miles less than the state of Rhode Island. Broward County has 23 miles of Atlantic Ocean beach frontage, and it extends 50 miles inland to the west. A coastal ridge rising in places to 25 feet above sea level separates the coastal lowlands from the interior lowlands of the Everglades.

Broward County is named for Napolean Bonaparte Broward, Florida's governor 1905–09. His drainage schemes around the turn of the century opened much of the marshy Everglades region for farming, ranching, and settlement. In fact, the first successful efforts at large-scale Everglades drainage took place within Broward County's boundaries.

Fort Lauderdale's first known white settler, Charles Lewis, established a plantation along the New River in 1793. The city is named for a fort which Major William Lauderdale built at the river's mouth in 1838 during the Seminole Indian wars.

The area was still a remote frontier when Frank Stranahan arrived in 1892 to operate an overnight camp on the river. Stranahan began trading with the Indians in 1901 and built a store, which later became his residence. It's now a museum.

Fort Lauderdale incorporated in 1911 with just 175 residents, but it grew rapidly during the Florida boom of the 1920s. Today the city's population of 160,000 remains relatively stable, while suburban areas bulge with growth. Broward County's population is expected to exceed 1.35 million by 1990—more than double its 1970 population of 620,000. The county has become a haven for retirees; more than a third of the new arrivals are over the age of 55.

New homes, offices and shopping centers have filled in the gaps between older communities along the coastal ridge. Now they're marching west along I-75, I-595, and the Sawgrass Expressway, transforming the Everglades. Meanwhile, Fort Lauderdale is building skyscrapers downtown to cement its position as the county's financial and commercial hub.

Broward County is developing a concentration of clean high-technology industries, including computer manufacturing, data processing, and electronics. Port Everglades, a major deep-water seaport, handles refined petroleum products and general cargo. A cruise terminal at Port Everglades caters to luxury liners, leaving the mass-market cruise business to the Port of Miami.

To accommodate the traffic that comes with all this growth, the Florida Department of Transportation is expanding Broward County's road system. During 1990, construction on I–95 and I–595 threatens to create gridlock during rush hours. Tri-Rail, a tri-county commuter train running through Broward County from Miami to West Palm Beach, will take some cars off the highways, but you should still expect traffic delays and allow extra time to move around the county.

Even when you're stuck in traffic, you can still enjoy Broward County's near-ideal weather. The average temperature is 75 degrees (winter average 66 degrees, summer average 84 degrees). Rainfall averages 65 inches a year, with 60% of the total occurring in afternoon thunderstorms June–October. The warm, relatively dry winters help to give the county about 3,000 hours of sunshine a year.

Arriving and Departing by Plane

Airport   **Fort Lauderdale-Hollywood International Airport (FLHIA),** four miles south of downtown Fort Lauderdale, is Broward County's major airline terminal. To get there off I–95, take the I–595 east exit to U.S. 1 and follow the signs to the airport entrance.

Between the Airport and Center City   Broward Transit's bus route No. 1 operates between the airport and its main terminal at N.W. 1st Street and 1st Avenue in the center of Fort Lauderdale. The fare is 75 cents. Limousine service is available from *Yellow Airport Limousine Service* (tel. 305/527–8690) to all parts of Broward County. Fares range from $6 to $13 or more per person, depending on distance. Fares to most Fort Lauderdale beach hotels are in the $6–$8 range. Pickup points are at each of the new terminals.

Arriving and Departing by Car, Train, and Bus

By Car   The access highways to Broward County from the north or south are Florida's Turnpike, I–95, U.S. 1, and U.S. 441; for a more scenic—and slower—drive, Rte. A1A, which generally parallels the beach area. The primary access road to Broward County from the west is Rte. 84.

By Train   **Amtrak** provides daily service to Broward County, with stops at Hollywood, Fort Lauderdale, and Deerfield Beach. *Fort Lauderdale station, 200 S.W. 21st Terr., tel. 305/463–8251; reservations, tel. 800/872–7245.*
Tri-Rail, which connects Broward, Dade, and Palm Beach counties, has six stations in Broward. All stations are west of I–95; the location of the FLHIA station may change in 1990. *Tel. 305/ 728–8445 or 800/TRI–RAIL (in Dade, Broward, and Palm Beach counties).*

By Bus   **Greyhound** Bus Lines (513 N.E. 3rd St., Ft. Lauderdale, tel. 305/764–6551 or 800/872–6242).

Getting Around

By Car In 1988 the Florida Department of Transportation (FDOT) began to build the last stage of the I–595/Port Everglades Expressway Project, which runs east-west through the middle of Broward County. By 1991, 15 interchanges will be improved and local roads will be linked to I–595, which follows the Rte. 84 corridor from I–75 east to the port.

At the same time, I–95 is being widened, disrupting north-south traffic for 46 miles from Yamato Road, in southern Palm Beach County, through Broward County to Rte. 836, in northern Dade County.

If you're driving into Florida, stop at a visitor center near the state line for a traveler advisory card on the current status of I–95 construction. Ask for current information on travel time and alternative routes.

FDOT officials urge you to take Florida's Turnpike or the Sawgrass Expressway through Broward County to avoid I–95. A new interchange at S.W. 10th Street in Deerfield Beach connects the Sawgrass Expressway directly to I–95. Other alternatives include crowded local roads such as A1A, U.S. 1, U.S. 441, and University Drive (Rte. 817).

Listen to radio traffic reports on the status of I–95 construction. Your hotel clerk should know which stations have them.

Try to avoid driving anywhere in Broward County—and especially on I–95—in the morning and evening rush hours (7–9 AM and 3–6 PM). Allow plenty of time to get where you're going, be patient, and stay calm. South Florida drivers can be among the world's worst.

FDOT has set up a consumer service organization to issue free publications and to provide traffic reports by phone. *Gold Coast Commuter Services, 6261 N.W. 6th Way, Suite 100, Fort Lauderdale, tel. 305/771–9500 or in FL 800/234–7433. Open 8–5.*

By Bus **Broward County Mass Transit** serves the entire county. The fare is 75 cents plus 10 cents for a transfer, with some bus routes starting as early as 5 AM; most end at 10 PM. Call for route information (tel. 305/357–8400). There are also special seven-day tourist passes for $8 that are good for unlimited use on all county buses. These are available at most major hotels.

By Taxi It's difficult to hail a taxi on the street; sometimes you can pick one up at a major hotel. Otherwise, phone ahead. Fares are not cheap; meters run at the rate of $2.20 for the first mile and $1.50 for each additional mile. The major company serving the area is **Yellow Cab** (tel. 305/565–5400).

By Water Taxi **Water Taxi** (tel. 305/565–5507) provides service along the Intracoastal Waterway between Port Everglades and Commercial Boulevard 10 AM–3 AM. The boats stop at 20 restaurants, hotels, and nightclubs; the fare is $2.50 one way.

Important Addresses and Numbers

Tourist Information The main office of the Greater Fort Lauderdale Convention & Visitors Bureau (tel. 305/765–4466) is at 500 E. Broward Boulevard, Suite 104. The office is open weekdays 8:30–5. A new information booth—the first of four—has been established at the Delta Terminal of the Fort Lauderdale International Airport and is open daily 10–10. Other communities in Broward County also have individual chambers of commerce, including Dania (Box 838, Dania 33004, tel. 305/927–3377), Hollywood (330 N. Federal Hwy., Hollywood 33020, tel. 305/776–1000), Oakland Park–Wilton Manors (181 N.E. 32nd Ct., Oakland Park 33334, tel. 305/564–8300), and Pompano Beach (2200 E. Atlantic Blvd., Pompano Beach 33062, tel. 305/941–2940).

Tickets Call **Ticketmaster** to order tickets for performing arts and sports events (tel. 800/446–3939 or tel. 305/523–3309).

Emergencies Dial 911 for **police** and **ambulance** in an emergency.

Poison Control (tel. 800/282–3171).

Hospitals. The following hospitals have a 24-hour emergency room: **Holy Cross Hospital** (4725 N. Federal Hwy., Fort Lauderdale, tel. 305/771–8000; physician referral, tel. 305/776–3223) and **Broward General Medical Center** (1 Corporate Plaza, Fort Lauderdale, tel. 305/355–4400; physician referral, tel. 305/466–2411).

24-Hour Pharmacies. Eckerd Drug (1385 S.E. 17th St., Fort Lauderdale, tel. 305/525–8173; and 154 University Dr., Pembroke Pines, tel. 305/432–5510). **Walgreens** (2855 Stirling Rd., Fort Lauderdale, tel. 305/981–1104; 71 S.E. 17th St., Fort Lauderdale, tel. 305/467–5448; and 289 S. Federal Hwy., Deerfield Beach, tel. 305/481–2993.)

24-Hour Doctors House Calls. Many Broward hotels use this referral service, which will send a physician to you. Medical services available include general medicine, pediatrics, and geriatrics. In-office dental referrals and translators are available. *3801 N. University Dr., Suite 507, Sunrise 33321, tel. 305/ 522–1522. MC, V.*

Telecommunications for the Hearing-Impaired. United Hearing and Deaf Services (4850 W. Oakland Park Blvd., Suite 207, Lauderdale Lakes, tel. 305/731–7208).

Guided Tours

The Voyager Sightseeing Train offers nine different tram tours, including a city tour of Fort Lauderdale. *600 Seabreeze Blvd., Fort Lauderdale, tel. 305/463–0401 (Broward County), tel. 305/944–4669 (Dade County).*

The *Jungle Queen,* built to resemble an old-time steamboat, travels day and night up the New River through the heart of Fort Lauderdale. Dinner cruises are available. The same company sends boats to Miami's Bayside Marketplace. All cruises leave from the Bahia Mar dock on Rte. A1A (*see* Hotels, below). *Tel. 305/462–5596 (Broward County), 305/947–6597 (Dade County).*

The *Paddlewheel Queen,* a flat-bottom luncheon and sightseeing cruise boat, visits major spots along Fort Lauderdale's Intracoastal Waterway. Four sailings daily. *2950 N.E. 30th St., a block south of Oakland Park Boulevard bridge, two blocks west of Rte. A1A, tel. 305/564–7659. AE, MC, V.*

Exploring Fort Lauderdale

*Numbers in the margin correspond with points of interest on
the Fort Lauderdale Area map.*

Central Fort Lauderdale is diverse, picturesque, and surpris-
ingly compact. Within a few blocks you'll find modern high-rise
office buildings; a historic district with museums, restaurants
and antique shops; a scenic riverfront drive; upscale shopping;
and the only tunnel in Florida—all within two miles of the
beach.

This tour begins on the beach at Las Olas Boulevard and Rte.
A1A. Go north on Rte. A1A along **the beach,** with hotels, restaurants and shops on your left, the ocean on your right. Turn
❶ left at Sunrise Boulevard, then right into **Hugh Taylor Birch
State Recreation Area.** Amid the 180-acre park's tropical green-
ery, you can stroll along a nature trail, picnic, and canoe. *3109
E. Sunrise Blvd., tel. 305/564–4521; concessions tel. 305/563–
1714. Open 8–sundown. Admission: $1 per car and driver, 50¢
per passenger; (out of state): $2 per car and driver, $1 per passenger.*

Leaving the park, go south on Birch Road to Las Olas Boulevard, turn right, and cross the Intracoastal Waterway. You're
❷ now westbound through **The Isles,** Fort Lauderdale's most expensive and prestigious neighborhood, where the homes line a
series of canals with large yachts beside the seawalls. When
you reach the mainland, Las Olas becomes an upscale shopping
street with Spanish-Colonial buildings housing high-fashion
boutiques, jewelry shops, and art galleries. The heart of the
Las Olas Shopping District is from S.E. 12th Avenue to S.E. 6th
Avenue.

❸ Turn left on S.E. 6th Avenue, and visit **Stranahan House,** home
of pioneer businessman Frank Stranahan. He arrived in 1892
and began trading with the Seminole Indians. In 1901 he built
this building as a store, and later made it his home. Now it's a
museum with many of the Stranahans' furnishings on display. *1
Stranahan Pl. (S.E. 6th Ave.), tel. 305/524–4736. Open Wed.,
Fri., Sat. 10–4. Admission: $3, $2 children under 12.*

Return to Las Olas Boulevard, go to S.W. 1st Avenue, and turn
left beside the *News & Sun-Sentinel* building. Go a block south
to New River Drive, where you can park and stroll a portion of
❹ the palm-lined **River Walk,** a linear park with walkways and
sidewalk cafes along both banks of the New River. As part of a
$44-million redevelopment program, Fort Lauderdale is im-
proving and extending the River Walk. Unlike the Miami River,
which carries a heavy load of commercial shipping, New River
traffic is primarily recreational yachts and tour boats. This
portion of New River Drive returns you to Las Olas Boulevard
at S.W. 5th Avenue.

Turn left, and go to the **Museum of Art,** which features a major
collection of works from the CoBrA (Copenhagen, Brussels,
and Amsterdam) movement, plus American Indian, Pre-
Columbian, West African, and Oceanic ethnographic art. Edward Larabee Barnes designed the museum building, which
opened in 1986. *1 E. Las Olas Blvd., tel. 305/525–5500. Open
Tues. 11–9, Wed.–Sat. 10–5, Sun. noon–5. Admission: $3.25*

Fort Lauderdale Area

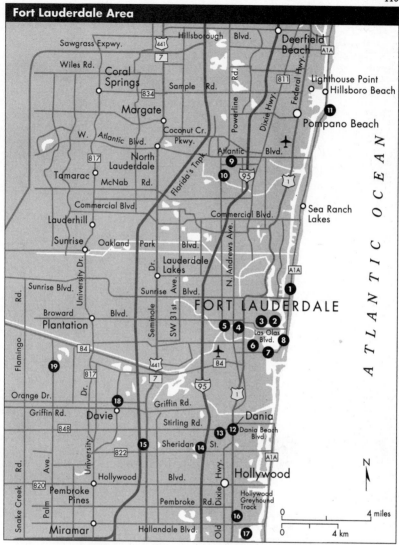

Brooks Memorial Causeway, **7**

Broward County Museum of Archaeology, **5**

Dania Jai-Alai Palace, **12**

Davie, **18**

Flamingo Gardens, **19**

Gulfstream Park, **17**

Hillsboro Lighthouse, **11**

Hollywood Dog Track, **16**

Hugh Taylor Birch State Recreation Area, **1**

The Isles, **2**

Ocean World, **6**

Pompano Harness Track, **9**

Quiet Waters Park, **10**

River Walk, **4**

Seminole Okalee Indian Village, **15**

Six Flags Atlantis, **13**

Stranahan House, **3**

Swimming Hall of Fame Museum, **8**

Topeekeegee Yugnee Park, **14**

adults, $2.75 seniors, $1.25 students, free under 12. Free 1-hour highlight tours Tues. noon and 6:30 PM, Wed.–Sat. noon, Sun. 2 PM. Parking nearby in municipal garage.

Go west on Las Olas Boulevard to S.W. 1st Avenue, and stop at
⑤ the **Broward County Museum of Archaeology.** Featured here are a 2,000-year-old skeleton of a Tequesta Indian girl, remains of Ice Age mammals, a diorama of Indian life, and information on archaeological techniques. Special shows display artifacts of African, pre-Columbian, and other cultures. *203 S.W. 1st Ave., tel. 305/525–8778. Open Tues.–Sat. 10–4, Sun. 1–4. Admission: $1 adults, 50¢ children and seniors.*

Take S.W. 1st Avenue north to S.W. 2nd Street, turn left, cross the Florida East Coast Railway tracks, and turn left onto S.W. 2nd Avenue. You're now in **Himmarshee Village,** an eight-square-block historic district. Park and walk to explore several fascinating museums.

The **Fort Lauderdale Historical Society Museum** surveys the city's history from the Seminole Indian era to World War II. A model in the lobby depicts old Fort Lauderdale. The building also houses a research library and a bookstore. *219 S.W. 2nd Ave., tel. 305/463–4431. Open Tues.–Sat. 10–4, Sun. 1–4. Admission by donation.*

The **Discovery Center** includes a science museum in the three-story **New River Inn,** Fort Lauderdale's first hotel, and a pioneer residence museum in the restored **King-Cromartie House.** The Discovery Center Museum is a child-oriented place with hands-on exhibits that explore optical illusions and bend rays of light, an insect zoo, a glass-front beehive, a loom, a computer center, and a small planetarium. *229 and 231 S.W. 2nd Ave., tel. 305/462–4115. Open Tues.–Fri. 2–5, Sat. and school holidays 10–5, Sun. 1–5. Admission (includes both museums): $3, under 3 free.*

A brick drive between the King-Cromartie House and the New River Inn brings you one block west to S.W. 3rd Avenue. On your left is the **Bryan House,** a 1904 dwelling which is now a restaurant.

Go north on S.W. 3rd Avenue past an assortment of antique shops and restaurants in some old commercial buildings that are also part of the Himmarshee Village historic district. At Broward Boulevard, turn right and go east to Federal Highway (U.S. 1). Turn right and go south through the **Henry E. Kinney Tunnel,** named for a founder of Fort Lauderdale; it dips beneath Las Olas Boulevard and the New River.

Continue south on Federal Highway to S.W. 17th Street, then
⑥ turn left. About a mile east is the entrance to **Ocean World.** Continuous shows daily feature trained dolphins and sea lions. Display tanks hold sharks, sea turtles, alligators, and river otters. You can feed and pet a dolphin here. *1701 S.E. 17th St., tel. 305/525–6611. Open 10–6, last show starts 4:15. Admission: $8.95 adults, $6.95 children 4–12, under 4 free. Boat tour admission: $5 adults, $4 children 4–12, under 4 free.*

⑦ Go east on S.E. 17th Street across the **Brooks Memorial Causeway** over the Intracoastal Waterway, and bear left onto Seabreeze Boulevard (Rte. A1A). You'll pass through a neighborhood of older homes set in lush vegetation before emerging at the south end of Fort Lauderdale's beachfront strip. On your left at **Bahia Mar Resort & Yachting Center,** novelist John McDonald's fictional hero, Travis McGee, is honored with a plaque at the marina where he allegedly docked his houseboat (*see* Lodging). *801 Seabreeze Blvd., tel. 305/764-2233 or 800/327-8154.*

8 Three blocks north, visit the **Swimming Hall of Fame Museum,** featuring photos, medals, and other souvenirs from major swimming events around the world. Included are memorabilia from Johnny Weissmuller, Mark Spitz, and other swimming champions. An Olympic-size pool hosts special events and is open to the public for swimming at other times. *501 Seabreeze Blvd., museum tel. 305/462-6536, pool tel. 305/523-0994. Open Mon.–Sat. 10–5, Sun. 11–4. Museum admission: $4 adults, $2 children 6–21 and seniors, $10 family. Pool admissions: $3 nonresident adults, $1.50 nonresident students.*

This concludes the central Fort Lauderdale tour. To return to the starting point, continue north on Seabreeze Boulevard to Las Olas Boulevard.

Exploring North Beach

The northeast section of Broward County includes the communities of Pompano Beach, Sea Ranch Lakes, Lighthouse Point, Deerfield Beach, and Hillsboro Beach.

9 Exit I-95 at Atlantic Boulevard and go west to Power Line Road, which will lead you to the popular **Pompano Harness Track.** The Top 'O The Park restaurant overlooks the finish line. Post time: 7:30; call for dates, tel. 305/972-2000.

10 A unique water skiing cableway is at **Quiet Water Park,** just south of the racetrack, on Power Line Road. **Ski Rixen** offers lessons for beginners, plus skis and life vests. A cable pulls the skiers. If you're skilled enough, there are all sorts of variations to the two-hand, two-ski way of skimming across the water. *Tel. 305/421-3133. Open weekdays 10–sunset, weekends 9:30–sunset. Admission: weekdays free, weekends 50 cents. Children under 5 free at all times.*

11 Take Hillsboro Boulevard east to Rte. A1A, turn right, and go south to Hillsboro Beach and the **Hillsboro Lighthouse,** a major historic landmark since 1907 and one of the most powerful lighthouses in the United States. It marks the eastern tip of the Hillsboro inlet, which provides easy access to the ocean from the Intracoastal Waterway.

Exploring Southern Broward

In southern Broward County, an exploration can include native Indian crafts and lifestyles, high-stakes pari-mutuel wagering, and a unique natural park, all within the same driving loop.

12 Start with the **Dania Jai-Alai Palace** (301 E. Dania Beach Blvd., Dania, tel. 305/428-7766), offering one of the fastest games on the planet from early November through April.

13 Take Dania Beach Boulevard west to U.S. 1, turn left, go south to Sterling Road, turn right, and go west to **Atlantis,** one of the world's largest water-theme parks. It has 2 million gallons of water in 45 pools and water slides up to 7 stories high, plus seven amusement rides, and water ski and diving shows. Highlights include a wave pool and an activity pool with trollies, slides, and rope ladders. Riders on Thunderball, the steepest water slide, reach speeds near 40 mph. The park sets minimum and maximum height requirements for participants in some activities. *2700 Stirling Rd., Box 2128, Hollywood, tel. 305/926–1000. Summer hours 10 AM–10 PM; phone for hours at other times of year. Admission: $11.95 adults, $4.95 seniors over 55, $9.95 children 3–11.*

⑭ Take Dania Beach Boulevard west to I–95, and go south to the Sheridan Street exit, then west to **Topeekeegee Yugnee Park.** Rentals include sailboats, Windsurfers, paddleboats, and canoes. *Open daily 8–8. Admission weekends and holidays: $1 car and driver, 50 cents each passenger, children under 5 free, tel. 305/961–4430.*

⑮ Take Sheridan Street west to U.S. 441/Rte. 7, turn right, and go north through the **Seminole Okalee Indian Village,** a reservation of the never-conquered Seminole Indian tribe. The Indians sell native arts and crafts and run a high-stakes bingo parlor (4150 N. Rte. 7, tel. 305/961–5140 or 305/961–3220). Three bingo games daily; call recording for information. Continue north to **Anhinga Indian Museum and Art Gallery,** where Joe Dan and Virginia Osceola display a collection of artifacts from the Seminoles and other American Indian tribes. They also sell contemporary Indian art and craft objects. *5791 S. Rte. 7, tel. 305/581–8411. Open daily 9–6. V.*

⑯ Take U.S. 441/Rte. 7 south to Pembroke Road and go east to Federal Highway to the **Hollywood Dog Track** (831 S. Federal Highway, Hallandale, tel. 305/454–7000). Call for race dates.

⑰ Take Federal Highway south to **Gulfstream Park Race Track** (901 S. Federal Hwy., tel. 305/454–7000), home of the Florida Derby, one of the southeast's foremost horse racing events. Call for race dates.

Exploring Inland

Between the coastal cities and the watery wilderness of the Everglades, urban sprawl is rapidly devouring Broward County's citrus groves and cow pastures. If you go inland, you can still find vestiges of the county's agricultural past.

⑱ The **Davie Rodeo Complex** at Orange Drive and Davie Road (6591 S.W. 45th St., Davie 33314, tel. 305/797–1166) holds rodeos in March and December. Just north on Davie Road is the **Buehler Planetarium,** where star-studded skies are on view regardless of the weather. *On the Central Campus of Broward Community College, 3501 S.W. Davie Rd., tel. 305/475–6680 (recording) or 305/475–6681. Main feature Sat. 3 and 8:30, family show Fri. 7, Sat. 1:30. Admission: $2.50 adults, $1.50 children and seniors. Reservations required.*

Take Davie Road south past Orange Drive, cross the South New River Canal, and turn right on Griffin Road. Go west to **Spykes Grove & Tropical Gardens,** where the entire family can hop aboard a tractor-pulled tram for a 15-minute tour of working citrus groves. *7250 Griffin Rd., tel. 305/583–1987. Tours hourly. Admission free. Open daily Oct.–June 9–5:30.*

⑲ Head west on Griffin Road and turn right onto Flamingo Road to **Flamingo Gardens.** There are crocodiles, alligators, monkeys, pink flamingoes, and other exotic birds, along with a petting zoo, a mini botanical garden, 60 acres of orange groves, antique car and historical museums, and a tram ride. *3750 Flamingo Rd., tel. 305/473–2955. Open daily 9–5:30. Admission: $6.50 adults, $3.25 children 4–14.*

Return to Griffin Road and go west until the road ends at the edge of the Everglades. There you'll find **Everglades Holiday Park and Campground,** which offers a 45-minute narrated airboat tour and an alligator-wrestling show featuring Seminole Indians. The park has a 100-space campground that accommodates recreational vehicles and tents. *21940 Griffin Rd., Ft. Lauderdale 33332, tel. 305/434–8111 (Broward County), 305/621–2009 (Miami). Tour: $11 adults, $5.50 children. MC, V.*

Fort Lauderdale for Free

Manatees   During the winter, manatees frolic in the warm-water discharge from Florida Power & Light Company's Port Everglades power plant. The massive marine mammals, which may be 15 feet long and weigh three-quarters of a ton, are susceptible to cold and congregate around the outfall when the temperature in local waters falls below 68 degrees.

An observation deck at the plant's intake pipe is open to the public, without charge, at all times. There you may see angelfish, reef fish, and sea turtles as well as manatees. Take Rte. 84 east to its end inside the port, turn right at Eisenhower Boulevard, and look on your right near some railroad tracks for the observation deck and a nearby parking area.

One weekend a year, usually in late January, FP&L invites the public onto the plant grounds for a closer look at the manatees. Hourly viewings, film showings. *For schedule information, phone the Broward Parks & Recreation Division's recorded special-events number, tel. 305/563–PARK, or the administrative office, tel. 305/357–8100.*

What to See and Do with Children

Butterfly World. This attraction in Tradewinds Park South is a screened-in tropical rainforest on 2.8 acres of land, where thousands of caterpillars pupate and emerge as butterflies. Up to 150 species flit through the shrubbery. Many are so tame they will land on you. Best time to go is in the afternoon; school groups fill the place in the mornings. *3600 W. Sample Rd., Coconut Creek, tel. 305/977–4400. Open Mon.–Sat 9–5, Sun. 1–5. Admission: $6 adults, $4 children 3–12 and senior citizens.*

Shopping

Shopping Districts   **Major malls:** *Galleria Mall* on Sunrise Boulevard, just west of the Intracoastal Waterway, occupies more than one million square feet and includes Neiman-Marcus, Lord & Taylor, Saks Fifth Avenue, and Brooks Brothers (open 10–9 Mon.–Sat., noon–5:30 Sun.). *Oceanwalk* in the Hollywood Beach Hotel (101 N. Ocean Dr., Hollywood) is in a seashore environment with shops, restaurants, food, and entertainment. The building is a historic landmark.
Antiques: More than 75 dealers line U.S. 1 (Federal Hwy.) in

Dania, a half mile south of the Fort Lauderdale International Airport and a half mile north of Hollywood. Open 10–5 every day but Sunday. Exit Griffin Road East off I–95.

Boutiques and Specialty Shops: *Las Olas Boulevard.* From S.E. 5th Avenue to a block east of the Himmarshee Canal. A tree-lined boulevard with a divided grassy median and bricked crosswalks, with some of the finest shops in Fort Lauderdale.

Beaches

The Fort Lauderdale area boasts an average temperature of 75.5 degrees and 25 miles of oceanfront beach. Parking is readily available, often at parking meters. At the southern end of Broward County, **John U. Lloyd Beach State Recreation Area** (6503 N. Ocean Dr., Dania) offers a beach for swimmers and sunners, but also 251 acres of mangroves, picnic facilities, fishing, and canoeing. *Open 8 AM–sunset. Park tel. 305/923–2833. Admission: nonresident $2 car and driver, $1 per passenger. Concessions tel. 305/922–7320. Open: weekdays 9–3, weekends 9–4. Canoes not rented at low tide.*

Throughout Broward County, each municipality along the Atlantic has its own public beach area. Hollywood also has a 2.5-mile boardwalk, edged with shops and eateries. Dania, Pompano Beach, Deerfield Beach, and Lauderdale-by-the-Sea have fishing piers in addition to the beaches. The most crowded portion of beach in this area is along the **Fort Lauderdale "Strip,"** which runs from Las Olas Boulevard north to Sunrise Boulevard.

In past years, there have been some serious oil spills and dumpages by freighters and tankers at sea, and the gunk has washed ashore in globules and become mixed with the beach sand. The problem has been somewhat eased, but some hotels still include a tar-removal packet with the toilet amenities. If you're concerned, ask at the desk of your hotel or motel.

Participant Sports

Biking Bicycling is popular throughout Greater Fort Lauderdale. Young children should ride accompanied by their parents because of heavy traffic and older drivers who have difficulty in seeing children on low bicycles. Some south Florida auto drivers resent bike riders. Ride defensively to avoid being pushed off the road.

Diving Good diving can be enjoyed within 20 minutes of shore along Broward County's 25-mile coast. Among the most popular of the county's 80 dive sites is the two-mile-wide, 23-mile-long Fort Lauderdale Reef.

South of Port Everglades Inlet, experienced divers can explore Barracuda and Hammerhead reefs. North of the port, three parallel coral reefs extend most of the way to the Palm Beach County line. The reef closest to shore comes within 100 yards of the beach a block north of Commercial Boulevard; the most distant is in 100 feet of water about a mile offshore. Snorkelers and beginning divers should stay on the first reef.

Dive Boats and All **Force E** stores rent scuba and snorkeling equipment. In-
Instruction struction is available at all skill levels. Dive boat charters are available. *2700 E. Atlantic Blvd., Pompano Beach, tel. 407/943–*

3488 or 800/527–8660 (answered by West Palm Beach store). Open winter weekdays 10–8:30, Sat. 8–7, Sun. 8–5; summer weekdays 8 AM–9 PM, Sat. 8–2, Sun. 8–5. 2104 W. Oakland Park Blvd., Oakland Park, tel. 305/735–6227. Hours same as Pompano Beach store.

Spas If you watch "Lifestyles of the Rich and Famous" on TV, you'll recognize the names of Greater Fort Lauderdale's two world-famous spas, the Bonaventure Resort & Spa and Palm-Aire Spa Resort. At each resort, women comprise 75%–80% of the spa clientele.

Both resorts offer single-day spa privileges to non-guests. Price and availability of services vary with seasonal demand; resort guests have priority. At each resort, day users may receive a body massage, exercise class, facials, herbal wrap, spa-cuisine lunch, and other spa facilities and services.

Bring your own sneakers and socks. The spa provides everything else you'll need. Each spa will help you design a personal exercise-and-diet program tied to your lifestyle at home. If you already have an exercise program, bring it with you. If you have a medical problem, bring a letter from your doctor.

Bonaventure Resort & Spa (250 Racquet Club Rd., Fort Lauderdale, tel. 305/389–3300) is part of a hotel and convention complex near the Sawgrass Expressway interchange with I–595 in western Broward County. Free caffeine-free herbal teas served in the morning, fresh fruit in the afternoon. Staff nutritionist follows American Heart Association and American Cancer Society guidelines, and can accommodate macrobotic and vegetarian diets. Full-service beauty salon open to the public.

Palm-Aire Spa Resort (2501 Palm-Aire Drive N., Pompano Beach, tel. 305/968–2700 or 800/327–4960). This health, fitness and stress-reduction spa offers exercise activities, personal treatments, and calorie-controlled meals. Fifteen minutes from downtown Fort Lauderdale.

Spectator Sports

Baseball The New York Yankees hold spring training in 7,000-seat Lockhart Stadium (5301 N.W. 12th Ave., Fort Lauderdale, tel. 305/776–1921).

Rugby The Fort Lauderdale Knights play rough and ready on the green at Holiday Park. *Off of Federal Hwy., 2 blocks south of Sunrise Blvd., Fort Lauderdale, tel. 305/561–5263 for a recorded message. Games Sat. 2 PM Sept.–Apr. Admission free.*

Dining

The list below is a representative selection of independent restaurants in Fort Lauderdale and Broward County, organized geographically, and by type of cuisine within each region of the county. Unless otherwise noted, they serve lunch and dinner.

The most highly recommended restaurants are indicated by a star ★.

The following credit card abbreviations are used: AE, American Express; CB, Carte Blanche; DC, Diners Club; MC, MasterCard; and V, Visa.

Category	Cost*
Very Expensive	over $55
Expensive	$35–$55
Moderate	$15–$35
Inexpensive	under $15

*per person, excluding drinks, service, and 6% sales tax

American **Boodles.** In Sheraton Design Center Hotel, you may dine on a "porch" with a fountain, overlooking the lobby; or in a wine room, an intimate "plum room," or the main dining room. Specialties include a spicy-sweet alligator chili; Boodles's house salad of field greens with goat cheese, sun-dried tomatoes, and vinaigrette dressing; and mesquite-grilled salmon with basil Key-lime butter. *1825 Griffin Rd., tel. 305/920–3500. Dress: informal. Reservations accepted. Nonsmoking seating available. AE, CB, DC, MC, V. Expensive.*

★ **Cafe Max.** As you enter Cafe Max, you're greeted by the aroma of fragrant spices issuing from the open theater kitchen. The decor includes art deco-style black wood chairs, original art work, and cut flowers. Booth seating is best; the tables are quite close together. Owner-Chef Oliver Saucy combines the best of new American cuisine with traditional *escoffier* cooking. Specialties include Anaheim chili peppers stuffed with Monterey Jack cheese; mushroom duxelles served with goat-cheese sauce; duck and smoked mozzarella ravioli with sun-dried tomatoes and basil butter; soft-shell crab with fresh tomato-jicama relish; and grilled veal chops. Daily chocolate dessert specials include hazelnut chocolate capuccino torte and white-chocolate mousse pie with fresh raspberries. Other desserts include fresh fruit sorbets and homemade ice cream served with sauce *Anglais* and fresh raspberries. *2601 E. Atlantic Blvd., Pompano Beach, tel. 305/782–0606. Jacket preferred. Dinner only. Reservations advised. AE, DC, MC, V. Expensive.*

The Garden. Coral-rock walls, earth-tone rattan furnishings, and terraced seating gives this restaurant in the Bonaventure Resort and Spa an inviting, outdoorsy appearance. It's a relaxed family restaurant, catering primarily to a resort clientele but welcoming others as well. Specialties include seafood salad appetizer (shrimp, crab, scallops) served with mustard sauce on a bed of greens, veal Milanese (medallion of veal sautéed in egg batter, with a sauce containing tomatoes, ham, mushrooms, dill pickles, and cream), and tall cheesecake (chocolate, marble, blueberry, strawberry, and plain). *250 Racquet Club Rd., tel. 305/389–3300 or 800/327–8090. Dress: informal. Reservations not accepted. AE, DC, MC, V. Moderate.*

Shorty's Bar-B-Q. A clone of the original Shorty's on U.S. 1 in Miami, opened at the request of a loyal Broward following. The food's the same, and the decor resembles the original log cabin with long wooden tables—but the new building is air-conditioned! *5989 S. University Dr., Davie 33028, tel. 305/680–9900. Reservations not accepted. Dress: informal. Closed Christmas and Thanksgiving. No credit cards. Inexpensive.*

Continental **Down Under.** When Al Kocab and Leonce Picot opened Down Under in 1968, the Australian government sent them a boomer-

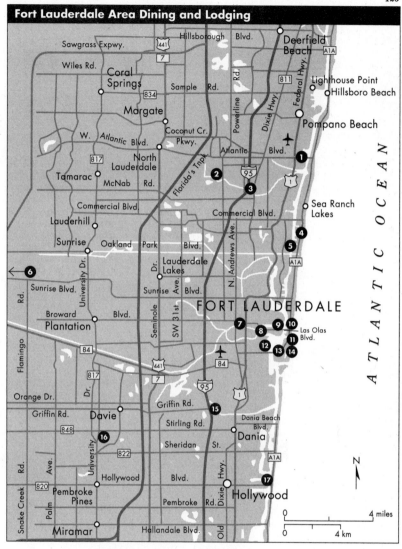

Fort Lauderdale Area Dining and Lodging

Lodging

Bahia Mar Resort & Yachting Center, **11**

Bonaventure Resort and Spa, **6**

Casa Alhambra, **10**

De Vito by the Sea, **17**

Fort Lauderdale Marriott Hotel & Marina, **12**

Marriott's Harbor Beach Resort, **14**

Palm-Aire Spa/Resort, **2**

Pier 66 Hotel and Marina, **13**

Riverside Hotel, **8**

Royce Resort Hotel, **4**

Sheraton Design Center Hotel, **15**

Westin Cyprus Creek, **3**

Dining

Boodles, **15**

Cafe Max, **1**

Casa Vecchia, **9**

Down Under, **5**

The Garden, **6**

Renaissance, **6**

Shirttail Charlie's, **7**

Shorty's Bar-B-Q, **16**

Spa Restaurant, **6**

ang as a gift. The name actually describes the restaurant's location, below a bridge approach at the edge of the Intracoastal Waterway. The two-story structure was built to look old, with walls of antique brick deliberately laid off-plumb. Specialties include fresh Belon oysters and littleneck clams from Maine; Florida blue crab cakes; Brutus salad (Down Under's version of Caesar salad); fresh Idaho trout lightly sautéed and topped with Florida blue crab and Hollandaise sauce; and Florida lobster and stone crab in season. Desserts include Key-lime pie with meringue, crème brûlée, and pecan squares. *3000 E. Oakland Park Blvd., tel. 305/563-4123. Jackets preferred. Reservations advised. AE, CB, MC, V. Expensive.*

Italian **Casa Vecchia.** This old house (*casa vecchia*) stands beside the
★ Intracoastal Waterway, surrounded by a formal garden where you can watch boats cruise past. The garden also grows herbs which flavor the restaurant's fare. Casa Vecchia was built in the late 1930s. Diners are encouraged to roam through the building to admire antique furnishings and original statuary and paintings. Spanish tiles decorated Casa Vecchia's walls and many tabletops. Specialties include canneloni, fettuccine funghi (mushroom-flavored noodles tossed with butter, basil, and porcini), and *granchio* Casa Vecchia (Maryland lump crabmeat served with scallions, a splash of cognac, and red linguine). Desserts include full-flavored sorbets of fresh seasonal fruit prepared on the premises and poached pear with mascarpone cheese. *209 N. Birch Rd., tel. 305/463-7575. Jacket preferred. Reservations advised. AE, CB, MC, V. Expensive.*

Natural **Spa Restaurant.** In the Bonaventure Resort and Spa, this 70-seat restaurant caters primarily to spa guests. Menus state the number of calories in each item. Tropical pastels and white rattan furniture seem to match the healthful, low-calorie natural fare prepared in a separate kitchen by chefs attuned to special dietary needs. Specialties include cream of cauliflower soup, a broad variety of salads, medallions of turkey Santa Barbara with a tangy-sweet apricot-lingonberry sauce, peach cobbler topped with granola, and strawberry-rhubarb crustless pie. *250 Racquet Club Rd., tel. 305/389-3300 or 800/327-8090. Dress: informal. Breakfast, lunch, dinner. Reservations advised. Nonsmoking seating available. Closed last 2 weeks in Aug. AE, DC, MC, V. Moderate.*

Seafood **Shirttail Charlie's.** You can watch the world go by from the out-
★ door deck or upstairs dining room of Shirttail Charlie's. Boats glide up and down the New River. Sunday–Thursday diners may take a free 45-minute after-dinner cruise on the 24-passenger launch *Cavalier*, which chugs upriver past an alleged Al Capone speakeasy. Charlie's itself is built to look old, with 1920s blue-and-white five-sided tile on a floor that leans toward the water. The menu reflects Caribbean cuisine. Specialties include an alligator-tail appetizer served with Tortuga sauce (a béarnaise with turtle broth and sherry); conch served four ways; crab balls; shark bites; blackened tuna with Dijon mustard sauce; crunchy coconut shrimp with a not-too-sweet piña colada sauce; and a superbly tart Key-lime pie with graham-cracker-crust. *400 S.W. 3rd Ave., tel. 305/463-3474. Jacket preferred upstairs, casual downstairs. Reservations advised upstairs. AE, MC, V. Moderate.*

Seafood **Renaissance Seafood Grill.** This gourmet restaurant, in the Bonaventure Resort and Spa, 5-star-rated by the Confrerie de

la Chaine des Rotisseurs, features mesquite-grilled seafood
and California cuisine with Florida adaptations. You dine in a
rain forest, with views of a waterfall surrounded by palm and
fiscus trees, ferns and blooming flowers, and a pond with variegated foot-long carp. Specialties include chilled cream of
avocado and cucumber soup; hot cream of popleno pepper soup
with chunks of brie cheese; a spinach-and-beansprout salad
with pickled eggs and rosemary vinaigrette dressing;
wholewheat fettuccine sautéed with chunks of Maine lobster,
scallops, and chives in a lobster sauce; mako shark in a lime-
parsley-butter sauce. *250 Racquet Club Rd., tel. 305/389–3300
or 800/327–8090. Jacket preferred. Dinner only. Reservations
required. AE, DC, MC, V. Expensive.*

Lodging

In Fort Lauderdale, Pompano Beach, and the Hollywood-
Hallandale area, dozens of hotels line the Atlantic Ocean
beaches. You can find a full spectrum of accommodations, from
economy motels to opulent luxury hotels with posh, pricey
suites.

Inland, the major chain hotels along I–95 north and south of the
airport cater primarily to business travelers and overnight visitors en route to somewhere else.

Wherever you plan to stay in Broward County, reservations
are a good idea throughout the year. Tourists from the northern United States and Canada fill up the hotels from
Thanksgiving through Easter. In summer, southerners and
Europeans create a second season that's almost as busy.

The list below is a representative selection of hotels and motels,
organized geographically. The rate categories in the list are
based on the all-year or peak-season price; off-peak rates may
be a category or two lower.

The most highly recommended hotels are indicated by a star
★.

Category	Cost*
Very Expensive	over $120
Expensive	$90–$120
Moderate	$50–$90
Inexpensive	under $50

**All prices are for a standard double room, excluding 6% state
sales tax and nominal tourist tax.*

The following credit card abbreviations are used: AE, American Express; CB, Carte Blanche; DC, Diners Club; MC,
MasterCard; V, Visa.

Bahia Mar Resort & Yachting Center (a Clarion hotel). Naval
architect J. H. Phillpot designed the Bahia Mar marina in 1949;
it was the first in Fort Lauderdale to accommodate boats longer
than 30 feet. Travis McGee, fictional hero of mystery author
John McDonald, "lived" at Bahia Mar aboard a boat called *The
Busted Flush.* Two months after McDonald died in December
1986, the Literary Landmark Association dedicated a plaque at

slip F-18 in memory of McDonald and McGee. Ironically, McDonald never stayed on the premises. Marina wing rooms are furnished in tropical decor; tower rooms have a soft blue-white color scheme. Upper floors of the 16-story tower provide spectacular views of the ocean and Intracoastal Waterway. *801 Seabreeze Blvd., Fort Lauderdale 33316, tel. 305/764–2233 or 800/327–8154. 298 rooms with bath, including 9 suites, 30 non-smokers rooms, 3 rooms for handicapped guests. Facilities: outdoor freshwater swimming pool, 350-slip marina where 15 deep-sea-fishing charter boats dock, power-boating and sailing instruction, dive boat and shop, 4 tennis courts, conference center, shopping arcade, restaurants. AE, CB, DC, MC, V. Expensive.*

Bonaventure Resort and Spa. Mid-rise resort with spa and conference center on 1,250 acres, 17 miles west of Fort Lauderdale. The hotel lobby is light and airy, with colorful angelfish and a cuddly-looking sand shark in a large aquarium just inside the front entrance. All guest rooms are in nine four-story buildings. Room views look out on the pools, lake, and golf courses. Bathroom amenities include bidets in many rooms, heat lamps, and full-size bath towels. *250 Racquet Club Rd., Fort Lauderdale 33326, tel. 305/389–3300 or 800/327–8090. 504 rooms include 8 suites. Facilities: 5 outdoor solar-heated freshwater swimming pools; 2 18-hole golf courses; 24 tennis courts, 43,000-square-foot spa with separate facilities for men and women (see* Participant Sports*); canoes, paddleboats, and a small sailboat on a half-mile-long lake which winds through the resort; bicycles and bicycle paths, saddle club, bowling alley, roller-skating rink, 4 restaurants, 2 lounges. AE, DC, MC, V. Expensive.*

★ **Casa Alhambra Bed & Breakfast Inn.** Victoria Feaman, co-owner and manager of this guest house, lives on the premises and treats customers as honored guests in her home. In fact, Casa Alhambra was a private home, built in 1932–36 and restored in 1986–87. The white-stucco dwelling retains such charming touches as a red-tile roof, stained-glass windows, hardwood floors, and a working brick fireplace. Vicky serves a complimentary Continental breakfast each morning. The large upstairs bedroom has a medium-firm king-size bed overlooking the tile roof and deck; two smaller bedrooms upstairs share a bath, an arrangement ideal for a foursome. *3029 Alhambra St., Fort Lauderdale 33304, tel. 305/467–2262. 5 rooms with bath. Facilities: outdoor freshwater hot tub with Jacuzzi, bicycles, piano, library, refrigerator privileges. No children under 10. AE. Moderate.*

Di Vito By the Sea. This eccentric low-rise beachfront hotel was built by Anthony Di Vito to express his love for his wife and exalt their Italian origins. Its architecture incorporates a reproduction of the Leaning Tower of Pisa with sea-horses, mermaids, and friezes with mythological heroes. Most guests rent by the week. There is no lobby, just an office and a patio facing the boardwalk in front of the building. *3500 N. Boardwalk, Hollywood 33019, tel. 305/929–7227. 20 rooms with bath, 4 yearly-rental apartments in an adjoining building. Facilities: 200 feet of beach frontage, efficiency kitchens in some rooms. No credit cards. Moderate.*

Fort Lauderdale Marriott Hotel & Marina. This hotel's 13-story tower beside the Intracoastal Waterway commands a striking view of the beach and the entrance to Port Everglades. Most

rooms have balconies overlooking the water and standard
Marriott furnishings in natural dark woods with pink, mauve,
and green fabrics and wall coverings. *1881 S.E. 17th St., Fort
Lauderdale 33316, tel. 305/463–4000 or 800/228–9290. 583
rooms with bath, including 19 suites, 26 nonsmokers rooms, 17
rooms for handicapped guests. Facilities: outdoor freshwater
swimming pool and whirlpool, free shuttle to beach, 32-slip
marina for yachts up to 200 feet long, 4 tennis courts, fitness
center, game room, in-room minibars and safes, pay-TV movies, AE, CB, DC, MC, V. Very Expensive.*
Marriott's Harbor Beach Resort. Fort Lauderdale's only AAA-
rated 5-diamond hotel is a 14-story tower on 16 acres of oceanfront. Built in 1984, its guest rooms were renovated in 1989.
The free-form pool has a cascading waterfall. Room furnishings
are light wood with mauve, pink, blue, and green hues; each
room has a balcony facing either the ocean or the Intracoastal
Waterway. *3030 Holiday Dr., Fort Lauderdale 33316, tel. 305/
525–4000 or 800/228–9290. 645 rooms with bath, including 36
suites, 45 nonsmokers rooms, 7 rooms for handicapped guests.
Facilities: 1,100 ft of beach frontage, cabanas, windsurfing,
Hobie cats, 65-foot catamaran, parasailing, outdoor heated
freshwater swimming pool and whirlpool, 5 tennis courts, fitness center, men's and women's saunas, masseuse, 3
boutiques, 5 restaurants, 3 lounges, in-room minibars, HBO,
TV movies. AE, DC, MC, V. Very Expensive.*
Palm-Aire Spa Resort. This mid-rise resort with spa and conference center on 1,500 acres 15 miles north of Fort Lauderdale is
lushly landscaped, and planters on each terrace make the four-
story main building resemble a hanging garden. The rooms
have big closets, a separate dressing alcove, and choice of soft
or firm pillows. *2501 Palm-Aire Dr. N, Pompano Beach 33069.
tel. 305/972–3300 or 800/327–4960. 192 rooms with bath and
private terrace, 4 outdoor freshwater swimming pools, 5 golf
courses, half-mile jogging trail with exercise stations, 37 tennis courts, Continental and spa restaurants, boutique. AE,
DC, MC, V. Very Expensive.*
★ **Pier 66 Resort and Marina.** Phillips Petroleum built Fort
Lauderdale's original high-rise luxury hotel on the eastern
bank of the Intracoastal Waterway. An octagonal rooftop cocktail lounge rotates slowly, offering patrons a spectacular view.
Rooms are attractively furnished in tropical pastels. *2301 S.E.
17th St., Fort Lauderdale 33316, tel. 305/525–6666, in FL 800/
432–1956, rest of USA 800/327–3796. 388 rooms, including 8
suites. Facilities: water taxi and van shuttle to beach, outdoor
heated freshwater swimming pool, full-service marina with
142 wet slips for boats up to 200 ft long, scuba diving,
snorkling, parasailing, small boat rentals, waterskiing, fishing and sailing yacht charters, 2 hard-surface tennis courts,
indoor and outdoor health clubs with saunas and exercise
equipment, men's and women's saunas, massage therapy. AE,
CB, DC, MC, V. Very Expensive.*
Plaza Beach Resort. Built in 1966, this nine-story former Royce
hotel came under new management in 1989. All rooms have balconies, air-conditioners, and triple dressers. In some, the color
scheme is off-white and pastels; others have burgundy carpet-
ing with mauve curtains and matching bedspreads. *4060 Galt
Ocean Mile, Fort Lauderdale Beach 33308, tel. 305/565–6611 or
800/678–9022. 220 rooms with bath, including 14 suites, 4
rooms for handicapped guests. Facilities: 225 ft of beach front-*

age on Atlantic Ocean, outdoor heated freshwater swimming pool, complete water sports program, 2 restaurants, nightclub, ice cream shop, free cable TV, pay-TV movies. *AE, DC, MC, V. Expensive.*

★ **Riverside Hotel.** This six-story hotel, on For Lauderdale's most fashionable shopping thoroughfare, was built in 1936, and was extensively remodeled in 1987. An attentive staff includes many veterans of two decades or more. Each room is unique, with antique oak furnishings, framed French prints on the walls, in-room refrigerators, and European-style baths. Best rooms face south, overlooking the New River; worst rooms, where you can hear the elevator, are the 36 series. *620 E. Las Olas Blvd., Fort Lauderdale 33301, tel. 305/467–0671, in USA 800/325–3280, in FL 800/421–7666. 117 rooms with bath, including 5 suites, 15 nonsmokers rooms. Facilities: kidney-shaped heated outdoor freshwater swimming pool beside the New River, 540 ft of dock with mooring space available by advance reservation, volleyball court, two restaurants, poolside bar. AE, DC, MC. Expensive.*

Sheraton Design Center Hotel. This high-rise business hotel is near the airport, across a landscaped plaza from the interior-design showrooms in Design Center of the Americas. The hotel's color theme is mauve, with variations of peach, wine, and pink. In the two-story atrium lobby, art deco-style hanging chandeliers with double-round diffusers hang from a skylight; pale beige, peach, and gray fabrics predominate. *1825 Griffin Rd., Dania 33004, tel. 305/920–3500 or 800/325–3535. 250 rooms with bath, including 5 suites, 20 nonsmokers rooms, 20 rooms for handicapped guests. Facilities: outdoor heated freshwater swimming pool and whirlpool, 2 lighted tennis courts, fitness center, men's and women's saunas, 2 racquetball courts, 2 restaurants, 2 lounges, complimentary shuttle to airport, AE, CB, DC, MC, V. Very Expensive.*

Westin Cypress Creek. Built in 1986, this high-rise business hotel is in Radice Corporate Park, a suburban office complex surrounding a lagoon with a fountain in the center. The hotel's three-story atrium lobby was inspired by the Great Temple at Karnak, Egypt; eight weathered-looking concrete columns with a rough pink-stucco finish rise to a skylight through which you can see the building's facade. Best rooms are on the 14th and 15th floors, where concierge service includes a Continental breakfast and a cocktail hour. *400 Corporate Dr., Fort Lauderdale 33334, tel. 305/772–1331 or 800/228–3000. 294 rooms with bath, including 25 suites, 34 nonsmokers rooms, 19 rooms for handicapped guests. Facilities: outdoor heated freshwater swimming pool and Jacuzzi, poolside bar with lunchtime barbecue, health club with Nautilus equipment, men's and women's saunas, jogging trail, volleyball, basketball, 2 restaurants, 2 lounges, in-room minibars. AE, CB, DC, V. Very Expensive.*

The Arts and Nightlife

For the most complete weekly listing of events, read the "Showtime!" entertainment insert and events calendar in the Friday *Fort Lauderdale News/Sun Sentinel.*

Tickets are sold at individual box offices and through Ticketmaster, a computerized statewide sales system (tel. 305/

523–3309 in Broward County or 800/446–3939 statewide).
Broward also has a concert information line (tel. 305/493–
8811).

The Arts **Sunrise Musical Theatre** (5555 N.W. 95th Ave., Sunrise, tel.
Theater 305/741–7300) stages Broadway musicals, some dramatic plays
with name stars, and concerts by well-known singers throughout the year. The theater is 14 miles west of Fort Lauderdale
Beach via Commercial Boulevard.

Concerts **Bailey Concert Hall** is a popular place for classical music concerts, dance, drama, and other performing arts activities,
especially October–April. *On the Central Campus of Broward
Community College, 3501 S.W. Davie Rd., tel. 305/475–6500
for reservations.*
The Philharmonic Orchestra of Florida, South Florida's only
fully professional orchestra, is Broward-based but performs in
eight locations in Broward, Dade, and Palm Beach counties. It
offers a variety of series and individual-performance tickets;
write for schedule. *1430 N. Federal Hwy., Ft. Lauderdale
33304, tel. 305/561–2997 (Dade County), 305/945–5180
(Broward County), 407/392–5443 (Boca Raton), 407/659–0331
(Palm Beach), 800/446–3939 (Ticketmaster statewide). Office
open weekdays 9–5. AE, MC, V.*
The Fort Lauderdale Opera Guild presents the current production of the Greater Miami Opera in War Memorial Auditorium
(800 N.E. 8th st., Fort Lauderdale). For tickets, contact the
Guild office. *333 S.W. 2nd St., Fort Lauderdale 33312, tel. 305/
728–9700. Office open weekdays 9–5.*

Nightlife **Musician Exchange Downtown Cafe.** This 200-seat club fea-
Bars and tures an eclectic mix of blues, jazz, and rock-and-roll, with
Nightclubs reggae on Sundays. Performers include local bands as well as
leading musicians like Woodie Herman, Buddy Rich, Carmen
McCrae, and Stan Getz. *729 W. Sunrise Blvd., Fort Lauderdale,
305/764–1912. Admission price varies with show. National big-
name acts Fri. and Sat. Call for schedule and reservations.*
Shirttail Charlie's Downstairs Bar. A scenic place to have a beer
or snack and watch boat traffic on the New River through
downtown Fort Lauderdale. No entertainment. Informal. *400
S.W. 3rd Ave., Fort Lauderdale, tel. 305/463–3474. Open
Mon.–Fri. 11:30–10, Sat. 11:30–10, Sun. 11:30–9.*
Peppers. High-energy nightclub with art-deco decor in Westin
Cypress Creek Hotel. Features rock-and-roll DJs most weekend nights, with videos produced in-house; occasional live jazz.
Wood dance floor, pool table. *400 Corporate Dr., Fort Lauderdale, tel. 305/772–1331. Open Mon.–Thurs. 5 PM–1:30 AM with
complimentary buffet 5–7 PM, Fri.–Sat. 7 PM–1:30 AM. No cov-
er or minimum.*

Comedy Clubs **The Comic Strip.** Stand-up comedians from New York work
surrounded by framed old newspaper funnies—Katzenjammer
Kids, Superman, Prince Valiant, L'il Orphan Annie, Hubert,
etc. Full restaurant menu, two-drink minimum, alcoholic and
nonalcoholic beverages. Amateur night Sunday and Monday,
phone ahead to sign up. *1432 N. Federal Hwy., Fort Lauderdale, tel. 305/565–8887. Showtime Sun.–Thurs. 9:30, Fri. 10,
Sat. 8:30 and 11:30.*

Country/Western **Do-Da's Country Music Emporium.** The Frontier Room seats
800 at buckboard tables and has a 2,100-square-foot wood dance
floor; the smaller pecky-board Tennessee Room seats 100.

Glass-and-brick arches enclose the Tex-Mex dining area, Rosa's Cantina. The shoot-'em-down corral bar in the Frontier Room has an old-fashioned barber chair. Free international buffet during happy hour, weekdays 5–8 PM. *700 S. U.S. 441, Plantation, tel. 305/791–1477. Open 11 AM–4 AM. Live country/ western music, with name bands on weekends 8 PM–3 AM.*

5   Palm Beach

Introduction

Wealth has its privileges. That's the continuing reality of Palm Beach. Those privileges include the finest homes, cars, food, wine, furniture, jewelry, art, clothing, and toys that money can buy—and the right to stare back at the tourists who visit this elegant barrier-island enclave 70 miles north of Miami.

Henry Morrison Flagler created Palm Beach in 1894. He helped John D. Rockefeller establish the Standard Oil Company, then retired and put his money into Florida railroads and real estate. He bought a small railroad between Jacksonville and St. Augustine, renamed it the Florida East Coast Railroad, and extended it southward. Along the rail line he built hotels to generate traffic, including a huge wooden structure, the 2,000-room Royal Poinciana, beside a tidal bay called Lake Worth.

Flagler created an international high-society resort at Palm Beach, attracting the affluent for the Season, December 15 to Washington's Birthday (Feb. 22). Then they departed for Europe, extolling Palm Beach's virtues and collecting great art to ship back to the mansions they were building on the island.

A workman told Flagler that people liked to picnic along the beach "down by the breakers," so he built a second hotel there in 1896. It burned, was rebuilt, and burned again. The third structure to bear the name The Breakers rose in 1926 and stands today as the grande dame of Palm Beach hostelries.

Socialites and celebrities still flock to The Breakers for charity galas. They browse in the stores along Worth Avenue, regarded as one of the world's classiest shopping districts. They swim on secluded beaches that are nominally public but lack convenient parking and access points. They pedal the world's most beautiful bicycle path beside Lake Worth. And what they do, *you* can do—if you can afford it.

Despite its prominence and affluence, the Town of Palm Beach occupies far less than 1% of the land area of Palm Beach County, which is 521 square miles larger than the state of Delaware and is a remarkably diverse political jurisdiction.

West Palm Beach, on the mainland across Lake Worth from Palm Beach, is the city Flagler built to house Palm Beach's servants; today it's the county seat and commercial center of Palm Beach County, with a population of about 70,000.

Lantana, to the south, has a large Finnish population and is the headquarters of the *National Enquirer*. Delray Beach began as an artists' retreat and a small settlement of Japanese farmers, including George Morikami, who donated the land for the beautiful Morikami Museum of Japanese Culture to the county park system (4000 Morikami Park Rd., Delray Beach 33446. tel. 407/499–0631. Open Tues.–Sun. 10–5. Donation). Boca Raton, an upscale community developed by pioneer architect Addison Mizner as a showcase for his Spanish Revival style, retains much of its 1920s ambience through strict zoning.

To the north, Palm Beach Gardens is a golf center, home of the Professional Golfer's Association. Jupiter boasts the Burt Reynolds Jupiter Theater and a dune-fringed beach that remains largely free of intrusive development.

Many visitors to Palm Beach County don't realize that it extends 50 miles inland to encompass the southeastern quadrant of 448,000-acre Lake Okeechobee, the fourth-largest natural lake in the United States. Its bass and perch attract fishermen; catfish devotees prize the hearty flavor of succulent Okeechobee "sharpies."

Marinas at Pahokee and Belle Glade provide lake access. Pahokee has a 125-foot tower, which you can climb for a view of the lake. In Lake Harbor, about as far west as you can go in Palm Beach County, the state is restoring a lock and lockmaster's house built early in the 20th century on the Miami Canal.

Palm Beach County is also the main gateway to the Treasure Coast, consisting of Martin, St. Lucie, and Indian River counties along the Atlantic coast to the north.

Arriving and Departing by Plane

Airport **Palm Beach International Airport (PBIA)** (Congress Ave. and Belvedere Rd., West Palm Beach) expanded to 24 gates in 1988 and handled just over 5 million passengers. It will add up to 24 more gates by 1993.

Between the Airport and City Center Route No. 10 of **Tri-Rail Commuter Bus Service** joins PBIA and Tri-Rail's Palm Beach Airport station during weekday rush hours only. For schedule, call 800/TRI–RAIL. For connections with CoTran (Palm Beach County Transportation Authority) routes, call 407/686–4560 or 407/686–4555 in Palm Beach, 407/272– 6350 in Boca Raton–Delray Beach.

Palm Beach Transportation (tel. 407/689–4222) provides taxi and limousine service from PBIA. Reserve at least a day in advance for a limousine.

Arriving and Departing by Train and Car

By Train **Amtrak** (201 S. Tamarind Ave., West Palm Beach, tel. 800/872–7245 or 407/832–6169) connects West Palm Beach with cities along Florida's east coast daily.

Tri-Rail has six stations in Palm Beach County. For details, tel. 800/TRI–RAIL or tel. 305/728–8445.

By Car Most visitors explore Palm Beach County by car. I–95 runs north-south, to link West Palm Beach with Miami and Fort Lauderdale to the south. To get to central Palm Beach, exit at Belvedere Road or Okeechobee Boulevard. Southern Boulevard (U.S. 98) runs east-west. From West Palm Beach, take I–95 south to Boca Raton and Delray Beach, north to Palm Beach Gardens and Jupiter.

Getting Around

By Bus CoTran buses require exact change (80 cents, plus 15 cents for a transfer). Service is provided from 6 AM to 9 PM. For details, tel. 407/686–4560 or 407/686–4555 (Palm Beach), 407/272–6350 (Boca Raton-Delray Beach).

By Taxi **Palm Beach Transportation** (tel. 407/689–4222). Cab meters start at $1.25. Each mile is $1.50. Some cabs may charge more.

Important Addresses and Numbers

Tourist Information	**Palm Beach County Convention & Visitors Bureau** (1555 Palm Beach Lakes Blvd., Suite 204, West Palm Beach 33401, tel. 407/471–3995) is open weekdays 8:30–5.

Chamber of Commerce of the Palm Beaches (501 N. Flagler Dr., West Palm Beach, tel. 407/833–3711) is open weekdays 8:30–5.

Deaf Service Center of Palm Beach County (5730 Corporate Way, Suite 210, West Palm Beach 33407, TDD tel. 407/478–3904, voice tel. 407/478–3903) is open weekdays 8:30–5.

Tickets Call **Ticketmaster** to order tickets for performing arts and sports events. *Tel. 800/446–3939 or 407/588–3309. MC, V.*

Emergencies Dial 911 for **police** and **ambulance** in an emergency.

Hospitals Two hospitals in West Palm Beach with 24-hour emergency rooms are **Good Samaritan Hospital** (Flagler Dr. and Palm Beach Lakes Blvd., tel. 407/655–5511; doctor-referral, tel. 407/650–6240) and **St. Mary's Hospital** (901 45th St., tel. 407/844–6300; doctor-referral, tel. 407/881–2929).

24-Hour Pharmacy **Eckerd Drugs** (3343 S. Congress Ave., Palm Springs, southwest of West Palm Beach, tel. 407/965–3367). **Walgreen Drugs** (1688 Congress Ave., Palm Springs, tel. 407/968–8211).

Exploring Palm Beach and West Palm Beach

Numbers in the margin correspond with points of interest on the Palm Beach and West Palm Beach map.

Palm Beach is an island community 12 miles long and no more than a quarter-mile across at its widest point. Three bridges connect Palm Beach to West Palm Beach and the rest of the world. This tour takes you through both communities.

● Begin at Royal Palm Way and County Road in the center of Palm Beach. Go north on County Road past **Bethesda-by-the-Sea Church,** built in 1927 by the first Protestant congregation in southeast Florida. Inspiring stained-glass windows and a lofty, vaulted sanctuary grace its Spanish-Gothic design. A stone bridge with an ornamental tile border spans the pond; bubbling fountains feed it. *141 South County Rd., Palm Beach, tel. 407/655–4554. Gardens open 8–5. Services Sun. 8, 9, and 11 AM in winter, 8 and 10 June–Aug.; phone for weekday schedule.*

❷ Continue north on County Road past **The Breakers** (1 S. County Rd., Palm Beach), an ornate Italian Renaissance hotel built in 1926 by railroad magnate Henry M. Flagler's widow to replace an earlier hotel, which burned (*see* Lodging). Explore the elegant public spaces—especially on a Sunday morning, when you can enjoy the largest champagne brunch in Florida at The Beach Club.

❸ Continue north on County Road to Royal Poinciana Way. Go inside the **Palm Beach Post Office** to see the murals depicting Seminole Indians in the Everglades and royal and coconut palms. *95 N. County Rd., Palm Beach, tel. 407/832–0633 or 1867. Open weekdays 8:30–5.*

Continue north on County Road to the north end of the island,
④ past the very-private **Palm Beach Country Club** and a neighborhood of expansive (and expensive) estates.

⑤ You must turn around at **E. Inlet Drive,** the northern tip of the
island, where a dock offers a view of Lake Worth Inlet, the U.S.
Coast Guard Reservation on Peanut Island, and the Port of
Palm Beach across Lake Worth on the mainland. Observe the
no-parking signs; Palm Beach police will issue tickets.

Turn south and make the first right onto Indian Road, then the
first left onto Lake Way. You'll return to the center of town
through an area of newer mansions, past the posh, private Sail-
fish Club. Lake Way parallels the **Palm Beach Bicycle Trail**
⑥ along the shoreline of Lake Worth, a palm-fringed path
through the backyards of some of the world's priciest homes.
Watch on your right for metal posts topped with a swatch of
white paint, marking narrow public-access walkways between
houses from the street to the bike path.

Lake Way runs into Country Club Road, which takes you
⑦ through the **Canyon of Palm Beach,** a road cut about 25 feet
deep through a ridge of sandstone and oolite limestone.

As you emerge from the canyon, turn right onto Lake Way and
continue south. Lake Way becomes Bradley Place. You'll pass
⑧ the **Palm Beach Biltmore Hotel,** now a condominium. Another
flamboyant landmark of the Florida boom, it cost $7 million to
build and opened in 1927 with 543 rooms.

As you cross Royal Poinciana Way, Bradley Place becomes Co-
⑨ conut Row. Stop at **Whitehall,** the palatial 73-room mansion
that Henry M. Flagler built in 1901 for his third wife, Mary Lily
Kenan. After the couple died, the mansion was turned into
a hotel. In 1960, Flagler's granddaughter, Jean Flagler
Matthews, bought the building. She turned it into a museum,
with many of the original furnishings on display. The art collection includes a Gainsborough portrait of a girl with a pink sash,
displayed in the music room near a 1,200-pipe organ. Exhibits
also depict the history of the Florida East Coast Railway.
Flagler's personal railroad car, "The Rambler," is parked behind the building. A tour by well-informed guides takes about
an hour; afterwards, you may browse on your own. *Coconut
Row at Whitehall Way, Palm Beach, tel. 407/655–2833. Open
Tues.–Sat. 10–5, Sun. noon–5; closed Mon. Admission: $3.50
adults, $1.25 children.*

Turn left on leaving Whitehall. Take Coconut Row back north
⑩ to Royal Poinciana Way, turn left, and cross the **Flagler Memorial Bridge** into West Palm Beach. On the mainland side of the
bridge, turn left onto Flagler Drive, which runs along the west
⑪ shore of Lake Worth. A half-mile south of the **Royal Palm
Bridge,** turn right onto Acteon Street, which is the north edge
⑫ of a sloping mall leading up to the **Norton Gallery of Art.**

Founded in 1941 by steel magnate Ralph H. Norton, the Norton Gallery boasts an extensive permanent collection of French
impressionist and 20th-century American paintings, Chinese
bronze and jade sculptures, a sublime outdoor patio with sculptures on display in a tropical garden, and a library housing
more than 3,000 art books and periodicals. The Norton also se-
cures many of the best traveling exhibits to reach south

Palm Beach and West Palm Beach

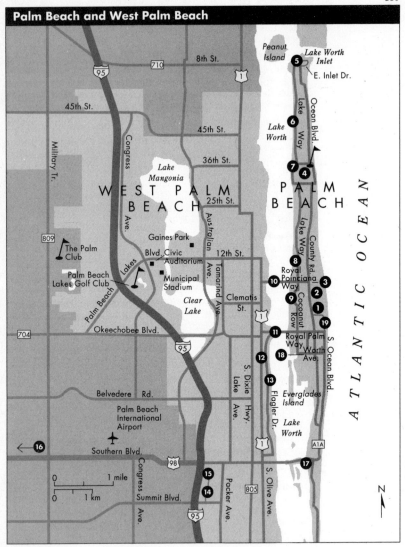

Ann Norton Sculpture Gardens, **13**

Bethesda-by the-Sea Church, **1**

The Breakers, **2**

Canyon of Palm Beach, **7**

Dreher Park Zoo, **14**

E. Inlet Drive, **5**

Flagler Memorial Bridge, **10**

Lion Country Safari, **16**

Mar-A-Lago, **17**

Norton Gallery of Art, **12**

Palm Beach Bicycle Trail, **6**

Palm Beach Biltmore Hotel, **8**

Palm Beach Country Club, **4**

Palm Beach Post Office, **3**

Public beach, **19**

Royal Palm Bridge, **11**

South Florida Science Museum, **15**

Whitehall, **9**

Worth Ave., **18**

Florida. *1451 S. Olive Ave., West Palm Beach, tel. 407/832–5194. Open Tues.–Sat. 10–5, Sun. 1–5. Admission free; donations requested.*

Return to Flagler Drive down Diana Street at the south edge of the mall, turn right, go a half-mile south to Barcelona Road, and turn right again. You're at the entrance to the **Ann Norton Sculpture Gardens,** a monument to the late American sculptor Ann Weaver Norton, second wife of Norton Gallery founder Ralph H. Norton. The gardens display, in a tropical jungle, seven granite figures and six brick megaliths. The brick forms reflect their creator's girlhood in Selma, Alabama, in a pre-World War I southern landscape dotted with the brick chimneys of burned-out farmhouses and haunted by memories of General Sherman's Civil War march to the sea. The garden also contains native plants and 132 different kinds of palms. Other sculptures in bronze, marble, and wood are on display in Norton's studio. *253 Barcelona Rd., West Palm Beach, tel. 407/832–5328. Open Tues.–Sat. noon–4 or by appointment. Admission: $2 adults, children under 12 free.*

Return again to Flagler Drive and continue south to Southern Boulevard (U.S. 98). Turn left and go west almost a mile, turn left onto Parker Avenue, and go south about a mile. Turn right onto Summit Boulevard, and right again at the next stoplight into the parking lot at the **Dreher Park Zoo.** The 32-acre zoo has nearly 100 different species of animals, including an endangered Florida panther. Of special interest are the reptile collection and the petting zoo. *1301 Summit Blvd., West Palm Beach, tel. 407/585–2197 (recording) or 407/533–0887. Open daily 9–5. Admission: $4 adults, $2 children 3–12 and seniors over 60, under 3 free.*

As you leave the zoo parking lot, turn left and follow a winding road for about a quarter-mile to the **South Florida Science Museum.** Here you'll find hands-on exhibits, aquarium displays with touch-tank demonstrations and feedings daily at 4 PM, planetarium shows, and a chance to observe the heavens Friday nights through the most powerful telescope in south Florida. *4801 Dreher Trail N, West Palm Beach, tel. 407/832–1988. Open Tues.–Sun. 10–5, Fri. 6:30–10 PM. Admission: $3 adults, $2.50 seniors over 62, $1.50 children 4–12, $8 family. Planetarium admission: $1 extra.*

Leaving the science museum, retrace your path on Summit Boulevard and Parker Avenue to Southern Boulevard (SR 80), turn left, and go about 16 miles west to **Lion Country Safari,** where you drive (with car windows closed) on eight miles of paved roads through a 500-acre cageless zoo where 1,000 wild animals roam free. Lions, elephants, white rhinoceroses, giraffes, zebras, antelopes, chimpanzees, and ostriches are among the species in residence. Try to go early in the day, before the park gets crowded. If you have a convertible or a new car on which you don't want animals to climb, the park will rent you a zebra-stripe, air-conditioned sedan. An adjacent KOA campground offers campers a park discount. *Box 16066, West Palm Beach 33416, tel. 407/793–1084. Open daily 9:30–5:30. Admission: $12.14 adults, $10.45 children 3–16, $8.55 seniors over 65, under 3 free, car rental $5 per hour.*

Returning to town on Southern Boulevard, look for the Italianate towers of **Mar-A-Lago** (1100 S. Ocean Blvd., Palm Beach) silhouetted against the sky as you cross the bridge to Palm Beach. Mar-A-Lago, the former estate of breakfast-food heiress Marjorie Meriweather Post, is now owned by real estate magnate Donald Trump. It's closed to the public, but you can catch a glimpse as you drive past.

Turn north on Ocean Boulevard, one of Florida's most scenic drives. The road follows the dune top, with the beach falling away to surging surf on your right, and some of Palm Beach's most opulent mansions on your left. You will pass the east end

⑱ of **Worth Avenue,** regarded by many as the world's classiest shopping street (*see* Shopping).

⑲ As you approach Worth Avenue, the **public beach** begins. Parking meters along Ocean Drive between Worth Avenue and Royal Palm Way signify the only stretch of beach in Palm Beach with convenient public access.

This concludes the tour. To return to its starting point, turn left on Royal Palm Way and go one block west to County Road.

What to See and Do with Children

Gumbo Limbo Nature Center. At this unusual nature center, you can stroll a 1,628-foot boardwalk through a dense tropical forest and climb a 50-foot tower to overlook the tree canopy. The forest is a coastal hammock, with tropical species growing north of the tropics. One tree species you're sure to see is the gumbo-limbo, often called "the tourist tree" because of its red, peeling bark. Ask for a guide to the hammock's flora, with photos and brief text keyed to numbered posts along the trail. In the nature center building, a diorama depicts the nest of a loggerhead sea turtle along the nearby beach. The center's staff leads guided turtle walks to the beach to see nesting mothers come ashore and lay their eggs. *1801 N. Ocean Blvd., Boca Raton, tel. 407/338–1473. Open Mon.–Sat. 9–4, fall–spring; weekdays 4–8 PM in summer. Admission free. Turtle walks early June–late July Mon.–Thurs. 9 PM–12:30 AM. Admission: $2. Reservations required.*

Off the Beaten Track

Arthur R. Marshall Loxahatchee National Wildlife Refuge Loxahatchee Refuge is 221 square miles of saw-grass marshes, wet prairies, sloughs, and tree islands. You go there to stroll the nature trails, see alligators and birds (including the rare snail kite). You can also fish for bass and panfish, ride an airboat, or paddle your own canoe through this watery wilderness.

Loxahatchee refuge recently was renamed in memory of Art Marshall, a Florida environmental scientist instrumental in Everglades preservation efforts.

Refuge entrance fee: $3 per car, $1 per pedestrian. Open ½ hr before sunrise–½ hr after sunset.

The refuge has three access points, each with its own facilities and services:

Headquarters The ranger at the visitor center will show a seven-minute slide presentation on request. Walk both nature trails—a boardwalk through a dense cypress swamp, and a marsh nature trail to a 20-foot-tall observation tower overlooking a pond. A seven-mile canoe trail starts at the boat-launching ramp here. *Entrance off U.S. 441 between Boynton Blvd. (Rte. 804) and Atlantic Ave. (Rte. 806), west of Boynton Beach. Mailing address: Rte. 1, Box 278, Boynton Beach, tel. 407/732–3684 or 407/734–8303.*

Hillsboro Recreation Area A concessionaire offers airboat rides, boat rentals, guide services, and a store with snacks, fishing tackle, and bait. The airboat ride lasts a half hour, in a 20-passenger craft with a Cadillac engine. The driver will take you into the middle of the Everglades, then shut off the engine and explain the unique ecosystem around you. *Entrance off U.S. 441 on Lox Rd. (Rte. 827), 12 mi south of Headquarters and west of Boca Raton. Loxahatchee Recreation, Inc., Rte. 1, Box 642–S, Pompano Beach 33060, tel. 305/426–2474. Concessionaire open 6 AM–30 min before park closing. Airboat rides 9–4:30, $7.50 adults, $4 children under 12, under 3 free. Rental for 14-ft. boat with outboard engine $27.50 for 5 hours, $13.75 evening special for last 3 daylight hours; for rowboat, $10 for 5 hours. Fishing and hunting guide $150 per half-day, $200 per day. MC, V.*

20-Mile Bend Recreation Area Boat ramp and fishing area at north end of refuge. *Entrance off U.S. 98 and 441, due west of West Palm Beach. No services.*

Shopping

Worth Avenue One of the world's last strongholds for quality shopping, Worth Avenue runs a quarter-mile east–west across Palm Beach, from the beach to Lake Worth.

The street has more than 250 shops. The 300 block, with a maze of Italianate villas designed by Addison Mizner, retains a quaint charm. The 100 and 200 blocks are more overtly commercial. Most merchants open at 9:30 or 10 AM, and close at 5:30 or 6 PM. Summer hours may be shorter.

Parking on and around Worth Avenue is quite limited. On-street parking has a one- or two-hour limit, strictly enforced. An alternative is Apollo Valet Parking at Hibiscus and Peruvian avenues, a block off Worth Avenue. Merchants will stamp your parking ticket if you buy something (or if you look like a prospective customer); each stamp is good for an hour of free parking.

Apollo's parking deal is just one reason to look presentable when you tour Worth Avenue. Come dressed to feel comfortable, blend in, and indulge your fantasies.

The Worth Avenue Association has strict rules to keep the street classy: no renovations are allowed from October to May, and special sales are limited to 21 consecutive days anytime between April and October.

Many "name" stores associated with fine shopping have a presence on Worth Avenue, including Bonwit Teller, Brooks Brothers, Cartier, Elizabeth Arden, Gucci, Pierre Deux, Saks Fifth Avenue, and Van Cleef & Arpels. No other street in the world has such a dense concentration of these upscale firms—and they tend to send their best merchandise to Worth Avenue to appeal to the discerning tastes of their Palm Beach clientele.

Beaches

The best beaches in Palm Beach County are in the Jupiter area, on Singer Island, and in Boca Raton. Surfing isn't a major draw for this portion of the Atlantic, but wading and surf diving into the shallow waves are.

Participant Sports

Biking Because of traffic, bicycle with caution while on city and county roads. A nice bike path is in *John D. MacArthur Park* (alongside PGA Blvd.) as it runs east toward Singer Island. Rentals are available at **Palm Beach Bicycle Trail Shop.** *223 Sunrise Ave., Palm Beach, tel. 407/659-4583. Open 9-5. AE, MC, V.*

Diving You can drift-dive or anchor-dive along Palm Beach County's 47-mile Atlantic coast. Drift divers take advantage of the Gulf Stream's strong currents and proximity to shore—sometimes less than a mile. A group of divers joined by nylon line may drift across coral reefs with the current; one member of the group carries a large, orange float which the charter-boat captain can follow. Drift diving works best from Boynton Beach north. South of Boynton Beach, where the Gulf Stream is farther from shore, diving from an anchored boat is more popular.

Dive Boats and The following **Force E** stores rent scuba and snorkeling equip-
Instruction ment and have PADI affiliation. Instruction available at all skill levels. Dive-boat charters are also available.

1399 N. Military Trail, West Palm Beach, tel. 407/471-2676 or 800/527-8660. Open winter weekdays 10-9, summer weekdays 8-9, Sat. 8-7, Sun. 8-4.

155 E. Blue Heron Blvd., Riviera Beach, tel. 407/845-2333. Open weekdays year-round 8-7, Sat. 6:30-7, Sun. 6:30-5.

39 S. Ocean Blvd., Delray Beach, tel. 407/272-0311. Open Nov.-May. Contact store for hours.

877 E. Palmetto Park Rd., Boca Raton, tel. 407/368-0555. Hours same as West Palm Beach store.

7166 Beracasa Way, Boca Raton, tel. 407/395-4407. Hours same as West Palm Beach store.

Golf There are more than 130 public, private, and semiprivate golf courses in the Palm Beach County area. The **PGA Sheraton Resort** west of the city, has one of the most famous golf courses in the area (*see* Lodging, below).

Hunting **J. W. Corbett Wildlife Management Area.** You can hunt deer, wild hog, squirrel, and quail in season on this 57,892-acre state preserve. Access off Indiantown Road and Beeline Highway, west of Jupiter. For information on licensing, call the Florida Game and Fresh Water Fish Commission (tel. 407/683-0748).

Spas **Hippocrates Health Institute** (1443 Palmdale Ct., West Palm Beach, tel. 407/471-8876), was founded in Boston in 1963 by Ann Wigmore and moved to its present 10-acre site in 1987. Guests receive complete examinations by traditional and alternative health-care professionals. Personalized programs include juice fasts and the eating of raw foods.

Spectator Sports

The *Palm Beach Post*'s weekly "TGIF" section on Fridays carries information on sports activities.

Baseball The **Atlanta Braves** and the **Montreal Expos** both conduct spring training in West Palm Beach's Municipal Stadium, which is also home to the Palm Beach Expos, a Class-A team in the Florida State League. *1610 Palm Beach Lakes Blvd., Box 3087, West Palm Beach 33402, stadium tel. 407/683-6012. Expos tickets: Box 3566, West Palm Beach 33402, tel. 407/689-9121, AE, MC. Braves tickets: Box 2619, West Palm Beach 33402, tel. 407/683-6100. No credit cards.*

Greyhound Racing **Palm Beach Kennel Club** opened in 1932 and has 3,000 free seats. Dine in the Paddock Dining Room or watch and eat on the Terrace. Call for schedule. *1111 Congress Ave., 33409, tel. 407/683-2222. Admission: 50 cents general admission, $2 dining rooms. Free parking.*

Jai Alai **Palm Beach Jai Alai.** This jai alai fronton is the site of two world records: for the largest payoff ever, $988,325; and for the fastest ball ever thrown, 188 mph. *1415 45th St., West Palm Beach, ¼ mi east of I-95 off exit 54, tel. 407/844-2444 or 407/427-0009 (toll-free south to Pompano Beach. Admission: 50 cents to $5. Free parking. Sala Del Toro Restaurant. Open: Sept. to July. Schedule changes seasonally. No cameras.*

Equestrian Sports and Polo Many Olympic riders will come to Palm Beach county in 1990 to compete in world-class show-jumping events at the 12th annual **Winter Equestrian Festival.** It will take place in a new 125-acre equestrian complex at the Palm Beach Polo and Country Club (*see* Lodging).

Palm Beach county is the home of three major polo organizations. Seventy miles north in Vero Beach, the **Windsor Polo and Beach Club** held its first polo match in February 1989. Although only the affluent can support a four-member polo team, admission is free for some games and priced reasonably for others. If you like horses and want to rub elbows with the rich and famous, dress like the locals in tweeds or a good golf shirt and khakis and spend an afternoon watching some of the world's best professional polo players.

Polo teams play under a handicap system in which the U.S. Polo Association ranks each player's skills; a team's total handicap reflects its members' individual handicaps. The best players have a 10-goal handicap. The average polo game lasts about 90 minutes. Each game consists of 6 periods or *chukkers* of 7½ minutes each.

Gulf Stream Polo Club, the oldest club in Palm Beach, began in the 1920s and plays medium-goal polo (for teams with handicaps of 8–16 goals). It has six polo fields. *4550 Polo Rd., Lake Worth 33467, tel. 407/965-2057. Play Dec.–April. Games Fri. 3 PM and Sun. 1 PM. Admission free.*

Royal Palm Polo, founded in 1959 by Oklahoma oilman John T. Oxley, has a total sports complex open to the public. It includes seven polo fields with two stadiums, a fitness center with 13 clay tennis courts, racquetball courts, a swimming pool and three restaurants. The complex is home to the $100,000 International Gold Cup Tournament. *6300 Clint Moore Rd., Boca Raton 33496, tel. 407/994-1876. Winter season Jan.–Apr. Summer season June–Oct. Games Sun. 1 and 3 PM. General admission $5, box seats $15, $3 children and students.*

Palm Beach Polo and Country Club. Started in 1979, this is the site each April of the $100,000 Cadillac World Cup competition (*see* Lodging). *Stadium address: 13240 Southshore Blvd., West Palm Beach, 33414, tel. 407/798–7605. Games Sun. 3 PM. General admission reserve $10, lower level $14, upper level $17. AE, MC, V.*

Rugby **Boca Raton Rugby Club** practices on Tuesday and Thursday nights. Home games are played Saturday 2 PM at Boca Raton's Lake Wyman Park. *For information, contact Allerton "Bing" Towne, president, Florida Rugby Football Clubs, 1580 S.W. 6th Ave., Boca Raton 33432, tel. 407/395–3800 weekdays or 407/ 395–4259 weekends and nights.*

Dining

The list below is a representative selection of independent restaurants in Palm Beach County, organized geographically, and by type of cuisine within each region of the county. Unless otherwise noted, they serve lunch and dinner.

The most highly recommended restaurants are indicated by a star ★.

Category	Cost*
Very Expensive	over $55
Expensive	$35–$55
Moderate	$15–$35
Inexpensive	under $15

*per person, excluding drinks, service, and 6% state sales tax

The following credit card abbreviations are used: AE, American Express; CB, Carte Blanche; DC, Diners Club; MC, MasterCard; V, Visa.

Boca Raton **Gazebo Cafe.** The locals who patronize this popular restaurant
Continental know where it is, even though there is no sign. You'll probably circle the block three times. Look for the Barnett Bank in Sun Plaza, a block north of Spanish River Drive. Once you find the place, await your table in the open kitchen where Greek-born owner-chef William Sellas and his staff perform a gastronomic ballet. The main dining room has a high noise level. You may be happier in the smaller back dining room. Specialties include lump crabmeat with an excellent glaze of Mornay sauce on a marinated artichoke bottom; smoked spinach salad with *fresh* heart of palm, egg white, bacon, croutons, mushrooms, fruit garnish, and a dressing of olive oil and poupon mustard; Paul Sellas's (the chef's young son) "classic" bouillabaisse with Maine lobster, shrimp, scallops, clams, and mussel topped with julienne vegetables in a robust broth flavored with garlic, saffron, and tomatoes; and raspberries with a Grand Marnier-Sabayon sauce. The staff can accommodate travelers in seven languages. *4199 N. Federal Hwy., Boca Raton, tel. 407/395– 6033. Jacket preferred. Reservations advised. Closed Sun. and Aug.–mid-Sept. AE, DC, MC, V. Moderate.*

French **La Vieille Maison.** This elegant French restaurant occupies a
★ two-story dwelling, which architect Addison Mizner may have designed. The structure dates from the 1920s, hence the name, which means old house. It has been renovated repeatedly, but it retains features typical of Mizner's work. Closets and cubby-

holes have become intimate private dining rooms. You may order from a fixed-price or an à la carte menu throughout the year; in summer, a separate fixed-price menu available Sunday through Thursday offers a sampling of the other two at a more modest price. Specialties include saucisson chaud (pork-and duck sausage with pistachios, baked in a phyllo pastry and served with a truffle sauce), *l'endive Cyrille* (smoked salmon, onions, and Belgian endive with light vinaigrette), and fresh pompano sauteed with buttered pecans and deglazed with white wine. Dessert specialties include crepe soufflé au citron and a chocolate tart. *770 E. Palmetto Park Rd., tel. 407/391–6701 in Boca Raton, 407/737–5677 in Delray Beach and Palm Beach, 305/421–7370 in Ft. Lauderdale. Jackets required. Reservations required. Closed Memorial Day, Labor Day, July 4th. AE, CB, MC, V. Expensive.*

Jupiter
American

Sinclair's Grill. This 140-seat restaurant in the Jupiter Beach Hilton overlooks the ocean and hotel pool. It has a relaxed Key West atmosphere, with louvered shutters, paddle fans, ceramic banana-tree table lamps, light wood furnishings, and hanging plants. Most of the cooking takes place in an open theater kitchen with a French rotisserie. The menu favors Florida seafood and tropical fruits and vegetables in season. Seafood specialties include Florida seafood chowder, grilled Florida swordfish with pineapple and cilantro salsa, and yellowfin tuna grilled with tomato vinaigrette, tapenade, and artichoke aiolio. Nonseafood specialties include rack of lamb with an herb crust served with rosemary sauce; Ponchartrain pie (ice cream, crème de menthe, meringue, and chocolate sauce in a graham cracker crust); and Key-lime mousse. For grazers, half-portions are available at half the menu price plus $1. *Indiantown Rd. and Rte. A1A, Jupiter, tel. 407/746–2511, in FL 800/432–1420, elsewhere 800/821–8791. Dress: informal, jacket preferred. Reservations advised. AE, CB, DC, MC, V. Moderate.*

Seafood

Charley's Crab. A sister restaurant to the Palm Beach Charley's Crab, this one opened in March 1988, in a lofty tin-roofed Florida Cracker-style structure. Its high ceilings—with beams and air-conditioning ducts exposed and painted pale hues of blue, gray, and beige—evoke feelings of sea, sky, and sand. The restaurant's centerpiece—a gilded nude statue, *Women Bathing*, by Edward Kasprowicz—stands on a six-foot-high pedestal in the main dining room. Menus change daily. Specialties include chilled crab bisque; swordfish *picatta* (sautéed in a lemon and sherry sauce); seafood paella with salmon, swordfish, littleneck clams, mussels, sausage, chicken, and rice with saffron; a pungently spiced seviche; a tangy Key-lime pie rich with extra egg yolks; and a French apple tart with cinnamon ice cream. *1000 N. Federal Hwy., Jupiter, tel. 407/744–4710. (Also in Stuart at 423 S. Federal Hwy., tel. 407/288–6800.) Dress: informal in cafe; jackets preferred at night in restaurant. Reservations suggested. AE, CB, DC, MC, V. Moderate.*

Palm Beach
American

Chuck & Harold's. Boxer Larry Holmes and thespians Brooke Shields and Burt Reynolds are among the celebrities who frequent this combination power-lunch bar, celebrity sidewalk cafe, and nocturnal big-band/jazz garden restaurant. A blue-and-yellow tent on pulleys rolls back in good weather to expose the garden to the elements. Local business people wheel and deal at lunch in the bar area while quaffing Bass Ale and Harp

Lager on tap. Locals who want to be part of the scenery frequent the front-porch area, next to pots of red and white begonias mounted along the sidewalk rail. Specialties include a mildly spiced conch chowder with a rich flavor and a liberal supply of conch; an onion-crunchy gazpacho with croutons, cucumber spear, and a dollop of sour cream; an outrageous charcoal-grilled pizza topped with sun-dried tomato, smoked turkey, and grilled red onions; and a tangy Key-lime pie with a graham-cracker crust and a squeezable lime slice for even more tartness. *207 Royal Poinciana Way, Palm Beach, tel. 407/659–1440. Dress: casual. Reservations suggested. AE, CB, DC, MC, V. Moderate.*

Doherty's. This local restaurant-pub feels like an old shoe, comfortable and unpretentious. Specialties include chicken hash Doherty with a secret cream sauce and sherry or currant jelly, eggs Benedict, a creamy oyster stew, and fish and chips (Wed.–Fri. only). *288 County Rd., Palm Beach 33480, tel. 407/655–6200. Dress: Informal. Reservations not accepted. AE, MC, V. Moderate.*

Continental **The Breakers.** The main hotel dining area at The Breakers consists of the elegant Florentine Dining Room, decorated with fine 15th-century Flemish tapestries; the adjoining Celebrity Aisle where the maître d' seats his most honored guests; and the Circle Dining Room, with a huge circular skylight framing a bronze-and-crystal Venetian chandelier. Specialties include rack of lamb Dijonnaise; salmon *en croute* with spinach, herbs and sauce Véronique (a grape sauce); *vacherin glacé* (praline-flavored ice cream encased in fresh whipped cream and frozen in a baked meringue base); and Key-lime pie. The Breakers also serves less formally at its Beach Club, where locals flock for the most sumptuous Sunday champagne brunch in Florida, and at the Fairway Cafe in the golf-course clubhouse. *1 S. County Rd., Palm Beach, tel. 407/655–6611 or 800/833–3141. Jacket and tie required. Reservations required. AE, CB, DC, MC, V. Expensive.*

International **The Dining Room.** Since it opened in 1925, this formal hotel din-
★ ing room in the Brazilian Court has been a favorite with the Palm Beach elite. The 94-seat dining room, with Romanesque arches and a sunny yellow color scheme, opens onto the outdoor Fountain Court. David Woodward, executive chef, uses only fresh ingredients and prepares all sauces from scratch. Specialties include Brazilian black-bean soup, a hotel standard throughout its history; ragout of Maine lobster with mousseline of scallops; and baked escalope of salmon with a smoked-salmon crust served with a mint and parsley sauce; roast rack of baby lamb with a timbale of spinach and sweet roasted garlic; and kiwi, mango, and raspberry sorbet on a bed of cantalope puree. *301 Australian Ave., Palm Beach, tel. 407/655–7740 or 800/351–5656. Jacket and tie required. Reservations required. AE, CB, DC, MC, V. Very Expensive.*

Seafood **Charley's Crab.** Audubon bird prints, fresh flowers, and French posters accent the walls of this restaurant across the street from the beach. During the season, the dinner line forms early. The raw bar in front is noisy and crowded, the back dining rooms more relaxed. Menus change daily. Specialties include 8–10 daily fresh fish specials. *456 S. Ocean Blvd., Palm Beach, tel. 407/659–1500. Dress: informal. Reservations suggested. AE, DC, MC, V. Expensive.*

Palm Beach Gardens
Continental

The Explorers. You sit in red leather hobnail chairs at tables lit with small brass and glass lanterns. The à la carte menu includes a variety of international and American regional preparations. Specialties include a fresh sushi appetizer with soy, wasabi, and pickled ginger; loin of axis deer with lingonberry conserve; and almond snow eggs, an egg-shaped meringue poached in almond cream, plated between three-fruit coulees (boysenberry, mango, and tamarillo) and garnished with a nest of butter caramel. The Explorers Wine Club meets monthly for wine and food tastings and is open to the public for a one-time $5 membership. Contact the club for a schedule of events. *400 Ave. of the Champions, Palm Beach Gardens, tel. 407/627–2000. Jacket required. Reservations advised. Closed Sun.–Mon. May–Sept. AE, MC, V. Expensive.*

Lodging

The list below is a representative selection of hotels and motels in Palm Beach County. The rate categories in the list are based on the all-year or peak-season price; off-peak rates may be a category or two lower.

The most highly recommended hotels are indicated by a star ★.

Category	Cost*
Very Expensive	over $120
Expensive	$90–$120
Moderate	$50–$90
Inexpensive	under $50

*All prices are for a standard double room, excluding 6% state sales tax and nominal tourist tax

The following credit card abbreviations are used: AE, American Express; CB, Carte Blanche; DC, Diners Club; MC, MasterCard; V, Visa.

Very Expensive

Boca Raton Resort & Club. Architect and socialite Addison Mizner designed and built the original. The tower was added in 1961, the ultramodern Boca Beach Club, in 1981. Room rates during the winter season are based on the modified American plan (including breakfast and dinner). The rooms in the older buildings tend to be smaller and cozily traditional; those in the newer buildings are light, airy and contemporary in color schemes and furnishings. *501 E. Camino Real, Boca Raton 33432, tel. 407/395–3000 or 800/327–0101. 1,000 rooms: 100 in the original 1926 Cloister Inn, 333 in the 1931 addition, 235 in the 27-story Tower Building, 212 in the Boca Beach Club, 120 in the Golf Villas. Facilities: 1½ mi of Atlantic Ocean beach, 4 outdoor freshwater swimming pools, 22 tennis courts (2 lighted), health spa, 23-slip marina, fishing and sailing charters, 7 restaurants, 3 lounges, in-room safes. AE, DC, MC, V.*
Brazilian Court. Built in 1925, the Brazilian Court received new owners and an extensive renovation in 1984–85. The yellow Mediterranean-style buildings still surround a pair of courtyards, where much of the original landscaping survives today.

An open loggia with ceiling beams of exposed pecky cypress was enclosed to provide a gracious European-style lobby. A concierge at an antique desk greets you for check-in. All guest rooms feature gold-plated plumbing fixtures, firm mattresses, and valances above the beds and windows. However, no two rooms are alike. *301 Australian Ave., Palm Beach 33480, tel. 407/655–7740 or 800/351–5656. 134 rooms with bath, including 6 suites, rooms for nonsmokers and handicapped guests. Facilities: outdoor heated freshwater swimming pool, cable TV, two restaurants, lounge, 24-hr room service. AE, CB, DC, MC, V.*

The Breakers. This historic seven-story oceanfront resort hotel, built in 1926 and enlarged in 1968, is currently undergoing renovation. At this palatial Italian Renaissance structure, cupids wrestle alligators in the Florentine fountain in front of the main entrance. Inside the lofty lobby, your eyes rise to majestic ceiling vaults and frescoes. The hotel's proud tradition of formality remains. After 7 PM, men and boys must wear jackets and ties in the public areas. (Ties are optional in summer.) The new room decor comes in two color schemes: cool greens and soft pinks in an orchid-patterned English cotton chintz fabric; the other is in blue, with a floral and ribbon chintz. Both designs include white plantation shutters and wall coverings, Chinese porcelain table lamps, and original 1920s furniture restored to its period appearance. The original building has 15 different sizes and shapes of rooms, many a bit cramped by today's standards. If you like a lot of space, ask to be placed in the newer addition. *1 S. County Rd., Palm Beach 33480, tel. 407/655–6611 or 800/833–3141. 528 rooms with bath, including 40 suites. Facilities: ½ mi of Atlantic Ocean beachfront, outdoor heated freshwater swimming pool, 19 tennis courts, 2 golf courses, health club with Keiser and Nautilus equipment, men's and women's saunas, lawn bowling, croquet, shuffleboard, shopping arcade with upscale boutiques, 3 restaurants, lounge. AE, CB, DC, MC, V.*

The Colony. Located a block off Worth Avenue, this mid-rise luxury city hotel caters to an older, upscale clientele. The Duke and Duchess of Windsor stayed here. John Lennon once was turned away from the dining room because he arrived tieless. Hotel built in 1947, restored in 1987–88; low-rise maisonettes built in mid-1950s, apartments built in 1960s. A striking lobby mural by Phil Brinkman depicts turn-of-the-century Palm Beach. Room decor is tropical chic, with rattan furnishings and pink, blue, and tropical green pastel fabrics in floral patterns. *155 Hammon Ave., Palm Beach 33480, tel. 407/655–5430, fax 407/659–1793. 106 rooms, including 36 suites and apartments. Facilities: outdoor heated freshwater swimming pool, restaurant serves 3 meals daily, dancing nightly with live band, beauty parlor. AE, MC, V.*

PGA Sheraton Resort. This sportsperson's mecca at PGA National Golf Club underwent a $1.8-million renovation in 1987–88 by an interior designer who likes mauve, peach, and aqua. The resort is headquarters for the Professional Golfer's Association and the U.S. Croquet Association, and hosts many major golf, tennis, and croquet tournaments. *400 Ave. of the Champions, Palm Beach Gardens 33418, tel. 407/627–2000 or 800/325–3535. 413 rooms with bath, including 25 suites, 36 nonsmokers rooms, 14 handicapped rooms, 80 2-bedroom, 2-bath cottages with fully equipped kitchen. Facilities: 5 golf courses, 19 tennis courts (10 lighted), 5 croquet courts, 6 indoor racquetball* courts, outdoor freshwater swimming pool, sand beach on 26-acre lake, sailboats and aquacycles for rent, fitness center, sauna, whirlpool, aerobic dance studio, 4 restau-rants, 2 lounges, in-room minibars and safes. AE, DC, MC, V.

Palm Beach Polo and Country Club. Individual villas and condominiums are available in this exclusive 2,200-acre resort where Britain's Prince Charles comes to play polo. Arrange to rent a dwelling closest to the sports activity which interests you: polo, tennis, or golf. Each residence is uniquely designed and furnished by its owner according to standards of quality set by the resort. *13198 Forest Hill Blvd., West Palm Beach 33414, tel. 407/798-7000 or 800/327-4204. 140 privately owned villas and condominiums available for rental when the owners are away. Facilities: 10 outdoor freshwater swimming pools, 24 tennis courts, 2 18-hole golf courses and 1 9-hole course, men's and women's saunas, 10 polo fields, equestrian trails through a nature preserve, 5 stable barns, 2 lighted croquet lawns, squash and racquetball courts, sculling equipment and instruction, 5 dining rooms. AE, DC, MC, V.*

The Palm Court. A 66-room city hotel built in 1926, The Palm Court was restored by new owners in 1986 and reopened in November 1988. *363 Coconut Row, Palm Beach 33480, tel. 407/659-5800 or 800/233-8277. Facilities: outdoor swimming pool, restaurant, library. AE, MC, V.*

Expensive
★

The Jupiter Beach Hilton. This high-rise oceanfront resort hotel is frequented by celebrities and sea turtles. The sea turtles come ashore each summer to lay their eggs in the sand along this stretch of unspoiled beach. The Jupiter Beach Hilton's beach director leads turtle walks at night to look for nesting mothers. In the morning, he collects the eggs in a holding pen by the beach hut to protect them from predators. When the eggs hatch, he helps the baby turtles dig out and guards them as they scramble into the surf. Human guests are at least as well-pampered by a friendly and efficient staff. The nine-story hotel has interior decor of sophisticated informality. The lobby suggests Singapore, with wicker and bamboo furniture, white-washed wood floors, white ceiling fans, and a plethora of palms, orchids, and other tropical plants. *Indiantown Rd. and Rte. A1A, Jupiter 33477, tel. 407/746-2511, in FL 800/432-1420, elsewhere in the USA 800/821-8791, in Canada 800/228-8810. 197 rooms with bath, including 4 suites, 26 nonsmokers rooms, 2 rooms for handicapped guests. Facilities: outdoor heated freshwater swimming pool, 400 ft of beachfront, 60 cabanas, snorkeling, windsurfing, lighted tennis court, poolside snack bar, boutique, fitness center, restaurant, lounge, cable TV, in-room minibars. AE, CB, DC, MC, V.*

The Arts

The *Palm Beach Post*, in its "TGIF" entertainment insert on Fridays, lists all events for the weekend, including concerts. Admission to some cultural events is free or by donation.

Performing Arts Center

Mizner Park (Box 1695, Boca Raton 33429), a cultural center between Federal Highway and Mizner Boulevard, is scheduled to open in 1990. It will house a performing arts complex; art, science, and children's museums; and a specialty shopping center.

Theater **Caldwell Theatre Company.** This professional equity regional theater, part of the Florida State Theater system, moved to a temporary site in 1989 while awaiting completion of permanent quarters in the new Mizner Center. *7887 N. Federal Hwy., Boca Raton 33487, tel. 407/368–7509 (Boca Raton), 407/832– 2989 (Palm Beach), 305/462–5433 (Broward County).*

Royal Palm Dinner Theater. Equity cast performs five or six contemporary musicals each year. *303 Golfview Dr., Royal Palm Plaza, Boca Raton 33432, tel. 407/426–2211 or in FL, 800/841–6725. Tues.–Sat. 8 PM, Sun. 6 PM, Wed. & Sat. matinees 2 PM. AE, MC, V.*

Excursion: Treasure Coast

Numbers in the margin correspond with points of interest on the Treasure Coast map.

This excursion north from **Palm Beach** through the Treasure Coast counties of Martin, St. Lucie, and Indian River traverses an area that was remote and sparsely populated as recently as the late 1970s. Resort and leisure-oriented residential development has swollen its population. If you plan to stay overnight or dine at a good restaurant, reservations are a must.

The interior of all three counties is largely devoted to citrus production, and also cattle ranching in rangelands of pine-and-palmetto scrub. St. Lucie and Indian River counties also contain the upper reaches of the vast St. Johns Marsh, headwaters of the largest northward-flowing river in the United States. If you take Florida's Turnpike from Palm Beach north to the Orlando—Disney World area, you will dip into the edge of St. Johns Marsh about eight miles north of the Fort Pierce exit. Along the coast, the broad expanse of the Indian River (actually a tidal lagoon) separates the barrier islands from the mainland. It's a sheltered route for boaters on the Intracoastal Waterway, a nursery for the young of many saltwater game fish species, and a natural radiator keeping frost away from the tender orange and grapefruit trees that grow near its banks.

Completion of I–95's missing link from Palm Beach Gardens to Fort Pierce in 1987 eliminated the Treasure Coast's last vestiges of relative seclusion. Hotels, restaurants, and shopping malls already crowd the corridor from I–95 to the beach throughout the 70-mile stretch from Palm Beach north to Vero Beach. The Treasure Coast has become another link in the chain of municipalities that some Floridians call "the city of U.S. 1."

Of special interest in this area are the sea turtles that come ashore at night from April to August to lay their eggs on the beaches. Conservation groups, chambers of commerce, and resorts organize turtle-watches, which you may join.

Exploring Treasure Coast

❶ This tour takes you north from **Palm Beach** along the coast as far as Vero Beach, but you can break away at any intermediate point and return to Palm Beach on I–95.

❷ From downtown **West Palm Beach,** take U.S. 1 about five miles north to Blue Heron Boulevard (Rte. A1A) in Riviera Beach,

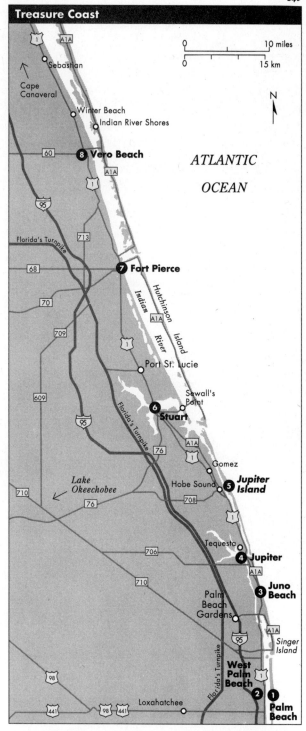

turn right, and cross the **Jerry Thomas Bridge** onto Singer Island. Sightseeing boats depart from **Phil Foster Park** on the island side of the bridge.

Continue on Rte. A1A as it turns north onto Ocean Boulevard, past hotels and high-rise condominiums to **Ocean Reef Park** (3900 N. Ocean Dr., Riviera Beach, tel. 407/964–4420), a snorkeling spot where the reefs are close to shore in shallow water. You may see angelfish, sergeant-majors, rays, robin fish, and occasionally a Florida lobster (actually a species of saltwater crayfish). Wear canvas sneakers and cloth gloves.

Go north on Rte. A1A to **John D. MacArthur State Park** (10900 Rte. A1A, North Palm Beach, tel. 407/964–4420), which offers more good snorkeling along almost two miles of beach, and access to the mangrove swamps in the upper reaches of Lake Worth.

North of MacArthur State Park, Rte. A1A rejoins U.S. 1, then veers east again 1½ miles north at Juno Beach. Take Rte. A1A ③ north to the **Children's Museum of Juno Beach,** established by Eleanor N. Fletcher, "the turtle lady of Juno Beach." Museum displays interpret the sea turtles' natural history; hatchlings are raised in saltwater tanks, tagged and released into the surf. The museum conducts guided turtle watches June 1–July 15, at the height of the nesting season. *1111 Ocean Dr., Juno Beach, tel. 407/627–8280. Admission free. Open Tues.–Sat. 10–3, Sun. 1–3.*

④ From Juno Beach north to **Jupiter,** Rte. A1A runs for almost four miles atop the beachfront dunes. West of the road, about half the land is undeveloped, with endangered native plant communities. The road veers away from the dunes at **Carlin Park** (400 Rte. A1A, Jupiter, tel. 407/964–4420), which provides beach frontage, covered picnic pavilions, hiking trails, two tennis courts, and fishing sites.

At the northwest corner of Indiantown Road and Rte. A1A is **Burt Reynolds Jupiter Theater.** Reynolds grew up in Jupiter; his father was Palm Beach County sheriff. More than 150 Broadway and Hollywood stars have performed here since the theater opened in 1979. In 1989 Reynolds gave the theater to Palm Beach Community College, which will run it as a not-for-profit regional theater. At press time it was scheduled to reopen early in 1990. *1001 E. Indiantown Rd., Jupiter, tel. 407/746–5566.*

Leave the theater grounds on Indiantown Road, go west to U.S. 1, and turn right. About a mile north of Jupiter Island, turn right into Burt Reynolds Park to visit the **Loxahatchee Historical Society Museum.** Permanent exhibits in preparation will emphasize Seminole Indians, the steamboat era, pioneer life on the Loxahatchee River, shipwrecks, railroads and modern-day development. A pioneer dwelling at the mouth of the river, the Dubois Home, is open Sunday 1–3:30 PM; ask for directions at the museum. *805 N. U.S. 1, Box 1506, Jupiter, tel. 407/747–6639. Open Tues.–Fri. 10–3, weekends noon–3, closed Mon. Admission by donation.*

Continue north on U.S. 1 across the Loxahatchee River. The 105-foot-tall **Jupiter Lighthouse,** east of the bridge, is the oldest structure in Palm Beach County, built 1855–59. To reach the lighthouse and a small museum of local history on the ground floor, turn east on Route 707, then take the first right into Lighthouse Park. *No phone. Admission by donation. Open Sun. noon–2:30.*

⑤ Take Rte. 707 north from the lighthouse onto **Jupiter Island.** Just north of the Martin County line, stop at the Nature Conservancy's 113-acre **Blowing Rocks Preserve,** with plant communities native to beachfront dune, strand (the landward side of the dunes), marsh, and hammock (tropical hardwood forest). Sea grape, cabbage palms, saw palmetto, and sea oats help to anchor the dunes. The floral beauty of Indian blanket, dune sunflower, and goldenrod carpets the ground. You may see pelicans, seagulls, ospreys, redbellied and pileated woodpeckers, and a profusion of warblers in spring and fall. A trail takes you over the dune to the beach. At high tide, spray shoots up through holes in the largest Anastasia limestone outcropping on the Atlantic coast. At dead low tide, you can walk on the seaward side of the rocks and peer into caves and solution holes. Best time to go is early morning, before the crowds. The parking lot holds just 18 cars, with room for three cars to wait; Jupiter Island police will ticket cars parked along the road shoulder. *Box 3795, Tequesta, tel. 407/575–2297. Open 6–5. Admission by donation. No food, drink, ice chests, pets, or spearfishing allowed. No rest rooms.*

Continue north through the town of Jupiter Island, a posh community where President Bush's mother and many other notables dwell in estates screened from the road by dense vegetation. At the north end of Jupiter Island, **Hobe Sound National Wildlife Refuge** has a 3½-mile beach where turtles nest and shells wash ashore in abundance. On the mainland at refuge headquarters, visit the **Elizabeth W. Kirby Interpretive Center.** Take Rte. 707 and County Road 708 through the town of Hobe Sound to U.S. 1, then turn left and go about two miles south. The center is on the left (east) side of the highway. An adjacent ½-mile trail winds through a forest of sand pine and scrub oak —one of Florida's most unusual and endangered plant communities. *13640 S.E. Federal Hwy., Hobe Sound 33455, refuge tel. 407/546–6141, nature center tel. 407/546–2067. Trail always open. Nature center open weekdays 9–11 and 1–3, group tours by appointment.*

From the interpretive center, go south 2½ miles to the entrance to **Jonathon Dickinson State Park.** Follow signs to Hobe Mountain, an ancient dune topped with a tower where you'll have a panoramic view across the park's 10,284 acres of varied terrain. It encompasses sand pine, slash pine and palmetto flatwoods, mangrove river swamp, and the winding upper northwest fork of the Loxahatchee River, which is part of the federal government's wild and scenic rivers program and populated by manatees in winter and alligators all year. *14800 S.E. Federal Hwy., Hobe Sound, tel. 407/546–2771. Open daily 8–sundown. Admission: $1 driver, 50 cents per passenger. Facilities: bicycle and hiking trails, campground, snack bar. Contact State Vending Corp., 16450 S.E. Federal Hwy., Hobe Sound 33455, tel. 407/746–1466 for information and reservations on cabins, rental canoes and rowboats. 2-hr narrated river cruise: $9 adults, $4 children under 12.*

⑥ Turn north and take U.S. 1 through some unavoidable commercial development to **Stuart,** then rejoin Rte. A1A northbound to Hutchinson Island. Stop at the pastel-pink **Elliott Museum,**

built in 1961 in honor of inventor Sterling Elliott. On display is an early model of his Elliott Addressing Machine, forerunner of today's Addressograph machines. Elliott also invented a four-wheel bicycle, the quadricycle; the mechanism that makes its wheels turn is the basis of the automobile differential. In addition to Elliott's inventions, the museum features antique automobiles, dolls and toys, and fixtures from an early general store, blacksmith shop, and apothecary shop. Children enjoy feeding coins to a voracious collection of 19th-century mechanical banks. *825 N.E. Ocean Blvd., Stuart, tel. 407/225–1961. Open daily 1–4. Admission: $2.50 adults, 50 cents children 6–13, under 6 free.*

A mile south of the Elliott Museum stands the **House of Refuge Museum,** built in 1875 and now restored to its original appearance. It's one of 10 such structures erected by the U.S. Life Saving Service (an ancestor of the Coast Guard) to aid stranded sailors along Florida's then-remote Atlantic Coast. The keeper here patrolled the beach looking for shipwreck victims whose vessels foundered on Gilbert's Bar, an offshore reef. Exhibits include antique lifesaving equipment, maps, ships' logs, artifacts from nearby wrecks, boatmaking tools, and six tanks of local fish from the ocean and the Indian River. A 35-foot watchtower in the front yard was used during World War II by submarine spotters. *301 S.E. MacArthur Blvd., Stuart, tel. 407/225–1875. Open Tues.–Sun. 1–4, closed Mon. and holidays. Admission: $1 adults, 50 cents children 6–13, under 6 free.*

Driving north on Rte. A1A, you will pass Florida Power & Light Company's St. Lucie nuclear power plant. As you approach the South Beach Causeway Bridge into **Fort Pierce,** stop at the **St. Lucie County Historical Museum** to see more artifacts of the region's history. Exhibits include treasure from a Spanish fleet wrecked in a 1715 hurricane and a diorama depicting a Seminole Indian encampment with a *chickee* (palm-thatched shelter) and dugout canoe. On the grounds is the Gardner House, a restored and furnished Cracker-style pioneer dwelling built in 1907. *414 Seaway Dr., Fort Pierce, tel. 407/464–6635. Open Tues.–Sat. 10–4, Sun. noon–4. Admission: $1 adults, 50 cents children 6–12, under 6 free.*

Cross the bridge into Fort Pierce for a mile on U.S. 1, bypassing Fort Pierce Inlet (which divides Hutchinson Island), then veer east on Rte. A1A across North Beach Causeway. About a mile east, as you approach the ocean, Rte. A1A turns left. Go right instead to visit **Fort Pierce Inlet State Recreation Area,** where a sand bottom creates the Treasure Coast's safest surfing conditions and a nature trail winds through a coastal hammock.

North on Rte. A1A at Pepper Park is the **UDT-Seal Museum,** beside the beach where more than 3,000 Navy frogmen trained during World War II. The museum traces the exploits of Navy divers from the 1944 Normandy invasion through Korea, Vietnam, and astronaut landings at sea. *Box 1117, Ft. Pierce, tel. 407/464–FROG (3764). Open Wed.–Sun. 10–4. Admission: $1 adults, 50¢ children 6–11, under 6 free.*

Within a mile north of Pepper Beach, turn left to the parking lot for the **Jack Island wildlife refuge,** accessible only by footbridge. The one-mile Marsh Rabbit Trail across the island traverses a mangrove swamp to a 30-foot observation tower overlooking the Indian River. You'll see ospreys, brown pelicans, great blue herons, ibis, and other water birds.

❽ Return to Rte. A1A and go north to **Vero Beach,** an affluent city of about 30,000; retirees comprise half the winter population. In the exclusive Riomar Bay section, north of the 17th Street Bridge, "canopy roads" shaded by massive live oaks cross the barrier island between Rte. A1A and Ocean Drive. **Painted Bunting Lane,** a typical canopy road, is lined with elegant homes—many dating from the 1920s.

The city provides beach-access parks with boardwalks and steps bridging the foredune. (Open daily 7 AM–10 PM, admission free.) From shore, snorkelers and divers can swim out to explore reefs 100–300 ft. off the beach. Summer offers the best diving conditions. At low tide you can see the boiler and other remains of an iron-screw steamer, *Breconshire,* which foundered in 1894 on a reef just south of Beachland Boulevard.

Along Ocean Drive near Beachland Boulevard, a specialty shopping area includes art galleries, antique stores, and upscale clothing stores. Also in this area is **The Driftwood Inn Resort** (3150 Ocean Dr., Vero Beach, tel. 407/231–0550), a unique beachfront hotel and restaurant built in the 1930s by Waldo Sexton, an eccentric plow salesman from Indiana. He used driftwood and other scavenged lumber as well as art treasures salvaged from Palm Beach mansions torn down during the Depression. Return to the mainland from Beachland Boulevard across the Merrill Barber Bridge or go 1½ miles south to the new high-rise 17th Street Bridge, which offers a sweeping view over the Indian River. At this point you can take Rte. 60 west through Vero Beach to I-95 for the return to Palm Beach.

Spectator Sports

Baseball   The **Los Angeles Dodgers** train each March in the 6,000-seat Holman Dodgertown Stadium near the Municipal Airport. *Box 2887, Vero Beach 32961, tel. 800/334–PLAY or 407/569–4900.*

The **New York Mets** hold spring training in the 7,400-seat St. Lucie County Sport Complex, home stadium for the Florida League's St. Lucie Mets. *North Peacock Blvd., Box 8808, Port St. Lucie 34985, tel. 407/879–7378.*

Polo   **Windsor Polo and Beach Club.** Geoffrey and Jorie Kent's new polo club featured England's Prince Charles in a special charity game, the Prince of Wales Cup, when it opened in February of 1989. For 1990 the Club plans an abbreviated season; the first complete season will be in 1991. *9300 North A1A, Suite 201, Vero Beach 32963, tel. 407/589–9800 or 800/233–POLO.*

Dining

The list below is a representative selection of restaurants on the Treasure Coast, organized geographically, and by type of cuisine within each community. Unless otherwise noted, they serve lunch and dinner.

Highly recommended restaurants in each price category are indicated by a star ★.

Category	Cost*
Very Expensive	over $55
Expensive	$35–$55
Moderate	$15–$35
Inexpensive	under $15

Average cost of a 3-course dinner, per person, excluding drinks, service, and 6% sales tax.

The following credit card abbreviations are used: AE, American Express; CB, Carte Blanche; DC, Diners Club; MC, MasterCard; and V, Visa.

Stuart
American

The Emporium. Indian River Plantation's coffee shop is an old-fashioned soda fountain and grill that also serves hearty breakfasts. Specialties include eggs Benedict, omelets, and fresh-baked pastries. *555 N.E. Ocean Blvd., Hutchinson Island, tel. 407/225–3700. Dress: informal. No reservations. AE, DC, MC, V. Inexpensive.*

The Porch. This casual indoor/outdoor restaurant overlooks the tennis courts at Indian River Plantation. Specialties include hearty clam chowder, a daily quiche, fried calamari, and two daily selections of fresh fish. *555 N.E. Ocean Blvd., Hutchinson Island, tel. 407/225–3700. Dress: informal. No reservations. AE, DC, MC, V. Inexpensive.*

Continental

★ **The Inlet.** This intimate 60-seat restaurant in the heart of Indian River Plantation features fine dining on gold-rimmed plates in a setting of ethereal pinks and earth tones. Specialties include oysters Rockefeller, creamy lobster bisque with cognac, steak Diane, and fresh snapper. *555 N.E. Ocean Blvd., Hutchinson Island, tel. 407/225–3700. Jacket and tie required. Reservations required. AE, DC, MC, V. No lunch. Closed Sun. Open July–Sept. Fri. and Sat. only. Expensive.*

★ **Scalawags.** Part of Indian River Plantation's new hotel complex, Scalawags can seat you on a terrace overlooking the marina, in a dining room decorated with original paintings of Florida birds, or in a private 20-seat wine room. Specialties include Caribbean conch soup, sea scallops with fresh dill sauce, seafood ravioli, and rack of lamb. The Sunday champagne brunch is superb. *555 N.E. Ocean Blvd., Hutchinson Island, tel. 407/225–3700. Jacket required. Reservations required. AE, DC, MC, V. Dinner only May–Sept. Expensive.*

Ft. Pierce
Seafood

Theo Thudpucker's Raw Bar. Businessmen in suits and ties mingle here with people off the beach in bathing suits. Specialties include oyster stew, smoked fish spread, conch salad and fritters, soft-shell crabs, fresh catfish, and alligator tail. *2025 Seaway Dr. (South Jetty), tel. 407/465–1078. Dress: informal. No reservations. No credit cards. Closed Christmas, New Year's Day, Easter, Mother's Day, and Thanksgiving. Inexpensive.*

Vero Beach
Continental

★ **The Black Pearl.** This small, intimate restaurant (19 tables) with red, pink, and green Art Deco furnishings offers entrées that combine fresh local ingredients with the best of the Continental tradition. Specialties include chilled leek-and-watercress soup, hearty conch-and-crab chowder, feta cheese and spinach fritters, mesquite-grilled swordfish, and dolphin brushed with lime juice and olive oil. *1409 Hwy. A1A, tel. 407/234–4426. Reservations advised. AE, MC, V. Dinner only. Closed Christmas, New Year's Day, and July 4th. Moderate.*

Seafood **Ocean Grill.** Opened as a hamburger shack in 1938, the Ocean Grill has since been refurbished and outfitted with antiques— Tiffany lamps, wrought-iron chandeliers, and Beanie Backus paintings of pirates and Seminole Indians. The menu has also changed with the times and now includes black bean soup, crisp onion rings, Indian River crab cakes, jumbo lump crabmeat salad, at least three kinds of fresh fish every day, prime rib, and a tart Key-lime pie. *Sexton Plaza (Beachland Blvd. east of Ocean Dr.), tel. 407/231–5409. Reservations accepted for parties of 5 or more. AE, MC, V. Closed 2 wks. after Labor Day. Moderate.*

Lodging

The list below is a representative selection of hotels and motels on the Treasure Coast. The rate categories in the list are based on the all-year or peak-season price; off-peak rates may be a category or two lower.

Highly recommended lodgings in each price category are indicated by a star ★.

Category	Cost*
Very Expensive	over $120
Expensive	$90–$120
Moderate	$50–$90
Inexpensive	under $50

**All prices are for a standard double room; excluding 6% state sales tax and nominal tourist tax.*

The following credit card abbreviations are used: AE, American Express; CB, Carte Blanche; DC, Diners Club; MC, MasterCard; and V, Visa.

Stuart **Indian River Plantation.** Situated on a 192-acre tract of land on
★   Hutchinson Island, this resort includes a three-story luxury hotel that is an architectural gem in the Victorian Beach Revival style, with tin roofs, shaded verandas, pink stucco, and much latticework. Some 70 new condos are scheduled to open in spring 1990. *555 N.E. Ocean Blvd., Hutchinson Island, 34996, tel. 407/225–3700 or 800/327–4873. 200 hotel rooms with bath, including 10 rooms for handicapped guests; 54 1- and 2-bedroom oceanfront condominium apartments with full kitchens. Facilities: 3 swimming pools, outdoor spa, 13 tennis courts, golf course, 77-slip marina, power boat and jet-ski rentals, 5 restaurants. AE, DC, MC, V. Very Expensive.*

Vero Beach **The Pickett Suite Resort.** Built in 1986, this five-story rose stucco hotel on Ocean Drive provides easy access to Vero Beach's specialty shops and boutiques. First-floor rooms have patios opening onto the pool. *3500 Ocean Dr., 32963, tel. 800/742–5388 or 407/231–5666. 55 1- and 2-bedroom suites with bath. Facilities: swimming pool, outdoor pool bar/restaurant, TV. AE, DC, MC, V. Very Expensive.*

6 The Florida Keys

Introduction

by George and Rosalie Leposky

The Florida Keys are a wilderness of flowering jungles and shimmering seas, a jade pendant of mangrove-fringed islands dangling toward the tropics. The Florida Keys are also a 110-mile traffic jam lined with garish billboards, hamburger stands, shopping centers, motels, and trailer courts. Unfortunately, you can't have one without the other. A river of tourist dollars gushes southward along the only highway—U.S. 1—to Key West. Many residents of Monroe County live by diverting some of that river's green flow to their own pockets, in ways that have in spots blighted the Keys' fragile beauty—at least on the 31 islands linked to the mainland by the 42 bridges of the Overseas Highway.

As you drive down U.S. 1 through the islands, the silvery blue and green Atlantic, with its great living reef, are on your left, and Florida Bay, the Gulf of Mexico and the back country are on your right. At points the ocean and the gulf are ten miles apart; on the narrowest landfill islands, they are separated only by the road.

The Overseas Highway varies from a frustrating traffic-clogged trap to a mystical pathway skimming across the sea. There are more islands than you will be able to remember. Follow the little green mile markers by the side of U.S. 1, and even if you lose track of the names of the islands, you won't get lost.

There are many things to do along the way, but first you have to remind yourself to get off the highway, which is lined with junk and has the seductive power of keeping you to itself. Once you leave this road, you can rent a boat and find a secluded anchorage at which to fish, swim, and marvel at the sun, sea, and sky. To the south in the Atlantic, you can dive to spectacular coral reefs or pursue dolphin, blue marlin, and other deep-water game fish. Along the Florida Bay coastline you can seek out the bonefish, snapper, snook, and tarpon that lurk in the grass flats and in the shallow, winding channels of the back country.

Along the reefs and among the islands are over 600 kinds of fish. Diminutive deer and pale raccoons, related to but distinct from their mainland cousins, inhabit the Lower Keys. And throughout the islands you'll find such exotic West Indian plants as Jamaica dogwood, pigeon plum, poisonwood, satinwood, and silver and thatch palms, as well as tropical birds like the great white heron, mangrove cuckoo, roseate spoonbill, and white-crowned pigeon.

Another Keys attraction is the weather: in the winter it's typically 10 degrees warmer in the Keys than on the mainland; in the summer it's usually 10 degrees cooler. The Keys also get substantially less rain, around 30 inches annually compared to 55–60 inches in Miami and the Everglades. Most of the rain falls in brief, vigorous thunderstorms on summer afternoons. In winter, continental cold fronts occasionally stall over the Keys, dragging temperatures down to the 40s.

The Keys were only sparsely populated until the early 20th century. In 1905, however, railroad magnate Henry Flagler began building the overseas extension of his Florida East Coast Railroad south from Homestead to Key West. His goal was to establish a rail link to the steamships that sailed between Key West and Havana, just 90 miles away across the Straits of Florida. The railroad arrived at Key West in 1912 and remained a lifeline of commerce until the Labor Day hurricane of 1935 washed out much of its roadbed. For three years thereafter, the only way in and out of Key West was by boat. The Overseas Highway, built over the railroad's old roadbeds and bridges, was completed in 1938.

Although the Keys on the surface seem homogenous to most mainlanders, they are actually quite varied in terms of population and ambience. Most of the residents of the Upper Keys, which extend from Key Largo to Long Key Channel, moved to Florida from the Northeast and Midwest; many are retirees. Most of the work force is employed by the tourism and service industries. Key Largo, the largest of the keys and the one closest to the mainland, is becoming a bedroom community for Homestead, South Dade, and even the southern reaches of Miami. In the Middle Keys, from Long Key Channel through Marathon to Seven-Mile Bridge, fishing and related services dominate the economy. Most residents are the children and grandchildren of migrants from other Southern states. The Lower Keys from Seven Mile Bridge down to Key West have a diverse population: native "Conchs" (white Key Westers, many of whom trace their ancestry to the Bahamas), freshwater Conchs (longtime residents who migrated from somewhere else years ago), gays (who now make up at least 20 percent of Key West's citizenry), black Bahamians, Hispanics (primarily Cubans), recent refugees from the urban sprawl of Miami and Fort Lauderdale, transient Navy and Air Force personnel, students waiting tables, and a miscellaneous assortment of vagabonds, drifters, and dropouts in search of refuge at the end of the road.

Important Addresses and Numbers

Tourist Information | **Florida Keys & Key West Visitors Bureau** (Box 1147, Key West 33041, tel. 305/296–3811 or 800/FLA–KEYS). Ask for their free accommodations guide.
Local chambers of commerce in Key Largo, Islamorada, Marathon, and Key West have visitor centers with information on accommodations, recreation, restaurants, and special events:
Key Largo Chamber of Commerce (MM 103.4, BS, 103400 Overseas Hwy., Key Largo 33037, tel. 305/451–1414 or 800/822–1088).
Islamorada Chamber of Commerce (MM 82.6, BS, Box 915, Islamorada 33036, tel. 305/664–5603 or 800/FAB–KEYS).
Greater Marathon Chamber of Commerce (MM 49, BS, 330 Overseas Hwy., Marathon 33050, tel. 305/743–5417 or 800/842–9580).
Lower Keys Chamber of Commerce (MM 30.5, OS, Box 511, Big Pine Key 33043, tel. 305/872–2411).
Greater Key West Chamber of Commerce (402 Wall St., Key West 33041, tel. 305/294–2587).

Emergencies | Dial 911 for ambulance and police.

Hospitals | The following hospitals have 24-hour emergency rooms: **Mariners Hospital** (MM 88.5, BS, 50 High Point Rd., Tavernier, Plantation Key 33070; physician-referral service, tel. 305/852–9222), **Fishermen's Hospital** (MM 48.7, OS, 3301 Overseas Hwy., Marathon, tel. 305/743–5533), **De Poo Hospital** (1200 Kennedy Dr., Key West 33040, tel. 305/294–4692 or 294–5183), and **Florida Keys Memorial Hospital** (MM5, BS, 5900 Junior College Rd., Stock Island, tel. 305/294–5531).

Late-Night Pharmacies The Keys have no 24-hour pharmacies. Hospital pharmacists will help with emergencies after regular retail business hours.

Arriving and Departing

By Plane Shuttle and connecting flights go to **Key West International Airport** (S. Roosevelt Blvd., tel. 305/296–5439) from the Miami and Orlando International airports. From Miami, you can fly direct to Key West on Piedmont Airlines, Eastern Express, and Delta Airlines. From Orlando, you must change planes in Miami if you fly on Piedmont or Eastern Express; Delta provides non-stop service.

Eastern Express also flies direct to the **Marathon Airport** (MM 52, BS, 9000 Overseas Hwy., tel. 305/743–2996) from the Miami and Ft. Lauderdale–Hollywood International airports.

Between Miami and the Keys **The Airporter.** Scheduled van and bus service is available from the lower level of MIA's Concourse E to major hotels in Key Largo and Islamorada. *701 S. Homestead Blvd., Homestead 33030, tel. 305/247–8874 (Miami) or 305/247–8876 (Keys). Reservations required.*

Island Taxi meets arriving flights at MIA. Reservations are required 24 hours in advance for arrivals, one hour for departures. Accompanied children ride free. *Tel. 305/852–9700 (Upper Keys), 305/743–0077 (Middle Keys), 305/872–4404 (Lower Keys). Fare: $4 for first 2 mi, then $1.50/mi.*

By Car If you want to avoid Miami traffic on the way to the Keys, take the Homestead Extension of Florida's Turnpike; although it's a toll road that carries a lot of commuter traffic, it's still the fastest way to go. From MIA, take LeJeune Road (SW 42nd Avenue) south, turn west on the Dolphin Expressway (Route 836) to the turnpike, then go south to the turnpike's southern end. If you prefer traffic to tolls, take LeJeune Road south to U.S. 1 and turn right.

Just south of Florida City, the turnpike joins U.S. 1 and the Overseas Highway begins. Once you cross the Jewfish Creek bridge at the north end of Key Largo, you're officially in the Keys.

From Florida City, you can also reach Key Largo on Card Sound Road. Go 13 miles south to the Card Sound Bridge (toll: $1), which offers a spectacular view of blue water and mangrove-fringed bays (and of Florida Power & Light Company's hulking Turkey Point nuclear power plant in the distance to your left). At low tide, flocks of herons, ibis, and other birds frequent the mud flats on the margin of the sound. Beyond the bridge, on north Key Largo, the road traverses a mangrove swamp with ponds and inlets harboring the exceedingly rare Florida crocodile. At the only stop sign, turn right onto Route 905, which cuts through some of the Keys' few remaining large tracts of tropical hardwood jungle. You'll rejoin U.S. 1 in north Key Largo 31 miles from Florida City.

Car Rentals All six of the rental-car firms with booths inside Miami International Airport also have outlets in Key West, which means you can drive into the Keys and fly out. Don't fly into Key West and drive out; the rental firms have substantial drop charges to leave a Key West car in Miami. Avis, Budget and Hertz also serve Marathon Airport.

Enterprise Rent-A-Car has offices at MIA, several Keys locations, and participating hotels in the Keys where you can pick up and drop off cars when the offices are closed. You can rent a car from Enterprise at MIA and return it there, or leave it in the Keys for a drop charge. *Tel. 305/576–1300 (Miami), 305/451–3998 (Key Largo), 305/664–2344 (Islamorada), or 305/325–8007. Key West and Marathon offices planned for 1990. Open weekdays 8–6, Sat. 9–noon. AE, DC, MC, V.*

By Bus **Greyhound/Trailways.** Buses traveling between Miami and Key West make 10 scheduled stops, but you can flag down a bus anywhere along the route. *Tel. 305/374–7222 (Miami) for schedule; 24-hr Miami Greyhound Station, tel. 305/871–1810; Big Pine Key, tel. 305/872–4022; Key West, 615½ Duval St., tel. 305/296–9072. No reservations.*

By Boat Boaters can travel to Key West either along the Intracoastal Waterway through Florida Bay, or along the Atlantic Coast. The Keys are full of marinas that welcome transient visitors, but they don't have enough slips for everyone who wants to visit the area. Make reservations in advance, and ask about channel and dockage depth—many Keys marinas are quite shallow.

Florida Marine Patrol (Marathon, tel. 305/743–6542).

Coast Guard Group Key West provides 24-hour monitoring of VHF-FM Channel 16. Safety and weather information is broadcast at 7 AM and 5 PM Eastern Standard time on VHF-FM Channel 16 and 22A. *Key West 33040, tel. 305/292–8727. 3 stations in the Keys: Islamorada, tel. 305/664–4404; Marathon, tel. 305/743–6778; Key West, tel. 305/292–8856.*

Getting Around

Directions and Maps The only address many people have is a mile marker (MM) number. The markers themselves are small green rectangular signs along the side of the Overseas Highway (U.S. 1). They begin with MM 126 a mile south of Florida City and end with MM 0 on the corner of Fleming and Whitehead streets in Key West. Keys residents also use the abbreviation BS for the Bay Side of U.S. 1, and OS for the Atlantic Ocean Side of the highway.

Florida Visitor Centers and the Florida Department of Commerce distribute *Florida's Official Transportation Map* free. Write to Florida Department of Commerce (Collins Bldg., Tallahassee 32304).

The best road map for the Florida Keys is published by the Homestead/Florida City Chamber of Commerce. You can obtain a copy at the Tropical Everglades Visitor Center in Florida City, or by mail. *160 U.S. Highway 1, Florida City 33034, tel. 305/245–9180. Open daily 8–6. Map costs $1.50; by mail add 25¢ in U.S., 75¢ elsewhere.*

Throughout the Keys, the local chambers of commerce, marinas, and dive shops will offer you the local **Teall's Guide**—a land and nautical map—for 50¢, which goes to build mooring buoys to protect living coral reefs from boat anchors. Separate guides in the *Teall's Miami and Keys Guides* series cover Miami to Key Largo, John Pennekamp Coral Reef State Park and Key

Largo National Marine Sanctuary, the Middle Keys, and Marathon–Key West. To order the entire series by mail, send $6.95 and your street address (not post office box) to Teall's Florida Keys Guides (111 Saguaro Ln., Marathon 33050, tel. 305/743–3942).

By Car The 18-mile stretch of U.S. 1 from Florida City to Key Largo is a hazardous two-lane road with heavy traffic (especially on weekends) and only two passing zones. Try to drive it in daylight, and be patient day or night. The Overseas Highway is four lanes wide in Key Largo and Marathon, but narrow and crowded elsewhere. Expect delays behind large tractor-trailer trucks, cars towing boats, and rubbernecking tourists. Allow at least five hours from Florida City to Key West on a good day. After midnight, you can make the trip in three hours—but then you miss the scenery.

In Key West's Old Town, parking is scarce and costly ($1.25/hour, $6 maximum at Mallory Square). Use a taxicab, bicycle, moped, or your feet to get around. Elsewhere in the Keys, however, having a car is crucial. Gas prices are higher in the Keys than on the mainland. Fill your tank in Miami and top it off in Florida City.

By Bus The **City of Key West Port and Transit Authority** operates three bus lines: Mallory Square (counterclockwise around the island), Old Town (clockwise around the island), and a free Shopping Center Shuttle (Key Plaza to Searstown). *Tel. 305/292–8165 or 292–8164. Exact fare: 75¢; monthly pass, $20.*

By Taxi **Island Taxi** offers 24-hour service from Key Largo to Boca Chica Key. Accompanied children ride free. There is no service to downtown Key West. *Tel. 305/852–9700 (Upper Keys), 305/743–0077 (Middle Keys), 305/872–4404 (Lower Keys). Fare: $4 for first 2 mi, then $1.50/mi.*
Maxi-Taxi (tel. 305/294–2222 or 296–2222) and **Sun Cab** (tel. 305/296–7777) offer 24-hour service in Key West. *Airport service: Maxi-Taxi $4/person, Sun Cab $4.50/person. Local service: Maxi-Taxi has zone rates and $7 group rate for 6 or more people. Sun Cab has meters, $1.40 first ½-mi, 35¢ each additional ¼-mi.*
Carriage Trade Limousine Service offers island tours in a 1980 stretch Cadillac. *tel. 305/296–0000. $40/hour, minimum 3 hrs.*

Guided Tours

Orientation Tours **The Conch Tour Train.** This 105-minute narrated tour of Key West travels 14 miles through Old Town and around the island. The driver pauses frequently to discuss points of historical interest and to chat with friends. *Boarding Locations: Mallory Sq. Depot on the half hr, Roosevelt Blvd. Depot on the hour, tel. 305/294–5161. Runs daily 9–4. Fare: $10 adults, $3 children. MC, V.*
Old Town Trolley. Key West has 11 trackless trolley-style buses that run every 30 minutes. The trolleys are smaller than the Conch Tour Train and go places the train won't fit. The narrated trolley tour lasts 90 minutes, passes more than 100 points of interest, and makes 16 stops all around the island. You may disembark at any stop and reboard a later trolley. *1910 N. Roosevelt Blvd., Key West 33040, tel. 305/296–6688. Runs 9 AM–4:30 PM. Admission: $10 adults, $4 children. MC, V.*

Special-Interest Tours
Canoe Tours

Canoeing Nature Tours. Stan Becker leads a full-day 5-mile canoe and hiking trip in the Key Deer National Wildlife Refuge. The trip includes three hours in canoes and four hours exploring Watson Hammock on Big Pine Key. *MM 28, BS, Box 62, Big Pine Key 33043, tel. 305/872–2620. Reservation required. Children welcome; no pets. Box lunch provided. 9 AM–4 PM. Fee: $60/person.*

Sunset and Harbor Boat Tours

Residents and tourists alike flock to west-facing restaurants, hotel docks, and bars to watch the glowing orb sink into the sea. Hundreds of people gather on Key West's Mallory Square Dock, where street performers and food vendors vie with the sunset for your attention. Throughout the keys, many motor yacht and sailboat captains take paying passengers on sunset cruises. Contact local chambers of commerce and hotels for information.

M/V *Miss Key West* offers a one-hour narrated cruise that explores Key West's harbor up to a half-mile from shore. The 45-passenger, 45-foot motor yacht passes Trumbo Point Navy Base, home of all six of the Navy's hydrofoil guided-missile destroyers. The sundown cruise includes live music. A morning cruise seeks dolphins, sea turtles, and birds. *Zero Duval St. (booth in front of Ocean Key House), tel. 305/296–8865, 800/328–9815 (USA), or 800/231–9864 (FL). Open 8 AM–11 PM. Tours: 10 AM, noon, 2 PM, 4 PM, and sundown. Admission: harbor and sunset cruise $8 adults, children under 12 free; dolphin watch and nature trip, $10 adults, children under 12 free. AE, MC, V.*

Walking Tours

Pelican Path is a free walking guide to Key West published by the **Old Island Restoration Foundation.** The tour discusses the history and architecture of 43 structures along 25 blocks of 12 Old Town streets. Pick up a copy at the Key West Chamber of Commerce.

Solares Hill's Walking and Biking Guide to Old Key West, by local historian Sharon Wells, contains eight walking tours of the city and a short tour of the Key West cemetery. Free copies are available from Key West Chamber of Commerce, many hotels and stores.

Exploring the Florida Keys

Attractions are listed by island or by mile marker (MM) number.

Numbers in the margin correspond with points of interest on the Florida Keys map.

The Upper Keys

This tour begins on Key Largo, the northeasternmost of the Florida Keys accessible by road. The tour assumes that you have come south from Florida City on **Card Sound Road** (Rte. 5). If you take the Overseas Highway (U.S. 1) south from Florida City, you can begin the tour with John Pennekamp Coral Reef State Park.

Cross the **Card Sound Bridge** onto **North Key Largo,** where Card Sound Road forms the eastern boundary of **Crocodile Lakes National Wildlife Refuge.** In the refuge dwell some 300 to 500 crocodiles, the largest single concentration of these shy, elusive reptiles in North America. There's no visitor center here—just 6,800 acres of mangrove swamp and adjoining upland jungle. For your best chance to see a crocodile, park on the shoulder of Card Sound Road and scan the ponds along the road with binoculars. In winter, crocodiles often haul out and sun themselves on the banks farthest from the road. Don't leave the road shoulder; you could disturb tern nests on the nearby spoil banks or aggravate the rattlesnakes.

Take Card Sound Road to Route 905, turn right, and drive for 10 miles through **Key Largo Hammock,** the largest remaining stand of the vast West Indian tropical hardwood forest that once covered most of the upland areas in the Florida Keys. The state and federal governments are busy acquiring as much of the hammock as they can to protect it from further development, and they hope to establish visitor centers and nature trails. For now, it's best to admire this wilderness from the road. According to law-enforcement officials, this may be the most dangerous place in the United States, a haven for modern-day pirates and witches. The "pirates" are drug smugglers who land their cargo along the ocean shore or drop it into the forest from low-flying planes. The "witches" are practitioners of voodoo, *santeria*, and other occult rituals. What's more, this jungle is full of poisonous plants. The most dangerous, the manchineel or "devil tree," has a toxin so potent that rainwater falling on its leaves and then onto a person's skin can cause sores that resist healing. Florida's first tourist, explorer Juan Ponce de León, died in 1521 from a superficial wound inflicted by an Indian arrowhead dipped in manchineel sap.

Time Out   Pause for a drink at the **Caribbean Club,** a friendly neighborhood bar on a historic site. Scenes from *Key Largo*, the 1948 Bogart-Bacall movie, were filmed in the original Caribbean Club, which burned down in the 1950s. *MM 104, BS, Key Largo, tel. 305/451–9970. Open daily 7 AM–4AM. No credit cards.*

Continue on U.S. 1 to Transylvania Avenue (MM 103.2) and turn left to visit the **Marine Resources Development Foundation.** The foundation expects by mid-1990 to have a 1-acre visitor center beside the Overseas Highway and to provide a minibus to transport visitors to its oceanside campus. There you'll find a museum devoted to the history of man and the sea, tanks for growing sea sprouts (a species of edible red algae), a 13-minute multimedia slide show, and a 280-foot moving sidewalk through a clear tube beneath the surface of a 30-foot-deep lagoon teeming with tropical fish. Also in the lagoon is **Jules' Undersea Lodge,** a two-room hotel for divers (*see* Participant Sports). *51 Shoreland Dr., Box 787, Key Largo, tel. 305/451–1139 or 800/858–7119 in FL. Phone for opening date, admission fees, and hours.*

❶ Return to U.S. 1, turn left, and left again into **John Pennekamp Coral Reef State Park.** The primary attraction here is diving on the offshore coral reefs (*see* Sports and Outdoor Activities), but even a landlubber can appreciate the superb interpretive aquarium in the park's visitor center. A huge central tank holds angelfish, stingrays, and Florida spiny lobsters. There's also a touch tank where you can fondle starfish, sponges, and various species of bivalves. A concessionaire rents canoes and sailboats and offers boat trips to the reef. The park also includes a nature trail through a mangrove forest, a swimming beach, picnic shelters, a snack bar, a gift shop, and a campground. *MM*

164

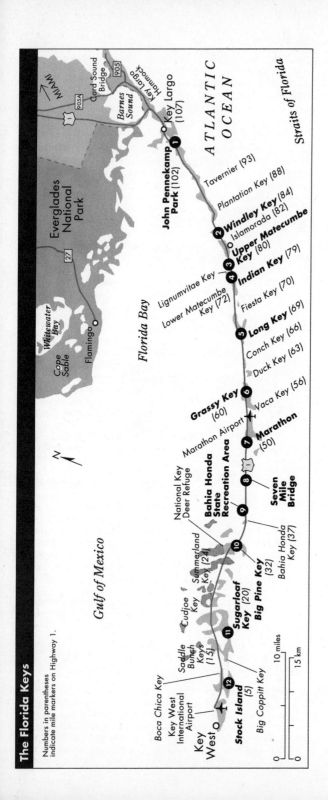

The Florida Keys

Numbers in parentheses indicate mile markers on Highway 1.

102.5, OS, Key Largo, tel. 305/451–1202. Admission: Florida residents $1.50/car and driver, $1/passenger; out-of-state visitors $2.50/car and driver, $1.50/passenger; children under 6 free. Open daily 8AM–sunset.

Return to U.S. 1 and turn left. At MM 100, turn left again into the parking lot of the Holiday Inn Key Largo Resort. In the adjoining Key Largo Harbor Canal you'll find the *African Queen,* the steam-powered workboat on which Katherine Hepburn and Humphrey Bogart rode in their movie of the same name. The 30-foot craft was built in England in 1912. James W. Hendricks, an attorney from Kentucky who owns the resort, bought the boat in 1982 and lovingly restored her. Hendricks also owns and displays at the resort the *Thayer IV,* a 22-foot mahogany Chris Craft built in 1951 and used by Ms. Hepburn and Henry Fonda in Fonda's last film, *On Golden Pond.*

② Continuing south on U.S. 1 you'll cross **Plantation Key** (MM 93–87), named for the plantings of limes, pineapples, and tomatoes cultivated here at the turn of the century. Next comes **Windley Key,** notable for **Theater of the Sea,** where seven dolphins, two sea lions, and an extensive collection of tropical fish swim in the pits of a 1907 railroad quarry. Allow at least two hours to attend the dolphin and sea lion shows and visit all the exhibits, which include a "bottomless" boat ride, touch tank, shark-feeding pool, and a 300-gallon "living reef" aquarium with invertebrates and small reef fishes. *MM 84.5, OS, Box 407, Islamorada, tel. 305/664–2431. Admission: $9.50 adults, $5.50 children 4–12. Open daily 9:30 AM–4 PM. Swim with dolphins (30-min orientation and 30 min in the water): $50. Reservations required with 50% deposit, minimum age 13, mask and swim fins recommended, life vests optional. Video or still photos: $49.95 additional.*

Time Out Stop at **Green Turtle Seafood Market & Cannery** on Upper Matecumbe Key. Owner Henry Rosenthal, who also operates the nearby **Green Turtle Inn** (*see* Dining), cans five kinds of chowder—turtle, conch, Manhattan clam, New England clam, and New England fish—plus turtle consomme and Key-lime pie filling. If the cannery is running when you visit, he'll show you the operation. Most of the fresh seafood on sale is local, right off the boats that dock behind the building, but the market also sells Key West shrimp, blue crabs from Maryland and Argentina, and oysters from Apalachicola Bay in North Florida. *MM 81.5, OS, Islamorada, tel. 305/664–4918. Open Tues.–Sun. 8–6.*

Just below the cannery, watch for the **Hurricane Memorial** (MM 81) beside the highway. It marks the mass grave of 423 victims of the 1935 Labor Day hurricane. Many of those who perished were veterans who had been working on the Overseas Highway; they died when a tidal surge overturned a train sent to evacuate them. The Art Deco–style monument depicts wind-driven waves and palms bowing before the storm's fury.

③ At the lower tip of **Upper Matecumbe Key** , stop at the **International Fishing Museum** in Bud n' Mary's Marina. The museum contains a collection of antique fishing tackle and a video library with information on fishing activities, fishery conservation, and the natural history of various species of local fishes. The videos don't circulate, but you can watch them in the museum. The museum staff can also help you find a charter captain for deep-sea or back-country fishing. *MM 79.5, OS. For information, contact Bob Epstein, 124 Gardenia St., Tavernier 33070, tel. 305/664–2767 (office), 852–8813 (home). Admission free. Open Mon.–Sat. 10–4.*

4 The dock on **Indian Key Fill** at MM 78, BS, is the closest point on the Overseas Highway to three unusual state parks accessible only by water. The newest of these parks, dedicated in 1989, is **San Pedro Underwater Archaeological Preserve** (*see* Sports and Outdoor Activities). State-operated boat tours aboard the M. V. *Monroe* will take you to the other two, **Indian Key State Historic Site** (OS) and **Lignumvitae Key State Botanical Site** (BS). Indian Key was a county seat town and shipwrecker's station until an Indian attack wiped out the settlement in 1840. Dr. Henry Perrine, a noted botanist, was killed in the raid. Today you'll see his plants overgrowing the town's ruins. A virgin hardwood forest still cloaks Lignumvitae Key, punctuated only by the home and gardens that chemical magnate William Matheson built as a private retreat in 1919. *MM 78. For information and tour boat reservations, contact Long Key State Recreation Area, Box 776, Long Key, tel. 305/664–4815. Indian Key open daily 8 AM–sunset; Lignumvitae Key open Thurs.–Mon. with 1-hr guided tour (admission: $1 adults, children under 6 free) at 10:30 AM, 1 and 2:30 PM for visitors from private boats. State tour boat admission: $6 adults, $3 children under 12, for 3-hr tours Thurs.–Mon. to Indian Key, 8:30 AM, to Lignumvitae Key, 1:30 PM.*

5 Return to U.S. 1 and turn right. Continue down to **Long Key** (MM 69), where you'll pass a tract of undisturbed forest on the right (BS) just below MM 67. Watch for a historical marker partially obscured by foliage. Pull off the road here and explore **Layton Trail,** named after Del Layton, who incorporated the city of Layton in 1963 and served as its mayor until his death in 1987. The marker relates the history of the Long Key Viaduct, the first major bridge on the rail line, and the Long Key Fishing Club that Henry Flagler established nearby in 1906. Zane Grey, the noted western novelist, was president of the club. It consisted of a lodge, guest cottages, and storehouses—all obliterated by the 1935 hurricane. The clearly marked trail leads through the tropical hardwood forest to a rocky Florida Bay shoreline overlooking shallow grass flats offshore.

Less than a mile below Layton Trail, turn left into **Long Key State Recreation Area,** then left again to the parking area for the **Golden Orb Trail.** This trail leads onto a boardwalk through a mangrove swamp alongside a lagoon where many herons and other water birds congregate in winter. The park also has a campground, a picnic area, a canoe trail through a tidal lagoon, and a not-very-sandy beach fronting on a broad expanse of shallow grass flats. Instead of a pail and shovel, bring a mask and snorkel here to observe the marine life in this rich nursery area. *Box 776, Long Key, tel. 305/664–4815. Admission: Florida residents $1.50/car and driver, $1/passenger; out-of-state visitors $2.50/car and driver, $1.50/passenger. Open daily 8 AM–sunset.*

The Middle Keys

Below Long Key, the Overseas Highway crosses Long Key Channel on a new highway bridge beside the railroad's **Long**

Key Viaduct. The second-longest bridge on the rail line, this two-mile-long structure has 222 reinforced-concrete arches. It ends at **Conch Key** (MM 63), a tiny fishing and retirement community. Below Conch Key, the causeway on your left at MM 61 leads to **Duck Key,** an upscale residential community where **Hawk's Cay Resort** (*see* Lodging) offers hotel guests a swim-with-the-dolphins experience at its Zoovet Dolphin Center.

6 Next comes **Grassy Key** (MM 59). Watch on the right for the **Dolphin Research Center** and the 35-foot-long concrete sculpture of the dolphin Theresa and her son Nat outside the former home of Milton Santini, creator of the original *Flipper* movie. The 17 dolphins here today are free to leave and return to the fenced area that protects them from boaters and predators. *MM 59, BS, Box Dolphin, Marathon Shores, tel. 305/289-0002. Admission: $5 donation. Visitor center open Wed.–Sun. 9 AM–3 PM, closed Christmas, New Year, and Thanksgiving. Walking tours at 9:30 and 11 AM, 1 and 3 PM. Swim with dolphins (20 min) $50. Children 5–12 swim with an accompanying swimming adult. Reserve for dolphin swim on the first day of the month before you plan to be in the Keys.*

Continuing down U.S. 1, you'll pass the road to **Key Colony Beach** (MM 54, OS), an incorporated city developed in the 1950s as a retirement community. It has a beach, golf course, and boating facilities. Soon after, you'll cross a bridge onto **Vaca**
7 **Key** and enter **Marathon** (MM 53–47), the commercial hub of the Middle Keys. Marathon is notorious for perpetual road construction along U.S. 1, which has resulted in the disappearance of mile markers beside the road. You must navigate here by means of numbered cross streets.

On your right (BS) at 55th Street is **Crane Point Hammock,** a 63-acre tract that includes the world's last undisturbed thatch-palm hammock. The Florida Keys Land Trust, a private, non-profit conservation group, paid $1.2 million to acquire the property in 1988. At least part of it should be open to the public in 1990. The tract also includes an exotic plant arboretum, an archaeological site, a Bahamian village with the oldest surviving example of Conch-style architecture outside Key West, and a children's museum in a historic 1925 house. Future plans include the opening of a marine science education center, interpretive tram rides, and nature trails. *For current information, contact Dr. Chuck Olson, Florida Keys Land Trust, Box 1432, Key West 33041, tel. 305/745-1110.*

Across the Overseas Highway from **Crane Point Hammock,** between the K-Mart and the Marine Bank, Sombrero Beach Road (55th Street) leads two miles south past Marathon High School to a free county beach on the ocean. **Sombrero Beach** has a modest stretch of sand, some limestone rock ledges at the water's edge, and picnic tables in covered shelters for sun and rain protection. Just offshore is the world's first underwater county park, **Marathon Marine Sanctuary** (*see* Sports and Outdoor Activities).

As you approach the new Seven Mile Bridge, turn right at MM 47 to the entrance to the **Old Seven Mile Bridge.** An engineering marvel in its day, the bridge rested on 546 concrete piers spanning the broad expanse of water that separates the Middle and Lower Keys. Monroe County maintains a two-mile stretch of the old bridge to provide access to **Pigeon Key** (MM 45), where the county's public schools and community college run marine-science classes in a railroad work camp built around 1908. The county has applied to place Pigeon Key on the National Register of Historic Places, a status the Old Seven Mile Bridge already enjoys. Other plans for Pigeon Key include restoration of its six wood buildings (four dormitories, an office, and a laboratory), a railroad museum with historic photos not previously on public display, and a tram to bring visitors from Marathon across the old bridge to Pigeon Key. *For information, contact James Lewis, Chairman, Pigeon Key Advisory Authority, 2945 Overseas Hwy., Marathon 33050, tel. 305/743–6040.*

❽ Return to U.S. 1 and proceed across the new **Seven Mile Bridge** (actually only 6.79 miles long!). Built between 1980 and 1982 at a cost of $45 million, the new Seven Mile Bridge is the world's longest segmental bridge, with 39 expansion joints separating its cement sections. Each April marathon runners gather in Marathon for the annual Seven Mile Bridge Run.

The Lower Keys

❾ At **Bahia Honda State Recreation Area** (MM 37) on Bahia Honda Key, you'll find a sandy beach most of the time. Lateral drift builds up the beach in summer; winter storms whisk away much of the sand. The park's Silver Palm Trail leads you through a dense tropical forest where you can see rare West Indian plants, including the Geiger tree, sea lavendar, Key spider lily, bay cedar, thatch and silver palms, and several species found nowhere else in the Florida Keys: the West Indies satinwood, Catesbaea, Jamaica morning glory, and wild dilly. The park also includes a campground, cabins, gift shop, snack bar, marina, and dive shop offering snorkel trips to offshore reefs. *MM 37, OS, Rte. 1, Box 782, Big Pine Key, tel. 305/872–2353. Admission: Florida residents $1.50/car and driver, $1/passenger; out-of-state visitors $2.50/car and driver, $1.50/passenger; children under 6 free. Open daily 8 **AM**–sunset.*

❿ Cross the Bahia Honda Bridge and continue past Spanish Harbor Key and Spanish Harbor Channel onto **Big Pine Key** (MM 32–30), where prominent signs warn drivers to be on the lookout for Key deer. Every year cars kill 50 to 60 of the delicate creatures. A subspecies of the Virginia white-tailed deer, Key deer once ranged throughout the Lower and Middle Keys, but hunting and habitat destruction reduced the population to fewer than 50 in 1947. Under protection in the **National Key Deer Refuge** since 1954, the deer herd grew to about 750 by the early 1970s. The government owns only about a third of Big Pine Key, however, and as the human population on the remaining land grew during the 1980s, the deer herd declined again until today only 250 to 300 remain.

To visit the refuge, turn right at the stoplight, then bear left at the fork onto Key Deer Boulevard (Rte. 940). Pass Road Prison No. 426 and a fire tower on the way to Watson Boulevard, then turn left and go about a mile to the **Refuge Headquarters** to see interpretive displays and obtain brochures.

The best place to see Key deer is on **No Name Key,** a sparsely populated island just east of Big Pine Key. To get there, take Watson Boulevard east to Wilder Road, and turn left. You'll go two miles from Key Deer Boulevard to the middle of the Bogie

Channel Bridge, which links Big Pine and No Name Keys, and 1½ miles from there across No Name Key. If you get out of your car at the end of the road to walk around, close all doors and windows to keep raccoons from wandering in. Deer may turn up along this road at any time of day—especially in early morning and late afternoon. Admire their beauty, but don't try to feed them—it's against the law. To resume your journey, take Wilder Road back to Key Deer Boulevard at the fork just before the stoplight on U.S. 1. Turn right at the stoplight, and continue on down the keys across **Big Torch, Middle Torch,** and **Little Torch Keys** (named for the torchwood tree, which settlers used for kindling because it burns easily even when green). Next comes **Ramrod Key** (MM 27.5), a base for divers in **Looe Key National Marine Sanctuary** five miles offshore (*see* Sports and Outdoor Activities).

⑪ On **Sugarloaf Key** (MM 20), you'll find the Sugar Loaf Lodge (MM 17, BS), an attractive motel known for its performing dolphin named Sugar, who lives in a lagoon behind the restaurant (*see* Lodging). Follow the paved road northwest from the motel for a half mile past an airstrip, and keep going on an unpaved spur. There, in bleak, gravel-strewn surroundings, you'll find a reconstruction of R. C. Perky's **bat tower.** Perky, an early real estate promoter, built the tower in 1929 to attract mosquito-eating bats, but no bats ever roosted in it.

Continue on through the Saddlebunch Keys and Big Coppitt Key to **Boca Chica Key** (MM 10), site of the Key West Naval Air Station. You may hear the roar of jet fighter planes in this vicinity.

⑫ At last you reach **Stock Island** (MM 5), the gateway to Key West. Pass the 18-hole **Key West Resort Golf Course,** then turn right onto Country Club Drive and pause at the **Key West Botanical Garden,** where the Key West Garden Club has labeled an extensive assortment of native and exotic tropical trees.

Key West

Numbers in the margin correspond with points of interest on the Key West map.

In April 1982, the U.S. Border Patrol threw a roadblock across the Overseas Highway just south of Florida City to catch drug runners and illegal aliens. Traffic backed up for miles as Border Patrol agents searched vehicles and demanded that the occupants prove U.S. citizenship. City officials in Key West, outraged at being treated like foreigners by the federal government, staged a mock secession and formed their own "nation," the so-called Conch Republic. They hoisted a flag and distributed mock border passes, visas, and Conch currency. The embarrassed Border Patrol dismantled its roadblock, and now an annual festival recalls the secessionists' victorious exploits.

The episode exemplifies Key West's odd station in life. Situated 150 miles from Miami and just 90 miles from Havana, this tropical island city has always maintained its strong sense of detachment, even after it was connected to the rest of the United States—by the railroad in 1912 and by the Overseas Highway in 1938. The U.S. government acquired Key West from Spain in 1818 along with the rest of Florida. The Spanish had named the island Cayo Hueso (Bone Key) in honor of Indian skeletons they found on its shores. In 1822, Uncle Sam sent Commodore David S. Porter to the Keys to chase pirates away.

For three decades, the primary industry in Key West was "wrecking"—rescuing people and salvaging cargo from ships that foundered on the nearby reefs. (According to some reports, when business was slow, the wreckers hung out lights to lure ships aground). Their business declined after 1852, when the federal government began building lighthouses along the reefs.

In 1845 the Army started to construct Fort Taylor, which held Key West for the Union during the Civil War. After the war, an influx of Cuban dissidents unhappy with Spain's rule brought the cigar industry to Key West. Fishing, shrimping, and sponge-gathering became important industries, and a pineapple-canning factory opened. Major military installations were established during the Spanish-American War and World War I. Through much of the 19th century and into the second decade of the 20th, Key West was Florida's wealthiest city in per-capita terms.

In the 1920s the local economy began to unravel. Modern ships no longer needed to stop in Key West for provisions, the cigar industry moved to Tampa, Hawaii dominated the pineapple industry, and the sponges succumbed to a blight. Then the depression hit, and even the military moved out. By 1934 half the population was on relief. The city defaulted on its bond payments, and the Federal Emergency Relief Administration took over the city and county governments.

Federal officials began promoting Key West as a tourist destination. They attracted 40,000 visitors during the 1934–35 winter season. Then the 1935 Labor Day hurricane struck the Middle Keys, sparing Key West but wiping out the railroad and the tourist trade. For three years, until the Overseas Highway opened, the only way in and out of town was by boat.

Ever since, Key West's fortunes have waxed and waned with the vagaries of world affairs. An important naval center during World War II and the Korean conflict, the island remains a strategic listening post on the doorstep of Fidel Castro's Cuba. Although the Navy shut down its submarine base at Truman Annex and sold the property to a real-estate developer, the nearby Boca Chica Naval Air Station and other military installations remain active.

As the military scaled back, city officials looked to tourism again to take up the slack. Even before it tried, Key West had much to sell—superb frost-free weather with an average temperature of 79°F, quaint 19th-century architecture, and a laid-back lifestyle. Promoters have fostered fine restaurants, galleries and shops, and new museums to interpret the city's intriguing past. There's also a growing calendar of artistic and cultural events and a lengthening list of annual festivals—including the Conch Republic celebration in April, Hemingway Days in July, and a Halloween Fantasy Fest rivaling the New Orleans Mardi Gras.

This tour begins at Front and Duval streets, near the Pier House hotel and Ocean Key House. Start by going west on ❶ Front Street to **Mallory Square,** named for Stephen Mallory, secretary of the Confederate Navy, who later owned the Mallory Steamship Line. On the nearby **Mallory Dock,** a nightly sunset celebration draws street performers, food vendors, and thousands of onlookers.

❷ Facing Mallory Square is the **Key West Aquarium,** which features hundreds of brightly colored tropical fish and other fascinating sea creatures from the waters around Key West. A touch tank enables visitors to handle starfish, sea cucumbers, horseshoe and hermit crabs, even horse and queen conchs—living totems of the Conch Republic. Built in 1934 by the Works Progress Administration as the world's first open-air aquarium, the building has been enclosed for all-weather viewing. *1 Whitehead St., tel. 305/296–2051. Admission: $5 adults, $2.50 children 8–15. Open daily, 10–6 (10–7 in winter). Guided tours 11 AM, 1 PM, 3 PM, 4:30 PM; shark feeding 3 PM.*

Return to Front Street and turn right to **Clinton Place,** where a Civil War memorial to Union soldiers stands in a triangle formed by the intersection of Front, Greene, and Whitehead streets. On your right is the **U.S. Post Office and Customs House,** a Romanesque Revival structure designed by prominent local architect William Kerr and completed in 1891. Tour guides claim that federal bureaucrats required the roof to have a steep pitch so it wouldn't collect snow.

❸ On your left is the **Mel Fisher Maritime Heritage Society Museum,** which displays gold and silver bars, coins, jewelry, and other artifacts recovered in 1985 from the Spanish treasure ships *Nuestra Señora de Atocha* and *Santa Margarita.* The two galleons foundered in a hurricane in 1622 near the Marquesas Keys, 40 miles west of Key West. In the museum you can lift a gold bar weighing 6.3 Troy pounds and see a 77.76-carat natural emerald crystal worth almost $250,000. One display replicates the hold of the *Atocha,* with smooth ballast stones, silver bars, and copper ingots for casting cannons and balls. A 20-minute video shows treasure being recovered from the wrecks. *200 Greene St., tel. 305/296–9936. Museum admission: $5 adults; $4 seniors, military, and Conch Train and trolley passengers with ticket stub; $1 children. Open daily 10–6; Christmas and New Year's Day 10–2; last video showing 4:30, last ticket sold 5:15.*

❹ Mel Fisher's museum occupies a former navy storehouse that he bought from Pritam Singh, the developer of **Truman Annex** (Key West 33040, tel. 305/296–5601), a decommisioned navy base. An American who embraced the Sikh religion, Singh speaks gently of his hope to "engender different forms of interaction" on the 103 acres the government sold him in 1986 for $17.25 million. Singh says people of modest means will be able to rub elbows with the wealthy in his planned development because 162 housing units will be sold at below-market rates, and restrictions will be imposed to prevent speculation and to foster a permanent community. Singh will keep 16 original structures (including six Victorian-style officers' houses) and several warehouses with 30,000 square feet of rentable space for art studios. The 1891 Customs House will become a yacht club. New construction will also include 93 condominiums in two waterfront complexes adjoining the deep-water harbor where submarines docked during World War II, 63 condominium town houses in four compounds, 60 single-family homes, a shopping village, and a 285-room Ritz-Carlton hotel. The Little

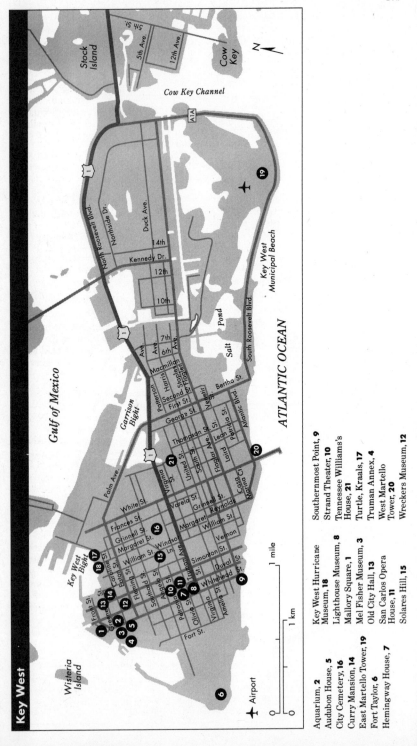

Key West

Gulf of Mexico

Wisteria Island

Key West Bight

Stock Island

Cow Key Channel

Cow Key

N

Northside Dr.
North Roosevelt Blvd.
Duck Ave.
14th
Kennedy Dr.
12th
10th

Key West Municipal Beach
South Roosevelt Blvd.

Salt Pond

ATLANTIC OCEAN

Garrison Bight

Palm Ave.
White St.
Frances St.
Grinnell St.
Margaret St.

7th Ave.
6th Ave.
MacMillan
Patterson
Second St.
First St.
Harris
Staples
Flagler
George St.
Thompson Ave.
South St.
Leon St.
Flagler Ave.
Patricia St.
Laird St.
Atlantic Blvd.
Bertha St.
Eisenhr

Virginia St.
Varela St.
Grinnell St.
Margaret St.
Reynolds
William St.
Vernon
Simonton St.
Duval St.
Whitehead
Amelia St.
Virginia St.
Olivia St.
Fort St.
Petronia Ave.
Truman Ave.
Angela St.
Southard St.
Fleming St.
Eaton St.
Caroline St.
Greene St.
Front St.
Windsor Ln.
Casa Ct.
Marina

Airport

0 ____ 1 mile
0 ____ 1 km

Aquarium, **2**
Audubon House, **5**
City Cemetery, **16**
Curry Mansion, **14**
East Martello Tower, **19**
Fort Taylor, **6**
Hemingway House, **7**

Key West Hurricane
Museum, **18**
Lighthouse Museum, **8**
Mallory Square, **1**
Mel Fisher Museum, **3**
Old City Hall, **13**
San Carlos Opera
House, **11**
Solares Hill, **15**

Southernmost Point, **9**
Strand Theater, **10**
Tennessee Williams's
House, **21**
Turtle, Kraals, **17**
Truman Annex, **4**
West Martello
Tower, **20**
Wreckers Museum, **12**

White House where President Harry Truman spent his vacations will become a museum, except for two presidential suites upstairs which the hotel will rent out to guests. Vehicular traffic in Truman Annex will be limited, but Singh intends to open the development to bicycle and pedestrian traffic daily from 8 AM to 9 PM. He also bought nearby **Tank Island,** where he plans to build 25 luxurious houses and 82 boat slips and 40 moorings. A ferry service will provide access from the mainland. Part of the island will be open to the public for a fee as a high-quality recreation area, with a beach, tennis center, concert pavilion, and perhaps an environmental center and aviary.

⑤ From Mel Fisher's museum, cross Whitehead Street to visit the **Audubon House and Gardens.** A museum in this two-story dwelling built in the mid-1840s commemorates ornithologist John James Audubon's 1832 visit to Key West. On display are several rooms of period antiques and a large collection of Audubon lithographs. A 12-minute video in the upstairs gallery describes Audubon's travels, and an exquisite collection of porcelains of American birds and foliage by Dorothy Doughty is on display in the upstairs sitting room off the front porch. *205 Whitehead St., tel. 305/294–2116. Admission: $4.50 adults, $1 children 6–12. Open daily 9:30–5.*

Continue up Whitehead Street past **Pigeonhouse Patio Restaurant & Bar** (301 Whitehead St., tel. 305/296–9600). This building was the first headquarters of Pan American World Airways, the first U.S. airline to operate scheduled international air service. The inaugural flight took off from Key West International Airport on Oct. 28, 1927. Passengers paid $9.95 for the 90-mile, 80-minute flight from Key West to Havana aboard *The General Machado,* a Fokker F-7 trimotor.

⑥ Turn right onto Southard Street and follow the signs to the **Fort Zachary Taylor State Historic Site.** Built between 1845 and 1866, the fort served as a base for the Union blockade of Confederate shipping during the Civil War. More than 1,500 Confederate vessels captured while trying to run the blockade were brought to Key West's harbor and detained under the fort's guns. What you will see at Fort Taylor today is a fort within a fort. In 1898 the army built poured-concrete gun emplacements for the Spanish-American War atop remnants of the original brick structure, burying the largest collection of Civil War cannons in the U.S. They are now being excavated and preserved for display. The concrete has been painted black as it was 90 years ago to absorb the muzzle flash and avoid disclosing the position of hideaway cannons that rolled forward to fire and then withdrew inside the walls. In 1989, the officers' kitchen became a 1,700-square-foot museum. Rangers give guided tours of the fort, including the museum and armament-preservation lab. *Box 289, tel. 305/292–6713. Admission: Florida residents $1.50/car and driver, $1/passenger; out-of-state visitors $2.50/car and driver, $1.50/passenger; children under 6 free. Park open daily 8–sunset, fort open 8–5. Free 90-min tour daily at 2 PM.*

Time Out   Pause for a libation at the **Green Parrot Bar.** Built in 1890, the bar is Key West's oldest, a sometimes-rowdy saloon where locals outnumber the tourists. *601 Whitehead St. (corner of Southard St.), tel. 305/294–6133. Open daily 10 AM–4 AM. No credit cards.*

Return to Whitehead Street, turn right, and go three blocks to the **Hemingway House,** now a museum dedicated to the novelist's life and work. Built in 1851, this two-story Spanish Colonial dwelling was the first house in Key West to have running water and a fireplace. Hemingway bought the house in 1931 and wrote about 70% of his life's work here, including *A Farewell to Arms* and *For Whom the Bell Tolls.* Three months after Hemingway died in 1961, local jeweler Bernice Dickson bought the house and its contents from Hemingway's estate and two years later opened it as a museum. Of special interest are the huge bed with a headboard made from a 17th-century Spanish monastery gate, a ceramic cat by Pablo Picasso (a gift to Hemingway from the artist), the handblown Venetian glass chandelier in the dining room, and the swimming pool. The museum staff gives guided tours rich with anecdotes about Hemingway and his family and feeds the 42 feline inhabitants (for the 42 bridges in the Keys), descendents of Hemingway's own 50 cats. Kitten adoptions are possible (for a fee), but there's a four-year waiting list. Tours begin every 10 minutes and take 35–40 minutes; then you're free to explore on your own. *907 Whitehead St., tel. 305/294–1575. Admission: $5 adults, $1 children. Open daily 9–5.*

Down the block and across the street from Hemingway House is the **Lighthouse Museum,** a 92-foot lighthouse built in 1847 and an adjacent 1887 clapboard house where the keeper lived. Both underwent extensive restoration in 1989. You can climb 88 steps to the top of the lighthouse for a spectacular view. On display in the keeper's quarters are vintage photographs, ship models, nautical charts, military uniforms, and a working submarine periscope. Note especially the old photos of the Key West Naval Air Station and the relics from the battleship U.S.S. *Maine,* which was blown up in Havana Harbor on February 15, 1898, precipitating the Spanish-American War. *938 Whitehead St., tel. 305/294–0012. Admission: $3 adults, $1 children 6–12. Open daily 9:30–5.*

Continue to the foot of Whitehead Street, where a huge concrete marker proclaims this spot to be the **Southernmost Point** in the United States. Most tourists snapping pictures of each other in front of the marker are oblivious to Key West's real southernmost point, on a nearby navy base off limits to civilians but visible through the fence to your right. Bahamian vendors of shells and straw hats line the sidewalk and blow a conch horn at passing Conch Tour Trains and Old Town Trolleys.

Turn left on South Street. To your right are two dwellings that both claim to be the **Southernmost House**—the Spanish-style home built in the 1940s at 400 South Street by Thelma Strabel, author of *Reap the Wild Wind,* a novel about the wreckers who salvaged ships aground on the reef in Key West's early days, and the adjoining cream-brick Queen Anne mansion at Duval and South streets. Neither is open to the public. Take the next right onto Duval Street, which ends at the Atlantic Ocean and the **Southernmost Beach.** *Admission free. Open daily 7 AM–11 PM.*

Time Out   **The Eatery,** adjoining the Southernmost Beach, serves carryouts and buffets for breakfast, lunch, and dinner. *Open daily 6 AM–9 PM. MC, V.*

Now go north on Duval Street towards downtown Key West. Pause at the **Cuban Club** (1108 Duval St., tel. 305/296-8997). The original building—a social club for the Cuban community —burned in 1983 and was replaced by shops and luxury condominiums; some of the original facade was retained. Continuing on Duval Street, you'll pass several art galleries from the 1100 block through the 800 block.

⑩ Pause to admire the colorful marquee and ornamental facade of the **Strand Theater,** built in 1918 by Cuban craftsmen. After a career as a movie theater, it now offers a variety of live entertainment: reggae, rock-and-roll, etc. *527 Duval St., tel. 305/ 294-6700 (recording).*

⑪ Continue on to the **San Carlos Opera House,** a Cuban-American heritage center, which houses a museum and research library focusing on the history of Key West and of 19th- and 20th-century Cuban exiles. The building is owned by the San Carlos Institute, which was founded in 1871 by Cuban immigrants who wanted to preserve their language, customs, and heritage while organizing the struggle for Cuba's independence from Spain. Cuban patriot Jose Martí delivered many famous speeches in Key West under the institute's auspices. Opera star Enrico Caruso sang in the 400-seat auditorium of the Opera House, which reportedly has the best acoustics of any concert hall in the South. After Cuba and the United States broke off diplomatic relations in 1961, the building deteriorated. It was saved from demolition when Miami attorney Rafael A. Penalver, Jr., secured a $1.7 million state grant for its restoration. At press time, the opera house was scheduled to be reopened in October 1989. A regular schedule of evening performances by internationally acclaimed artists is planned. *516 Duval St., Key West 33040. For information, contact Mr. Penalver at 1101 Brickell Ave., Suite 1700, Miami 33131, tel. 305/579-9000 (Miami) or call Key West Directory Assistance for local phone number. Admission: $3 adults, $1.50 children. Open daily 9-5. Guided tour, concluding with 30-min film.*

⑫ Continue north on Duval Street to the **Wreckers Museum,** which is alleged to be the oldest house in Key West. It was built in 1829 as the home of Francis Watlington, a sea captain and wrecker. He was also a Florida state senator, but resigned to serve in the Confederate Navy during the Civil War. Six of the home's eight rooms are now a museum furnished with 18th- and 19th-century antiques. In an upstairs bedroom is an eight-room miniature dollhouse of Conch architectural design, outfitted with tiny Victorian furniture. *322 Duval St., tel. 305/294-9502. Admission: $2 adults, 50¢ children 3-12. Open daily 10-4; closed Christmas.*

⑬ Take Duval Street to Front Street, turn right, go two blocks to Simonton Street, turn right again and go one block to Greene Street to see the **Old City Hall,** which has recently been restored. Designed by William Kerr, the architect also responsible for the Customs House, the Old City Hall opened in 1891. It has a rectangular tower with four clock faces and a fire bell. The ground floor, used as a city market for many years, now houses the **Historic Key West Shipwreck Museum.** Among the displays are relics from the *Isaac Allerton*, built at Portsmouth, New Hampshire, in 1838 and sunk off Key West in 1856. The second floor houses the city commission's meeting room and offices of the city government and the Historic Florida

Keys Preservation Board. *516 Greene St., tel. 305/292–9740. Museum admission: $4 adults, $2 children 10–16. Open daily 9–6.*

⑭ Return to Simonton Street, go one block south to Caroline Street, and turn right to the **Curry Mansion.** Built in 1899 for Milton Curry, the son of Florida's first millionaire, this 22-room Victorian mansion is an adaptation of a Parisian town house. It has the only widow's walk open to the public in Key West. The owners have restored and redecorated most of the house. Take an unhurried self-guided tour with a comprehensive brochure, which includes floor plans, full of detailed information about the history and contents of the house. *511 Caroline St., tel. 305/294–5349. Admission: $5 adults, $1 children under 12. Open daily 10–5.*

⑮ Return to Simonton Street, go south to Angela Street, and turn left. Before you rises **Solares Hill,** the steepest natural grade in Key West. Its summit, the island's loftiest elevation, is 18 feet above sea level.

⑯ Now cross Elizabeth Street and bear right onto Windsor Lane to the **City Cemetery.** Turn left onto Passover Lane to the entrance at Margaret Street. Clustered near a flagpole resembling a ship's mast are the graves of 22 sailors killed in the sinking of the battleship U.S.S. *Maine. Admission free. Open sunrise–sunset. Guided tours weekends 10 AM and 4 PM. Tour donation: $5.*

⑰ Go up Margaret Street to the harbor docks and visit the **Turtle Kraals,** where the Florida Marine Conservancy runs a hospital for sea creatures. Biologist Linda Bohl maintains a touch tank with horseshoe crabs, sea anemones, sea urchins, and other benign beasts you can fondle—but keep your fingers away from Hawkeye and Gonzo, a churlish pair of 150-pound, 30-year-old hawksbill turtles. A fishpond on the premises gives you a good look at live denizens of local waters, including barracuda, bluefish, lemon and nurse sharks, and yellowtail snapper. *1 Land's End Village, tel. 305/294–2640. Admission free; donations accepted. Open 11 AM–1 AM weekdays, weekends noon–1 AM.*

⑱ Half a block from the Turtle Kraals is the **Key West Hurricane Museum,** which opened in 1989 in the former Singleton Shrimp warehouse. Displays explain the origins and life cycle of hurricanes and the differences between regular storms, tornadoes, and hurricanes. A treasure map shows where Spanish galleons were sunk by hurricanes in the Florida Keys. A chart tracks the 10 hurricanes that have hit the Florida Keys since 1846, including the great hurricane of 1906, the Labor Day hurricane of 1935 (which destroyed the Overseas Railroad), Donna in 1960, Betsy in 1965, and Floyd in 1987. Additional displays, including a wind tunnel, are scheduled to open in late 1989. *201 William St., tel. 305/294–7522. Admission: $3.50 adults, children under 12 free. Open daily 10–6.*

Go one block south on Margaret Street or William Street to Eaton Street, turn left and continue east past White Street, where Eaton Street doglegs to the right into Palm Avenue. You'll cross a causeway and bridge across a corner of **Garrison Bight Yacht Basin,** where many charter-fishing boats dock.

Turn left onto North Roosevelt Boulevard (U.S. 1) and go east. Past the turnoff to Stock Island at the east end of Key West,

North Roosevelt Boulevard becomes South Roosevelt Boulevard and turns west. On your left is a small community of houseboats. On your right, just past the entrance to Key West ⑲ International Airport, stands **East Martello Tower,** one of two Civil War forts of similar design overlooking the Atlantic Ocean. The **Key West Art and Historical Society** operates a museum in East Martello's vaulted casemates. The collection includes Stanley Papio's "junk art" sculptures, Cuban primitive artist Mario Sanchez's chiseled and painted wood carvings of historic Key West street scenes, memorabilia from movies shot on location in the Keys, and a display of books by many of the 55 famous writers (including seven Pulitzer Prize winners) who live in Key West. In 1989, new historical exhibits were being developed to present a chronological history of the Florida Keys. A circular 48-step staircase in the central tower leads to a platform overlooking the airport and surrounding waters. *3501 S. Roosevelt Blvd., tel. 305/296-6206. Admission: $3 adults, $1 children. Open daily 9:30-5.*

Continue west on South Roosevelt Boulevard past Smathers Beach on your left. To your right are the **salt ponds,** where early residents evaporated seawater to collect salt. The area is now a wildlife sanctuary. Turn right where South Roosevelt Boulevard ends at Bertha Street, then make the first left onto Atlantic Avenue. Near White Street are **Higgs Memorial** ⑳ **Beach** (a Monroe County park) and **West Martello Tower,** a fort built in 1861 and used as a lookout post during the Spanish-American War. Within its walls the Key West Garden Club maintains an art gallery and tropical garden. *Tel. 305/294-3210. Donations accepted. Open Wed.-Sun. 10 AM-noon and 1-4 PM.*

Take White Street nine blocks north to Duncan Street, turn ㉑ right, and go three blocks to **Tennessee Williams' House** (1431 Duncan St., at the corner of Duncan and Leon Sts.), a modest Bahamian-style cottage where the playwright lived from 1949 until his death in 1983.

Shopping

Throughout the Keys many strip shopping centers cater to the basic needs of locals and visitors alike. In season, supermarkets and roadside stands sell tropical fruits. Look for Key limes (Apr.-Jan.), guavas (Aug.-Oct.), lychee nuts (June), and sapodillas (Feb.-Mar.).

Key West   In Key West's Old Town, you'll find specialty shops with international reputations:

Greenpeace. Opened in 1983, this is the only storefront in Florida operated by Greenpeace, an international conservation organization known for its efforts to prevent the killing of whales and seals. The store sells conservation-oriented educational materials, gift items, and T-shirts. The store planned to move to a new location on Duval Street in Key West late in 1989; phone for details. *Tel. 305/296-4442. Open Mon.-Sat. 10-9, Sun. 10-6. AE, MC, V.*

Key West Aloe. A company founded in a garage in 1971, Key West Aloe today produces some 300 perfume, sunscreen, and skin-care products for men and women. When you visit the factory store, you can watch the staff measure and blend ingredients, then fill and seal the containers. *Main store: 524 Front St., tel. 305/294-5592, 800/433-2563 (FL), 800/445-2563 (U.S.). Open Mon.-Sat. 9-8, Sun. 9-6. Factory store: Greene and Simonton Sts. Open 9-5, production weekdays 9-5. Free self-guided tour. AE, DC, MC, V.*

Key West Hand Print Fabrics. In the 1960s, Lilly Pulitzer's designs made Key West Hand Print Fabrics famous. Shoppers can watch workers making handprinted fabric on five 50-yard-long tables in the Curry Warehouse, a brick building erected in 1878 to store tobacco. *201 Simonton St., tel. 305/294-9535. Open daily 10-6. AE, MC.*

Key West Island Bookstore. You'll find a good selection of books on South Florida here and a rare book room to which you must request admittance. *513 Fleming St., tel. 305/294-2904. Open daily 10-6. AE, MC, V.*

Duval Books and Cards. Owned by the proprietors of Key West Island Bookstore, this shop specializes in new books and greeting cards. *817 Duval St., tel. 305/296-3508. Open Mon.-Sat. 9-9, Sun. 10-5. AE, MC, V.*

Tikal Trading Co. Since 1975, owners George and Barbara Webb have designed, produced, and sold double-stitched women's clothing of hand-woven Guatemalan cotton. *129 Duval St., tel. 305/294-6883. Open daily 10-9. AE, MC, V.*

The former Singleton Seafood, Inc., shrimp docks and warehouse along Key West Bight have been reincarnated as a row of marinas. One of these, **Key West Seaport,** a nautically oriented shopping area where boat builders work and charter-boat captains have booths to sign up customers. Merchants you might visit include the following:

Lazy Jake's Hammocks. Run by a man who describes himself as Key West's oldest beach bum, this establishment makes and sells hammocks of all shapes and sizes. *205 Elizabeth St., no phone. Open daily 8-5.*

Seafarers Heritage Library and Nautique. A storefront operated by the National Center for Shipwreck Research, Ltd., this shop sells maritime books and gift items. Its staff arranges archaeology dives, seminars, training programs, and other educational activities. *Seaport La., tel. 305/292-1301. Open daily 9 AM-8 PM. MC, V.*

Just east of Key West Seaport is Key West Bight. Popular stores there include the following:

Waterfront Baits & Tackle. This store sells bait and fishing gear. *201 William St., tel. 305/292-1961.*

Waterfront Fish Market, Inc. Fresh seafood is the draw here. *201 William St., tel. 305/294-8046.*

Waterfront Market. This store sells health and gourmet foods, deli items, fresh produce, and salads. *201 William St., tel. 305/294-8418.*

Ever since John James Audubon came to Key West in 1832, artists have flocked to the Florida Keys. Today's flourishing art community provides a rich array of merchandise for galleries throughout the Keys.

The Rain Barrel in Islamorada represents 300 local and national artists and has eight resident artists. *MM 86.7, BS, 86700 Overseas Hwy., Islamorada, tel. 305/852-3084. Open daily 9-5; closed Christmas. MC, V.*

Lane Gallery specializes in lesser-known local artists. *1000 Duval St., Key West, tel. 305/294–0067. Open winter, daily 10–6, in summer, daily noon–6. AE, MC, V.*

Gingerbread Square Gallery, owned by Key West Mayor Richard Heyman, represents Keys artists who have attained national prominence. *901 Duval St., Key West, tel. 305/296–8900. Open winter, daily 11–6; summer, Thurs.–Mon. AE, MC, V.*

Haitian Art Center sells the works of 175 Haitian artists. *600 Frances St., Key West, tel. 305/296–8932. Open daily 10–6. AE, CB, DC, MC, V.*

Sports and Outdoor Activities

Biking A bike path parallels the Overseas Highway from Key Largo through Tavernier and onto Plantation Key, from MM 106 (at the Route 905 junction) to MM 86 (near the Monroe County Sheriff's Substation). The **Marathon** area is popular with bikers. Some of the best areas include the paths along Aviation Boulevard on the bay side of Marathon Airport; the new four-lane section of the Overseas Highway through Marathon; Sadowski Causeway to Key Colony Beach; Sombrero Beach Road from the Overseas Highway to the Marathon public beach; the roads on Boot Key (across a bridge from Vaca Key on 20th Street, OS); and a two-mile section of the old Seven Mile Bridge that remains open to Pigeon Key, where locals like to ride to watch the sunset.

Key West is a cycling town, but many tourists aren't accustomed to driving with so many bikes around, so ride carefully. Some hotels rent bikes to their guests; others will refer you to a nearby bike shop and reserve a bike for you.

Key Largo Bikes stocks adult, children's and tandem bikes, all single-speed with coaster brakes. *MM 101.5 (RR 2, Box 19 C), Key Largo, tel. 305/451–1910. Open Mon.–Sat. 9:30–5:30. MC, V.*

KCB Bike Shop rents single-speed adult and children's bikes. *MM 53 (11518 Overseas Hwy.), Marathon, tel. 305/289–1670. Open weekdays 8:30–5, Sat. 8:30–2; closed Sun. MC, V.*

Holiday Rentals has moped and bicycle rentals for adults and children. *512 Greene St., Key West, tel. 305/296–1745. Open daily 8–6. No credit cards.*

Camping The State of Florida operates recreational-vehicle and tent campgrounds in **John Pennekamp Coral Reef State Park,** MM 102.5 (Box 487, Key Largo 33037, tel. 305/451–1202); **Long Key State Recreation Area,** MM 67.5 (Box 776, Long Key 33001, tel. 305/664–4815); and **Bahia Honda State Recreation Area,** MM 37 (Rte. 1, Box 782, Big Pine Key 33043, tel. 305/872–2353). Bahia Honda also has rental cabins.

The **Florida Campground Association** (1638 N. Plaza Dr., Tallahassee 32308, tel. 904/658–8878) publishes a free annual directory of over 200 member campgrounds in 11 regions. The Keys are in Region L, which lists 12 commercial campgrounds from Key Largo to Key West. The guide is available at Florida Welcome Centers or by mail.

Diving Although there are reefs and wrecks all along the east coast of Florida, the state's most extensive diving grounds are in the Keys. Divers come for the quantity and quality of living coral reefs within six or seven miles of shore, the kaleidoscopic beauty of 650 species of tropical fish, and the adventure of probing wrecked ships that foundered in these seemingly tranquil seas during almost four centuries of exploration and commerce. A popular dive destination is the nine-foot **Christ of the Deep** statue, a gift to the Underwater Society of America from an Italian dive equipment manufacturer. The statue is about six miles east-northeast of Key Largo's South Cut in about 25 feet of water. It's a smaller copy of the 50-foot Christ of the Abysses off Genoa, Italy.

Much of the Keys' expanse of coral reefs is protected in federal, state, and county parks and sanctuaries. From Key Biscayne south almost to Key Largo, **Biscayne National Park** (*see* The Everglades) encompasses most of Biscayne Bay, its barrier islands, and the patch reefs eastward to a depth of 60 feet. Biscayne National Park's southern boundary is the northern boundary of John Pennekamp Coral Reef State Park and Key Largo National Marine Sanctuary.

John Pennekamp Coral Reef State Park encompasses 78 square miles of coral reefs, seagrass beds, and mangrove swamps on the Atlantic Ocean side of Key Largo. The park is 21 miles long and extends to the seaward limit of state jurisdiction three miles offshore. Its reefs contain 40 of the 52 species of coral in the Atlantic Reef System. *MM 102.5, OS. Park admission: Florida residents $1.50/car and driver, $1/passenger; out-of-state residents $2.50/car and driver, $1.50/passenger. Park open daily 8 AM–sunset. Coral Reef Park Co., a concessionaire, offers glass-bottom boat, scuba, sailing, and snorkeling tours: Box 1560, Key Largo 33037, tel. 305/451–1621 or 800/432–2871. Concession open daily 8–5:30. AE, MC, V.*

The **Key Largo National Marine Sanctuary** (Box 1083, Key Largo 33037, tel. 305/451–1644) covers 103 square miles of coral reefs from the boundary of John Pennekamp Coral Reef State Park, three miles off Key Largo, to a depth of 300 feet some eight miles offshore. Managed by the National Oceanic and Atmospheric Administration (NOAA), the sanctuary includes Elbow, French, and Molasses reefs; the 1852 Carysford Lighthouse and its surrounding reefs; Christ of the Deep; Grecian Rocks, Key Largo Rocks, and the torpedoed WW II freighter *Benwood*.

San Pedro Underwater Archaeological Preserve. The state recently established this underwater park in 18 feet of water about a mile off the western tip of Indian Key. The *San Pedro* was part of a Spanish treasure fleet wrecked by a hurricane in 1733. You can get there on the *Coral Sea*, a 40-passenger glass-bottom dive and snorkel boat, from the dive shop at Bud 'n' Mary's Fishing Marina. *MM 78, OS, Box 1126, Islamorada, tel. 305/664–2211. 3-hr trips at 9 AM and 1 PM. Call for reservations. Cost: $13 adults, $7.50 children under 12. AE, MC, V.*

Marathon Marine Sanctuary. Monroe County recently established its first underwater park off the Middle Keys in Hawk Channel opposite MM 50, OS. It runs from Washerwoman Shoal on the west to navigation marker 48 on the east. The two-square-mile park contains a dozen patch reefs ranging from the size of a house to about an acre. *Greater Marathon Chamber of Commerce, MM 49, BS, 330 Overseas Hwy., Marathon, tel. 305/743–5417 or 800/842–9580.*

National Key Deer Refuge (Box 510, Big Pine Key 33043, tel. 305/872–2239) and **Great White Heron National Wildlife Refuge.** Reefs where the Keys' northern margin drops off into the Gulf of Mexico attract fewer divers than the better-known Atlantic Ocean reefs. A favorite Gulf spot for local divers is the Content Keys, off Big Pine Key (MM 30).

Looe Key National Marine Sanctuary (Rte. 1, Box 782, Big Pine Key, tel. 305/872–4039). Many divers say Looe Key Reef, five miles off Ramrod Key (MM 27.5), is the most beautiful and diverse coral community in the entire region. It has large stands of elkhorn coral on its eastern margin, large purple sea fans, and ample populations of sponges and sea urchins. On its seaward side, it has an almost-vertical dropoff to a depth of 50–90 feet. The reef is named for H.M.S. *Looe*, a British warship wrecked there in 1744.

From shore or from a boat, snorklers can easily explore grass flats, mangrove roots, and rocks in shallow water, almost anywhere in the Keys. You may see occasional small clusters of coral and fish, mollusks, and other sea creatures. Ask dive shops for snorkeling information and directions. Diving and snorkeling are prohibited around bridges and near certain keys.

Dive shops all over the state organize Keys dives and offer diving instruction. South Florida residents fill dive boats on weekends, so plan to dive Monday through Thursday, when the boats and reefs are less crowded.

Jules Undersea Lodge, the world's first underwater hotel, takes reservations a year in advance from divers who want to stay in its two-room lodge in 30 feet of water. A resort course for new divers is offered. PADI affiliation. *MM 103.2, OS, Box 3330, Key Largo 33037, tel. 305/451–2353. AE, MC, V.*

Dive Shops All of the dive shops listed below organize dives, fill air tanks, and sell or rent all necessary diving equipment. All have NAUI and/or PADI affiliation.

Quiescence Diving Service, Inc. Six people per boat. *MM 103.5, BS, 103680 Overseas Hwy., Key Largo, tel. 305/451–2440. Open daily 8–6; closed Thanksgiving and Christmas. MC, V.*
Capt. Corky's Diver's World of Key Largo. A reef and wreck diving package is available. Reservations accepted for wreck diving of the *Benwood*, Coast Guard cutters *Bibb* and *Duane*, and French and Molasses reefs. *MM 99.5, OS, Box 1663, Key Largo 33037, tel. 305/451–3200 or 800/445–8231. Open 8–5; closed Thanksgiving and Christmas. MC, V.*
Florida Keys Dive Center organizes dives from just south of John Pennekamp Coral Reef State Park to Alligator Light. This center has two Coast Guard–approved dive boats and offers training from introductory scuba through instructor course. Full-day "scuba safari" dives include complimentary on-board box lunch and barbecue afterward at the store. *MM 90.5, OS, 90500 Overseas Hwy., Box 391, Tavernier, tel. 305/842–4599 or 800/433–8946. Open 8–5. AE, MC, V.*
Treasure Divers, Inc., a full-service dive shop with instructors, arranges dives to reefs, Spanish galleons, and other wrecks. *MM 85.5, BS, 85500 Overseas Hwy., Islamorada, tel. 305/661–5111 or 800/356–9887. Open 8–5. AM, MC, V.*
Hall's Dive Center and Career Institute offers trips to Looe Key, Sombero Reef, Delta Shoal, Content Key, and Coffins Patch.

MM 48.5, BS, 1994 Overseas Hwy., Marathon, tel. 305/743–5929 or 800/331–4255. Open 9–6. AE, MC, V.

Looe Key Dive Center. This is the dive shop closest to Looe Key National Marine Sanctuary. *MM 27.5, OS, Box 509, Ramrod Key, tel. 305/872–2215. Open 7–6. AE, MC, V.*

Captain's Corner. Seven full-time instructors provide dive classes in English, French, German, and Italian. All captains are licensed divemasters. Reservations are accepted for regular reef and wreck diving, spear and lobster fishing, and archaeological and treasure hunting. Also has fishing charters. *Store at 201 William St., Key West, tel. 305/296–8918. Open 8–5. Booth at Zero Duval St., Key West, tel. 800/328–9815, 800/231–9864 (FL), or 305/296–8865. Booth open daily 8 AM–11 PM. AE, MC, V.*

Fishing and Boating
Fishing is popular throughout the Keys. You have a choice of deep-sea fishing on the ocean or the gulf or flat-water fishing in the mangrove-fringed shallows of the backcountry. Each of the areas protected by the state or federal government has its own set of rigorously enforced regulations. Check with your hotel or a local chamber of commerce office to find out what the rules are in the area you're staying. The same sources can refer you to a reliable charter-boat or party-boat captain who will take you where the right kind of fish are biting.

Glass-bottom boats, which depart daily (weather permitting) from docks throughout the Keys, are popular with visitors who want to admire the reefs without getting wet. If you're prone to seasickness, don't try to look through the glass bottom in rough seas.

Motor yachts, sailboats, Hobie Cats, Windsurfers, canoes, and other water-sports equipment are all available for rent by the day or on a long-term basis. Some hotels have their own rental services; others will refer you to a separate vendor.

Treasure Harbor Charter Yachts on Plantation Key rents bare sailboats, from 25-foot Watkins to 44-foot CSY. Captains and provisions available. No pets are allowed. *MM 86.5, OS, 200 Treasure Harbor Dr., Islamorada, tel. 305/852–9440 or 800/FLA–BOATS. Open 9–5. Reservations and advance deposit required; minimum 3-day rental; $100/day captain fee for boats returned elsewhere. No credit cards.*

Island Breeze Yacht Charters rents bare power boats from 32-foot Ranger Blaylinders to 42-foot Grand Banks. Captains and provisions available. No pets are allowed. *MM 103.5, OS, 51 Shoreland Dr., Box 815, Key Largo, tel. 305/451–4766 or 800/FLA–BOATS. Open 9–5. Reservations and advance deposit required; weekly charters; $100/day captain fee for boats returned elsewhere. No credit cards.*

Golf
Two of the five golf courses in the Keys are open to the public:

Key Colony Beach Par 3. Eight-hole course near Marathon. *MM 53.5, 8th St., Key Colony Beach, tel. 305/289–1533.*

Key West Resort Golf Course. Eighteen-hole course on the bay side of Stock Island. *6450 E. Junior College Rd., Key West, tel. 305/294–5232.*

The other three courses, open only to members and their guests, are the 18-hole **Ocean Reef Club** on Key Largo, the eight-hole executive course at **Cheeca Lodge** in Islamorada, and the 18-hole **Sombrero Country Club** course in Marathon.

Beaches

Keys shorelines are either mangrove-fringed marshes or rock outcrops that fall away to mucky grass flats. Most pleasure beaches in the Keys are manmade, with sand imported from the U.S. mainland or the Bahamas. There are public beaches in **John Pennekamp Coral Reef State Park** (MM 102.5), **Long Key State Recreation Area** (MM 67.5), **Sombrero Beach** in Marathon (MM 50), **Bahia Honda State Recreation Area** (MM 37), and at many roadside turnouts along the Overseas Highway. Many hotels and motels also have their own small shallow-water beach areas.

When you swim in the Keys, wear an old pair of tennis shoes to protect your feet from rocks, sea-urchin spines, and other potential hazards.

Key West **Smathers Beach** features almost two miles of sand beside South Roosevelt Boulevard. Trucks along the road will rent you rafts, Windsurfers, and other beach "toys."
Higgs Memorial Beach. Near the end of White Street, this is a popular sunbathing spot. A nearby grove of Australian pines provides shade and the **West Martello Tower** provides shelter should a storm suddenly sweep in.
Dog Beach. At Vernon and Waddell streets, this is the only beach in Key West where dogs are allowed.
Southernmost Beach. On the Atlantic Ocean at the foot of Duval Street, this spot is popular with tourists at nearby motels. It has limited parking and a nearby buffet-type restaurant.
Fort Zachary Taylor State Historic Site. The beach here, several hundred yards of shoreline near the western end of Key West, adjoins a picnic area with barbecue grills in a stand of Australian pines. In 1989, the beach was badly eroded and a renourishment program was planned. This beach is relatively uncrowded and attracts more locals than tourists.
Simonton Street Beach. At the north end of Simonton Street, facing the Gulf of Mexico, this is a great place to watch boat traffic in the harbor, but parking here is difficult.
Two hotels in Key West have notable beaches:
Marriott's Casa Marina Resort (1500 Reynolds St.) grants access to its 1,000-foot Atlantic Ocean beach to nonguests who rent a cabana for $10/day.
Pier House (1 Duval St.) has a beach club for locals and patrons of certain nearby guest houses.
Several hotels allow varying degrees of undress on their beaches. Pier House permits female guests on its beach to go topless, and nude bathing is acceptable at the **Atlantic Shores Motel** (510 South St.). Contrary to popular belief, the rangers at Fort Taylor beach do *not* allow nude bathing.

Dining

by Rosalie Leposky

Don't be misled by the expression *Key-easy*. Denizens of the Florida Keys may be relaxed and wear tropical-casual clothes, but these folks take food seriously. A number of young, talented chefs have settled here in the last few years to enjoy the climate and contribute to the Keys' growing image as a fine-dining center. Best-known among them is Norman Van Aken, who oversees the cuisine at two Key West restaurants, Louie's

Backyard and Mira. Van Aken's book, *Feast of the Sunlight* (Random House, 1988) describes the delights of Key West's "fusion cuisine," a blend of Florida citrus, seafood, and tropical fruits with Southwestern chilis, herbs, and spices.

The restaurant menus, the rum-based fruit beverages, and even the music reflect the Keys' tropical climate and their proximity to Cuba and other Caribbean islands. The better American and Cuban restaurants serve imaginative and tantalizing dishes that incorporate tropical fruits and vegetables, including avocado, carambola (star fruit), mango, and papaya.

Freshly caught local fish have been on every Keys menu in the past, but that is starting to change. The Keys' growing population has degraded the environment, disrupting the fishery and pricing fishermen out of the local housing market. Because many venerable commercial fish houses have abandoned the business in the past decade, there's a good chance the fish you order in a Keys restaurant may have been caught somewhere else. Since 1985, the U.S. government has protected the queen conch as an endangered species, so any conch you order in the Keys has come fresh-frozen from the Bahamas, Belize, or the Caribbean. Florida lobster and stone crab should be local and fresh from August through March.

Purists will find few examples of authentic Key-lime pie: a yellow lime custard in a Graham-cracker crust with a meringue top. Many restaurants now serve a version made with white-pastry crust and whipped cream, which is easy to prepare and hold for sale. The Pier House's **Market Bistro** and **Pier House Restaurant** serve the real thing with an extra-high meringue, almost as tangy and puckery as the truly homemade version at **Island Jim's** on Big Pine Key.

The list below is a representative selection of independent restaurants in the Keys, organized by mile marker (MM) number in descending order, as you would encounter them when driving down from the mainland. Small restaurants may not follow the hours listed here. Sometimes they close for a day or a week, or cancel lunch for a month or two, just by posting a note on the door.

The most highly recommended restaurants are indicated by a star ★.

Category	Cost*
Very Expensive	over $55
Expensive	$35–$55
Moderate	$15–$35
Inexpensive	under $15

per person, excluding service, drinks, tip, 6% state sales tax, and local tourist tax

Florida City   **Alabama Jack's.** In 1953 Alabama Jack Stratham opened his restaurant on two barges at the end of Card Sound Road, 13 miles south of Homestead in an old fishing community between Card and Barnes sounds. The spot, something of a no-man's-land, belongs to the Keys in spirit thanks to the Card Sound toll bridge, which joined the mainland to upper Key Largo in 1969. Regular customers include Keys fixtures such as balladeer Jimmy Buffett, Sunday bikers, local retirees, boaters who tie up at the restaurant's dock, and anyone else fond of dancing to country-western music and clapping for cloggers. You can also admire the tropical birds cavorting in the nearby mangroves and the occasional crocodile swimming up the canal. Specialties include peppery homemade crab cakes; light, fluffy conch fritters; crunchy breaded shrimp; homemade tartar sauce; and a tangy cocktail sauce with horseradish. *58000 Card Sound Rd., Florida City, tel. 305/248-8741 (Miami). Open 8:30-7. Live band Sat.-Sun. 2-7. Dress: casual. No reservations. No credit cards. Moderate.*

Key Largo **Crack'd Conch.** Foreign money and patrons' business cards festoon the main dining room, where vertical bamboo stakes support the bar. There's also a screened outdoor porch. Specialties include conch (cracked and in chowder, fritters, and salad), fried alligator, smoked chicken, and 88 kinds of beer. *MM 105, OS, Rte. 1, 105045 Overseas Hwy., tel. 305/451-0732. Open Mon., Tues., Thurs., Fri. 5-10; weekends noon-10; closed Wed. No credit cards. Inexpensive.*

Italian Fisherman. White plaster statues of a fisherman, Columbus, and a nude goddess welcome you to the Italian Fisherman. You can dine indoors, but the best seating is on a deck overlooking Florida Bay where an audience of seagulls awaits any morsel you may hurl in their direction. Chef Joseph Rotonda is particularly adept at pasta and rich tangy marinara sauce. Specialties include hearty minestrone soup with lots of vegetables and fresh garlic bread; linguine marechiaro with shrimp, scallops, and clams; and the catch of the day blackened New Orleans-style. *MM104, BS, tel. 305/451-4471. Dress: casual. Reservations accepted for parties of 10 or more. Closed Christmas and Thanksgiving. AE, M, V. Moderate.*

★ **Mrs. Mac's Kitchen.** Hundreds of beer cans, beer bottles, and expired auto license plates from all over the world decorate the walls of this wood-paneled, open-air restaurant. At lunchtime, the counter and booths fill up early with locals. Regular nightly specials are worth the stop: meatloaf on Monday, Mexican on Tuesday, Italian on Wednesday, and seafood Thursday through Saturday. The chili is always good, and the imported beer of the month is $1 a bottle or can. *MM 99.4, Rte. 1, tel. 305/451-3722. Dress: casual. No reservations. No credit cards. Closed Sun. Inexpensive.*

Islamorada **Marker 88.** The best seats in chef/owner Andre Mueller's main
★ dining room catch the last glimmers of sunset. Hostesses recite a lengthy list of daily specials and offer you a wine list with over 200 entries. You can get a good steak or veal chop here, but 75% of the food served is seafood. Specialties include a robust conch chowder; banana blueberry bisque; Salad Trevisana, made with radicchio, leaf lettuce, Belgium endive, watercress, and sweet-and-sour dill dressing (President Bush's favorite); sautéed conch or alligator steak meuniere; grouper Rangoon, served with chunks of papaya, banana, and pineapple in a cinnamon and currant jelly sauce; and Key-lime pie. *MM 88 on Overseas Hwy., BS, Plantation Key, tel. 305/852-9315. Dress: informal. Reservations advised. AE, DC, MC, V. Expensive.*

Whale Harbor Inn. This coral rock building has oyster shells cemented onto the walls and a water mark at the seven-foot mark as a reminder of Hurricane Donna's fury in 1960. Several restaurant employees rode out the storm in the building's lighthouse tower. The main attraction is a 50-foot-long all-you-can-eat buffet, which includes a stir-fry area for wok cookery and a plentiful supply of shrimp, rock shrimp, crayfish, and snowcrab legs. Special on Sunday are black beans and ham and Belgian waffles. The adjoining Dockside Restaurant and Lounge has a raw bar and grill and a catwalk overlooking a marina. *MM 83.5, OS, Upper Matecumbe Key, tel. 305/664–4959. Dress: casual. No reservations. AE, CB, DC, MC, V. Moderate.*

Green Turtle Inn. Photographs of locals and famous visitors dating from 1947 line the walls and stuffed turtle dolls dangle from the ceiling over the bar. Harry Rosenthal, the restaurant's third owner, retains the original menu cover and some of the original dishes. Specialties include a rich, spicy turtle chowder; conch fritters, nicely browned outside, light and fluffy inside; conch salad with vinegar, lime juice, pimento, and pepper; alligator steak (tail meat) sautéed in an egg batter; and Key-lime pie. Whole pies are available for carry-out. *MM 81.5, OS, tel. 305/664–9031. Dress: casual. No reservations. AE, CB, DC, MC, V. Closed Mon. and Thanksgiving Day. Moderate.*

Marathon **Ship's Pub and Galley.** The collection of historic photos on the restaurant walls depict the railroad era in the Keys, the development of Duck Key, and many of the notables who have visited here. Dinners include soup and a 40-item salad bar with all the steamed shrimp you can eat. Specialties include homemade garlic bread, Swiss onion soup, certified New York Angus beef, at least two fish specials, Florida stone crab claws (in season), and mile-high shoofly mudpie, a six-inch-high coffee ice cream pie with a whipped cream topping. The adjoining lounge has live entertainment and a dance floor. *MM 61, OS, tel. 305/743–7000, ext. 3627. Dress: casual. Reservations accepted. Early bird specials. AE, CB, DC, MC, V. Moderate.*

Grassy Key Dairy Bar. Look for the Dairy Queen–style concrete ice-cream cones near the road. Locals and construction workers stop here for quick lunches. Owner/chefs George and Johnny Eigner are proud of their fresh-daily homemade bread, soups and chowders, fresh seafood, and fresh-cut beef. *MM 58.5, OS, Grassy Key, tel. 305/743–3816. Dress: casual. Reservations accepted. No credit cards. Closed Sun. and Mon. Moderate.*

Herbie's Bar. A local favorite for lunch and dinner since the 1940s, Herbie's has three small rooms with two bars. Indoor diners sit at wood picnic tables or the bar; those in the screened outdoor room use concrete tables. Specialties include spicy conch chowder with chunks of tomato and crisp conch fritters with homemade horseradish sauce. Nightly specials. *MM 50.5, BS, 6350 Overseas Hwy., tel. 305/743–6373. Dress: casual. No reservations. No credit cards. Closed Sun. and Mon. Inexpensive.*

Kelsey's. The walls in this restaurant at the Faro Blanco Marine Resort are hung with boat paddles inscribed by the regulars. All entrees here are served with fresh-made yeast rolls brushed with drawn butter and Florida orange honey. Chef David Leeper serves only fresh local seafood and lobster. Specialties include broiled swordfish with dill sauce and grouper gourmet (lightly floured, dipped in egg batter, sautéed in white wine and fresh lemon, and topped with artichoke hearts, mushrooms, and toasted almonds). You can bring your own cleaned and filleted catch for the chef to prepare. Dessert offerings change nightly and may include German chocolate cake, Mrs. Kelsey's original macadamia pie, and Key-lime cheesecake. *MM 48, BS, 1996 Overseas Hwy., tel. 305/743–9018. Dress: casual. Reservations accepted. AE, MC, V. Dinner only. Closed Mon. Expensive.*

Mile 7 Grill. This open-air diner built in 1954 at the Marathon end of Seven Mile Bridge has walls festooned with mounted fish, sponges, and signs describing individual menu items. Specialties include grouper chowder, fresh fish sandwich of the day, and a foot-long chili dog on a toasted sesame roll. *MM 47.5, BS, 1240 Overseas Hwy., tel. 305/743–4481. No credit cards. Closed Wed.–Thurs. and when they want to in Aug.–Sept. Inexpensive.*

Big Pine Key **Island Jim's.** Good food comes out of this old 60-seat Conch-style building with screened windows, oilcloth-covered tables, and aerial photos of the Keys over the bar. The decor hasn't changed for decades, but the menu changes nightly, depending on what kind of fresh seafood is available. Specialties may include blacktip shark, conch, dolphin, shrimp, and tile fish, and steaks of midwestern beef. Owner Rita Ballard is especially proud of her meringue-topped Key-lime pie and Angel Strada pie (a semi-sweet cinnamon chocolate cream concoction), both made fresh daily by one of her waitresses. To order a whole pie, call a day ahead. *MM 31¼, BS, tel. 305/872–2017. Open lunch 11:30 AM–2 PM Mon.–Sat., dinner 5–9 PM, Sunday brunch 8 AM–1 PM. No reservations. Dress: casual. No credit cards. Inexpensive.*

Key West **American** ★ **Louie's Backyard.** This place is really two restaurants and a bar. The upstairs Cafe at Louie's has a coffered ceiling, an open-theater kitchen, louvered transom windows, and a balcony. Downstairs in Louie's Backyard, the walls are decorated with abstract art and old Key West paintings. Menus in both restaurants change regularly. The cafe serves what chef Norman Van Aken calls "nouveau Cuban." The menu may include pan-charred grouper with a dash of soy sauce, Myer's dark rum, and cracked black pepper; chicken livers pan-fried in olive oil with Spanish sherry vinegar, sweet peppers, red onion, chilies, and celery; and marinated roast pork served with black bean sauce, plantains, slices of red onion, sour cream, and lime. At Louie's Backyard, innovative selections include Bahamian conch chowder with bird-pepper hot sauce and grilled catch of the day with tomato-butter and red-onion marmalade and roasted peppers. *700 Waddell Ave., tel. 305/294–1061. Jackets required. Reservations advised. Dinner only at the Cafe. AE, DC, MC, V. Very Expensive.*

Pepe's Cafe and Steak House. Judges, policemen, carpenters, and fishermen rub elbows every morning in their habitual breakfast seats, at three tables and four pine booths under a huge paddle fan. Outdoors are more tables and an open-air bar under a canvas tarp. Pepe's was established downtown in 1919 and moved to the current site in 1962. The specials change nightly: barbecue chicken, pork tenderloin, ribs, potato salad, red or black beans, and corn bread on Sunday; meatloaf on Monday; seafood Tuesday and Wednesday; a full traditional Thanksgiving dinner every Thursday; filet mignon on Friday;

and prime rib on Saturday. *806 Caroline St., tel. 305/294–7192. Dress: casual. No reservations. MC, V. Inexpensive.*

★ **Pier House Restaurant.** Steamships from Havana once docked at this pier jutting out into the Gulf of Mexico. Now it's an elegant place to dine, indoors or out, and to watch boats gliding by in the harbor. At night the restaurant shines lights into the water, attracting schools of brightly colored parrot fish. The menu emphasizes tropical fruits, spices, and fish. Specialties include a peppery, cream-based conch chowder; fresh homemade conch ravioli on a bed of radicchio leaves; the daily gulf catch sautéed and served with fresh avocado and papaya in Key-lime sauce; and rack of lamb with apple jalapeño chutney and goat-cheese polenta. The dessert menu always includes a medium-tart Key-lime pie with a five-inch meringue topping. *1 Duval St., tel. 305/296–4600, 800/327–8340 (U.S.), or 800/432–3414 (FL). Jacket required. Reservations advised. AE, MC, V. Very Expensive.*

Cuban **El Siboney.** This family-style restaurant serves traditional Cuban food. Specials include chicken and rice every Friday, oxtail stew with rice and beans on Saturday. Always available are roast pork with *morros* (black beans and white rice) and cassava, paella, and *palomilla* steak. *900 Catherine St., tel. 305/296–4184. Dress: casual. No reservations. No credit cards. Closed Thanksgiving, Christmas, New Year's Day, 2 wks in June. Inexpensive.*

Delicatessen **Market Bistro.** The Pier House's deli and fine-dining snack shop sells the hotel's classic Key-lime pie by the slice. A cooler holds a respectable selection of fine wines, champagnes, and beers. Specialties include tropical fruit drinks, sandwiches, salads, and gourmet cheeses and pates. *1 Duval St. in the Pier House, tel. 305/296–4600. Dress: casual. No reservations. AE, MC, V. Moderate.*

French **Cafe des Artistes.** This intimate 75-seat restaurant occupies part of a hotel building constructed in 1935 by C. E. Alfeld, Al Capone's bookkeeper. Haitian paintings and Keys scenes by local artists decorate the walls. Skylights in one of the five rooms are open in good weather, and some seating is available in a secluded courtyard. Executive chef Frederic Debiasio presents a French interpretation of tropical cuisine, using fresh local seafood and produce and light, flour-free sauces. Specialties include sautéed scallops served with almond-curry-rum sauce, salade "Jessica" (avocado, hearts of palm, strawberries, and orange/ginger vinaigrette dressing), pear and Champagne cream soup with bits of fresh pear, a very light raspberry Cointreau cheesecake, and pear tart with passion fruit ice cream. *1007 Simonton St., tel. 305/294–7100. Jacket required. Reservations advised. No lunch. AE, MC, V. Very Expensive.*

Seafood **The Buttery.** The Buttery's waiters have come to be known as
★ buttercups, a nickname they share with the house's special drink, a blended frozen concoction of vodka, Kahlua, amaretto, coconut milk, and cream. Each of the restaurant's six rooms has its own character. The back room with the bar has wood paneling and skylights; a small private dining room in front has green-painted woodwork and floral wallpaper. The front rooms have green carpets and swag lamps, candles in large glass hurricane chimneys, and many plants. Specialties include yellowtail snapper baked with sliced bananas, walnuts, and banana liqueur; steak "Ricardo" (fillets of tenderloin sautéed

with mushrooms in Madeira-wine sauce), and chilled Senegalese cream-of-celery soup made with curry, heavy cream, and mango chutney, and, for dessert, Poor Richard's Super Rich, a creamy blend of Godiva and three other kinds of chocolate in a chocolate pie crust topped with fresh whipped cream, and crushed English walnuts. *1208 Simonton St., tel. 305/294–0717. Jacket required. Reservations advised. AE, CB, DC, MC, V. Closed 2–3 wks in Sept. No lunch. Expensive.*

Dockside Bar and Raw Bar. When the crowds get too thick on the Mallory Dock at sunset, you can come up here, have a piña colada and a snack, and watch the action from afar. This establishment, on a 200-foot dock behind Ocean Key House, has a limited but flavorful menu: freshly smoked fish, crunchy conch salad, crispy conch fritters, and fresh clams, oysters, and shrimp. Live island music is featured nightly. *Ocean Key House, Zero Duval St., tel. 305/296–7701. Dress: casual. No reservations. AE, CB, DC, MC, V. Inexpensive.*

Lodging

Some hotels in the Keys are historic structures with a charming patina of age; others are just plain old. Salty winds and soil play havoc with anything manmade in the Keys. Constant maintenance is a must, and some hotels and motels don't get it. Inspect your accommodations before checking in. The best rooms in the Keys have a clear bay or ocean view and a deep setback from the Overseas Highway.

The city of Key West offers the greatest variety of lodgings, from large resorts to bed-and-breakfast rooms in private homes. Altogether there are about 4,000 units (including about 1,500 rooms in close to 60 guest houses) as well as approximately 1,800 condominium apartments that are available for daily or weekly rental through their homeowners associations.

Accommodations in the Keys are more expensive than elsewhere in South Florida. In part this is due to the Keys' popularity and ability to command top dollar, but primarily it's because everything used to build and operate a hotel costs more in the Keys. All materials and supplies must be trucked in, and electric and water rates are among the steepest in the nation.

The Florida Keys and Key West Visitors Bureau provides a free accommodations guide (*see* Important Addresses and Numbers). The list below is a representative selection of hotels, motels, resorts, and guest houses. In the Upper, Middle, and Lower Keys outside Key West, we've listed hotels, motels, and resorts by mile marker (MM) number in descending order, as you would encounter them when driving down from the mainland.

Category	Cost*
Very Expensive	over $175
Expensive	$110–$175
Moderate	$75–$110
Inexpensive	under $75

*All prices are for a standard double room, excluding 6% state sales tax and local tourist tax.

Key Largo   **Largo Lodge.** No two rooms are the same in this vintage 1950s resort. A tropical garden with palm trees, sea grapes, and orchids surrounds the guest cottages. Late in the day, wild ducks, pelicans, herons, and other birds come looking for a handout. *MM 101.5, BS, 101740 Overseas Hwy., 33037, tel. 305/ 451–0424 or 800/IN–THE–SUN. 7 rooms with bath, including 1 efficiency. Facilities: 200 feet of bay frontage, public phone, boat ramp and 3 slips. No children under 16 or pets. AE, MC, V. Moderate.*

★ **Holiday Inn Key Largo Resort.** James W. Hendricks, the Kentucky attorney who restored the *African Queen* (*see* Exploring the Keys), completed renovations and new landscaping at this resort at the Key Largo Harbor Canal in 1989. The hotel was built in 1971, and a new wing was added in 1981. Decor includes blonde wood furniture and pink and green bedspreads. Provides onshore accommodations for guests coming to Jules Undersea Lodge and pickup service from Marathon Airport. *MM 100, OS, Box 708, U.S. 1, 33037, tel. 305/451–2121, 800/ HOLIDAY, 800/THE KEYS, or 800/247–2345 (FL). 132 rooms with bath, including 13 nonsmoker rooms and 2 rooms for handicapped guests. Facilities: 2 swimming pools (1 with waterfall), marina with 35 transient spaces, gift shop, dive and glass-bottom tour boats, boat rentals. AE, MC, V. Expensive.*

★ **Marina Del Mar Resort and Marina.** This resort beside the Key Largo Harbor Canal caters to sailors and divers. Two buildings opened in 1986, a third in 1988. All rooms contain original art by local artists Sue and Zita. The best rooms are suites 502, 503 and 504, each of which has a full kitchen and plenty of room for large families and dive groups. The fourth-floor observation deck offers spectacular sunrise and sunset views. Advance reservations are required for boat slips. To find the hotel, turn OS on U.S. 1 by the Texaco station at Laguna Avenue, and left at the first intersection onto Caribbean Boulevard. Marina Del Mar is about 100 yards on the left. *MM 100, OS, Box 1050, 33037, tel. 800/451–3483 (U.S.), 800/253–3483 (FL), 800/638– 3483 (Canada), or 305/451–4107. 76 rooms with bath, including 16 suites, 16 nonsmoker rooms and 3 rooms for handicapped guests. Facilities: in-room refrigerators, 46-slip full-service marina, showers and washing machines for live-aboards, swimming pool, 2 lighted tennis courts, weight room, washers and dryers on all floors, diver lockers, picnic tables, free Continental breakfast in lobby, restaurant and bar, dive packages, diving and snorkeling charters, fishing charters. No pets. AE, CB, DC, MC, V. Moderate.*

Sunset Cove Motel. Each room has one hard and one soft mattress plus a sleeper sofa, tile floors, and original hand-painted murals. Special discounts are offered to senior citizens and members of conservation groups. *MM 99.5, BS, Box 99, 33037, tel. 305/451–0705. 10 units with bath and a dormitory group house with kitchen for up to 15 people. Facilities: free watersports equipment (canoes, glass-bottom and regular paddle boat, sailboats, trimaran, and Windsurfers), 115-foot fishing pier, boat ramp. No children under 16. No pets. MC, V. Moderate.*

Bay Harbor Lodge. Owner Laszlo Simoga speaks German, Hungarian, and Russian and caters to an international clientele. Situated on two heavily landscaped acres, this resort has a rustic wood lodge and several concrete-block structures. Unit 14, a large efficiency apartment with a deck, has a wood ceiling, original oil paintings, and a dining table made from the hatch

cover of a World War II Liberty Ship. *MM 97.5, BS, Rte. 1, Box
35, 33037, tel. 305/852–5695. 12 rooms with bath. Facilities:
Jacuzzi, saltwater shower, Olympic weightlifting equipment,
individual outdoor barbecues, paddleboat, rowboats, canoes, 2
docks, cable TV, boat and trailer parking. No pets. MC, V. Inexpensive.*

Sheraton Key Largo Resort. This four-story hotel is nestled in
12½ acres of coastal hardwood hammock and mangrove swamp.
A modern interpretation of traditional Conch architecture, the
resort's three-story atrium lobby features a multitude of small
glass windowpanes separated by prominent mullions, a
Mexican-tile floor, coral-rock walls, and rattan furniture. *MM
97, BS, 97000 Overseas Hwy., 33037, tel. 305/852–5553, 800/325–
3535 (U.S.), 800/268–9393 (Eastern Canada), or 800/268–9330
(Western Canada). 200 rooms with bath, including 10 suites.
Facilities: minibars, 2 heated swimming pools, 2 lighted tennis
courts, 2,000-foot labeled nature trail, sailboat and
Windsurfer rental, fishing and dive charters, dive shop, 21-slip
dock for hotel guests, 2 restaurants, 3 lounges, beauty shop.
AE, CB, DC, MC, V. Expensive.*

Islamorada **Holiday Isle Resorts and Marina.** Situated near Theater of the
Sea, this is actually four separate resort motels under common
ownership and management—the original Holiday Isle Resorts and Marina, El Capitan, Harbor Lights, and Howard
Johnson's. All except El Capitan were renovated in 1988. Each
motel in the complex offers variety in price and location. On
weekends, the resort is popular with the under-30 set. Harbor
Lights, off on its own a half mile up the road, is quieter than the
rest. *MM 84.5, OS, Windley Key, 84001 Overseas Hwy., Box
588, 33036, tel. 305/664–2321. 800/432–2875 (FL), or 800/327–
7070 (U.S. and Canada). 171 rooms with bath, including 18
suites and 21 efficiencies, 3 nonsmoker rooms in Howard
Johnson's. Facilities: 3 swimming pools, 18-slip marina, 5 restaurants, Wave Runners charter fishing boats, Holiday
Princess glass-bottom sightseeing boat; Caribbean
Watersports, a concessionaire, rents Hobie 14s, jet skis, and
sailboats and offers parasailing. No pets. AE, CB, DC, MC, V.
Inexpensive–Very Expensive.*

Cheeca Lodge. Reminiscent of Miami Beach in the 1950s, this
27-acre resort on Upper Matecumbe Key appeals to affluent
northeasterners who appreciate ostentatious informality. It
reopened in 1989 after being closed for 17 months for a $30 mil-
lion total renovation and expansion. Lobby decor includes
cypress beams and Florida keystone floors. Two color schemes
were used for the guest rooms and suites: periwinkle blue and
strawberry, and hot orange and green. All guest units have
British Colonial–style furniture with bamboo and wicker headboards and chairs. Ocean Suite 102 features a cathedral ceiling
and a screened porch. Fourth-floor rooms in the main lodge
open onto a terrace with either an ocean or bay view. *MM 82,
Upper Matecumbe Key, Box 527, 33036, tel. 305/664–4651
(Islamorada), or 305/245–3755 (Miami), or 800/327–2888
(U.S. and FL). 203 rooms, including 64 suites, 160 nonsmoker
rooms, and 5 rooms for handicapped guests. Facilities: in-
room minibar, free golf-cart shuttle service around the resort,
9-hole par-3 executive golf course designed by Jack Nicklaus, 6
lighted tennis courts, 2 heated swimming pools and one saltwater tidal pool, 525-foot fishing pier, 2 restaurants, lounge.
Sun. brunch served in the Atlantic's Edge Dining Room.*

Beach Hut rents Hobie Cats, rafts, snorkeling and fishing gear, parasailing equipment, and power boats. All-year children's program. AE, CB, DC, MC, V. Very Expensive.

Long Key **Lime Tree Bay Resort** Four new rooms with cathedral ceiling were added in 1986 to this 2.5-acre resort built in 1972. Each room is decorated differently. A palm tree grows through the floor of "The Treehouse," a two-bedroom unit with kitchen that is popular with larger families. You can swim and snorkel in the shallow grass flats just offshore. *MM 68.5, BS, Box 839, Layton, 33001, tel. 305/664–4740. 28 rooms with bath. Facilities: outdoor swimming pool and Jacuzzi, tennis court, power and sailboat rentals, 2 restaurants. No pets. AE, MC, V. Moderate.*

Marathon **Hawk's Cay.** Morris Lapidus, architect of the Fontainebleau
★ Hilton hotel in Miami Beach, designed this rambling West Indies–style resort, which opened in 1959 as the Indies Inn and Marina. Over the years it has entertained a steady stream of politicians (including Harry Truman, Dwight Eisenhower, and Lyndon Johnson) and film stars who come to relax and be pampered by a friendly, low-key staff. Hawk's Cay retains the comfortable ambience it has always had, even after an $8 million renovation of rooms, public areas, meeting space, and landscaping completed in 1989. The new decor features wickerwork rattan, a sea-green and salmon color scheme, and original contemporary artwork in guest rooms and public areas. Most rooms face the water. New in 1990 will be 86 two-bedroom marina villas available to hotel guests; a new health club is scheduled to open in 1991. *MM 61, OS, 33050, tel. 305/743–7000, 800/432–2242 (FL) or 800/327–7775. 177 rooms with bath, including 16 suites, 4 rooms for handicapped guests. Facilities: heated swimming pool, 2 whirlpool spas, 1-mi fitness trail, 8 tennis courts, Tim Farwell's Tennis School, use of Sombrero Golf Course in Marathon, 70-slip full-service marina, PADI-certified dive boats, Club Nautico boat rentals, fishing and sailing charter boats, Zoovet Dolphin Center (where guests can swim with the dolphins), 4 restaurants, complimentary full-breakfast buffet, nightclub, 4 boutique and specialty shops, billiard room, video game room. Free summer children's program. AE, DC, MC, V. Very Expensive.*

Rainbow Bend Fishing Resort. First you notice the shocking-pink exterior, then the well-kept appearance of this 2.7-acre resort built in the late 1950s as a lumberyard and CIA base. Every room is different. The Main House has a series of interconnecting rooms that can accommodate up to 14 people. A restaurant offering complimentary breakfast overlooks an ample manmade beach, good bonefish flats just a few yards offshore, and a dock with boats available free to guests. *MM 58, OS, Grassy Key, Route 1, Box 159, 33050, tel. 305/289–1505. 21 rooms with bath, including 18 suites. Facilities: heated swimming pool and Jacuzzi, small fishing pier, 4 hrs free use of 15-foot Boston Whaler, free use of sailboards and canoe, complete bait and tackle shop, 2 charter boats, restaurant. Quarterly newsletter for guests. AE, MC, V. Expensive.*

Valhalla Beach Resort Motel. Watch for this resort's large sign along the Overseas Highway. The resort itself is a half mile off the road, surrounded by water on three sides. It's a 1950s motel that has been run by the same family for over 20 years. *MM 56.5, OS, Crawl Key, Rte. 1, Box 115, 33050, tel. 305/289–0616.*

12 rooms with bath, including 8 efficiencies. Facilities: boat ramp and dock, private beach. No credit cards. Inexpensive.

Sombrero Resort & Lighthouse Marina. You can choose from marina or pool views in this complex of buildings ranging in height from one to three stories. The original structure built in 1960 was renovated in 1985, and new rooms were opened in 1988 and 1989. Turn OS off the Overseas Highway by the K-Mart onto Sombrero Beach Road, then right at the first corner onto Sombrero Boulevard. The resort is to your left, across from the Sombrero Country Club. *MM 50, OS, 19 Sombrero Blvd., 33050, tel. 305/743–2250 or 800/433–8660. 154 rooms with bath, including 102 suites. Facilities: pool, sauna, 4 tennis courts, tennis pro, marine store, boat ramp, 54-slip marina, restaurant, bar. AE, MC, V. Moderate.*

Boot Key Seaport Resort. Opened in 1989, this houseboat resort consists of permanently anchored barges that move in the wind. By prior arrangement, yachtsmen with boats under 25 feet can tie their craft alongside their houseboat unit. The proprietor also operates Faro Blanco Marine Resort in Marathon. *MM 47.8, OS, 1000 15th St., 33050, tel. 305/743–4200 or 800/ 343–9091. 31 suites with bath on 19 houseboats, 1 room for handicapped guests. Facilities: ship's store, gift shop, raw bar and grill, full-service marina with 100 slips, boat rentals. Pets welcome with $18 fee and advance reservation. Dockage fee for guests' boats $7/night. AE, MC, V. Expensive.*

Little Torch Key
★

Little Palm Island. The lobby is just off the Overseas Highway on Little Torch Key, but the resort itself is a three-mile boat ride away on a palm-fringed island at the western end of the Newfound Harbor Keys. There you'll find 14 thatch-roof villas, each with two suites, and two additional suites in the Great House, a concrete fishing lodge built in 1928. Each suite has a Mexican-tile bath and dressing area, beds draped with mosquito netting, and Mexican and Guatemalan wicker and rattan furniture. Built on stilts nine feet above mean high tide, all villas afford good views of the water. The island is in the middle of Coupon Bight Aquatic Preserve and is the closest point of land to the Looe Key National Marine Sanctuary. *MM 28.5, Overseas Highway, Route 4, Box 1036, 33042, tel. 305/872–2524 or 800/343–8567. 30 suites, 1 for handicapped guests. Facilities: air conditioners, wet bars and stocked refrigerators, room safes, heated lagoon-style swimming pool, sauna, tiki bar, gift shop, restaurant, 12-slip marina for hotel and restaurant guests. Free launch service 7 AM–11 PM. Pickup from Marathon Airport and Key West International Airport. Guided tours and excursions. Full American plan—breakfast, lunch, dinner, Sun. brunch. No children under 9 or pets. Very Expensive.*

Ramrod Key

Looe Key Reef Resort and Dive Center. The rooms in this two-story divers' motel were refurnished in 1987. In the tiny lobby, the front desk doubles as a package liquor store. Rooms are spartan but comfortable, with firm mattresses and ocean-blue bedspreads and carpets. The least desirable rooms are the three singles without a canal view. Guests can make an appointment for free pickup from the private airstrip on Summerland Key. *MM 27.5, US 1, OS, Box 509, 33042, tel. 305/ 872–2215. 23 rooms with bath, 1 for handicapped guests. Facilities: air conditioners, cable TV, outdoor swimming pool, dive shop, 400 feet of boat dockage, two Coast Guard–certified dive* *boats, restaurant, poolside tiki bar and raw bar. AE, MC, V. Inexpensive.*

Sugarloaf Key   **Sugar Loaf Lodge.** This well-landscaped older motel overlooking mangrove islands and Upper Sugarloaf Sound has one building with soft beds and an eclectic assortment of furniture and another with high ceilings, wall murals, and balconies on the second floor. A friendly dolphin named Sugar inhabits a lagoon just outside the restaurant; diners can watch her perform through a picture window. *MM 17, BS, Box 148, 33044, tel. 305/ 745–3211. 55 rooms with bath. Facilities: swimming pool, tennis court, 18-hole miniature golf course, restaurant, lounge, free dolphin performances at 9 AM, 1 PM, and 5 PM. AE, CB, DC, MC, V. Moderate.*

Key West House and Condominium Rentals   **Key West Reservation Service** makes hotel reservations and helps visitors locate rental properties (condominiums and private homes). *628 Fleming St., Drawer 1689, 33040, tel. 305/294– 7713, 800/356–3567 (FL), 800/327–4813 (U.S.), 716/823–1061 (Canada). AE, MC, V.*

Property Management of Key West, Inc., offers lease and rental service for condominiums, town houses, and private homes, including renovated Conch homes. *1213 Truman Ave., 33040, tel. 305/296–7744. AE, MC, V.*

Hotels and Motels   **The Banyan Resort.** A time-share resort across the street from
★   the Truman Annex, the Banyan Resort includes five Victorian houses, a former cigar factory listed on the National Registry of Historic Places, and two modern buildings in the Victorian style. The award-winning gardens are a tropical cornucopia of avocado, Barbados cherry, eggfruit, papaya, Persian lime, and sapodilla. The rooms have a gray, maroon, and mauve color scheme and rattan and wicker furniture. *323 Whitehead St., 33040, tel. 305/294–9573 or 800/225–0639. 38 suites with bath. Facilities: 2 swimming pools (1 heated), 2 Jacuzzis, bar. No children under 16 or pets. AE, MC, V. Very Expensive.*

Hyatt Key West. A first for Hyatt, this "baby grand" resort consists of three four-story buildings surrounding a tropical piazza. The lobby has a Mexican terra-cotta tile floor and cherry wood fixtures; the room decor employs mint, lilac, peach, and teal blue hues with light-wood dressers and wicker chairs. All rooms except 2209 and 2110 have water views. *601 Front St., 33040, tel. 305/296–9900, 800/228–9000, or 800/233–1234. 120 rooms with bath, including 16 suites, 16 nonsmoker rooms, and 6 rooms for handicapped guests. Facilities: honor bar, in-room safe, swimming pool and Jacuzzi, hot tub, fitness room, small private manmade beach, bicycle and motor scooter rental, 6-slip marina. AE, CB, DC, MC, V. Very Expensive.*

Marriott's Casa Marina Resort. Henry Morrison Flagler built La Casa Marina in 1921 at the end of the Florida East Coast Railroad line. New wings were added in 1978 and 1986. The entire 13-acre resort revolves around an outdoor patio and lawn facing the ocean. The lobby has an elegant beamed ceiling, polished wood floor of Dade County pine, and wicker furniture. Rooms are decorated in purple, mauve, and green pastels and prints of fish and Key West scenes. Among the best rooms are the two-bedroom loft suites with balconies facing the ocean, and the lanai rooms on the ground floor of the main building with French doors opening directly onto the lawn. *1500 Reynolds St., 33040, tel. 305/296–3535, 800/235–4837 (FL), or 800/*

228–9290 (U.S.). 314 rooms with bath, including 63 suites, 16 nonsmoker rooms, 4 rooms for handicapped guests. Facilities: heated swimming pool, whirlpool, 600-ft. fishing pier, health club, massage studio and sauna, 3 tennis courts, 2 gift shops, activity center for children, game room, restaurant, poolside bar. Key West Water Sports, a concessionaire, offers deep-sea charter boats, light-tackle fishing, party-boat fishing, Hobie Cats, Sunfish, jet skis, scuba and snorkel trips, bicycle and moped rentals. AE, DC, MC, V. Very Expensive.

Ocean Key House. This newly refurbished five-story city resort hotel has large and comfortable rooms decorated in tasteful pastel colors and art-deco reproductions. The best rooms, penthouse suites 511 and 512, overlook the Gulf of Mexico. Ocean Key House is the closest hotel to Mallory Square. From its pool deck you can watch the sunset show while quaffing a piña colada from the outdoor bar. *Zero Duval St., 33040, tel. 305/296–7701, 800/231–9864 (FL), or 800/328–9815 (U.S.). 100 units with bath, including 52 1-bedroom suites and 16 2-bedroom suites. Suites have fully equipped kitchen, private Jacuzzi, full-size living room/dining room, minibar. Facilities: heated swimming pool, 6 boat slips, restaurant, pool bar, dive shop. AE, CB, DC, MC, V. Expensive.*

★ **Pier House.** This is the catbird seat for touring Key West—just off the intersection of Duval and Front streets and within easy walking distance of Mallory Square and downtown. Yet within the hotel grounds you feel the tranquility of a remote tropical island. Weathered-gray buildings flank a courtyard filled with tall coconut palms and hibiscus blossoms. Locals gather around a thatch-roof shelter at the Beach Club, a tiki bar. The complex's eclectic architecture includes an original Conch house. The entire hotel was renovated in 1989 and decorated in rich pastels. In an atrium just off the lobby, a trilevel waterfall plunges through a tropical rain forest. *1 Duval St., 33040, tel. 305/296–4600, 800/432–3414 (FL), or 800/327–8340 (U.S.). 120 rooms with bath, including 11 suites in 4 separate low-rise buildings. Facilities: heated swimming pool, 8 bars and restaurants. AE, MC, V. Expensive.*

Econo Lodge. Half the rooms of this six-story motel face the Gulf of Mexico, the rest face the pool. The sixth-floor penthouses have the best view of the Gulf's mangrove islands, grass flats, the nightly sunset, and Mount Trashmore on Stock Island. The rooms are decorated with Key West prints, floral-print bedspreads, and blonde-wood furniture. The trackless trolley stops in front of the main entrance. *3820 N. Roosevelt Blvd., 33040, tel. 305/294–5511, 800/533–9378 (FL), or 800/446–6900 (U.S.). 143 rooms with bath, including 4 1-bedroom suites with kitchenette and 4 penthouses with 2 bedrooms and 1½ baths. Facilities: swimming pool, restaurant, lounge, poolside tiki bar. AE, DC, MC, V. Inexpensive.*

★ **La Concha Holiday Inn.** This seven-story art-deco hotel in the heart of downtown Key West is the city's tallest building. It opened in 1926, was totally renovated and enlarged in 1986, and in 1987 was added to the National Register of Historic Places. Novelist Ernest Hemingway and playwright Tennessee Williams both stayed here. The lobby has a polished floor of pink, mauve, and green marble and a conversation pit with comfortable chairs. Rooms are large and furnished with 1920s-era antiques, lace curtains, and big closets. The restorers kept the old building's original louvered room doors, light globes, and floral trim on the archways. You can enjoy the sunset from "The Top," a restaurant and lounge that overlooks the entire island. *430 Duval St., 33040, tel. 305/296–2991 or 800/227–6151 (FL). 160 rooms with bath, including 8 suites, 18 nonsmoker rooms, and 8 rooms for handicapped guests. Facilities: pool and sun deck, whirlpool spa, fitness room, 2 restaurants, 3 bars, bicycle and motor scooter rentals. AE, CB, DC, MC, V. Moderate.*

★ **The Marquesa Hotel.** Key West architect Thomas Pope supervised the restoration of this four-story 1884 home and added onto it in a compatible style. The lobby resembles a Victorian parlor, with antique furniture, Audubon prints, fresh flowers, and a bowl of apples for nibbles. Rooms have French Provincial furnishings and dotted Swiss curtains. There are marble vanities in some baths, marble floors in others. Continental breakfast prepared by the Mira restaurant's pastry chef is served poolside ($5 extra). *600 Fleming St., Key West 33040, tel. 305/292–1919. 15 rooms with private bath. Facilities: solar-heated swimming pool, room service, 24-hr staff, in-room safe. AE, MC, V. Very Expensive.*

Guest Houses **The Curry Mansion Inn.** Careful dedication to detail by Key
★ West architect Thomas Pope and owners Al and Edith Amsterdam have produced a near-perfect match between the Victorian Curry Mansion (1899) and its modern bed-and-breakfast addition. Each room has a different color scheme of tropical pastels; all rooms have carpeted floors, wicker headboards and furnishings, and quilts from the Cotton Gin Store at MM 94.5 in Tavernier. Rooms 1 and 8 are honeymoon suites with canopy beds and balconies. *511 Caroline St., Key West 33040, tel. 305/294–5349. 15 rooms with bath, 4 rooms for handicapped guests. Facilities: wheelchair lift, swimming pool, in-room safes, wet bars. Guests have privileges at Pier House Beach Club. AE, CB, DC, MC, V. Expensive.*

★ **Eaton Lodge.** Built just after the great fire of 1886, the lodge has eight rooms in the main house and four in the adjoining coach house. The common parlor and guest rooms are furnished with fine antiques. The upstairs Jonquil Springfield suite (two rooms with a connecting bath and adjoining veranda) has white metal hospital-style beds, rag and sissal rugs, and London underground wall posters from the 1930s. A peahen named Matilda struts along brick walks in the tropical garden in search of cocktail peanuts. *511 Eaton St., Key West 33040, tel. 305/294–3800. 12 rooms with bath. Facilities: refrigerators in bathroom, whirlpool spa. Airport pickup service in London taxi. AE, MC, V. Expensive.*

Island City House. This guest house is actually three separate buildings: the vintage-1880s Island City House and Arch House (a former carriage house) and a 1970s reconstruction of an old cigar factory that once stood on the site. Guests share a private tropical garden. *422 William St., Key West 33040, tel. 305/294–5702 or 800/634–8230. 24 parlor suites with bath and kitchen. Facilities: swimming pool and Jacuzzi, bike rental. AE, MC, V. Expensive.*

Authors of Key West. This complex is made up of two turn-of-the-century Conch cottages and seven rooms in a 1940s main house. Each unit is named for a writer linked to Key West and decorated with appropriate posters and furnishings. *725 White St. (at Petronia St.), Key West 33040, 305/294–7381. 9 rooms with bath. No children under 18 or pets. AE, MC, V. Moderate.*

The Mermaid & The Alligator. This is a homey bed-and-breakfast convenient to the center of town. The original 1904 structure of Dade County pine recently underwent extensive restoration. The Garden Room, the only downstairs room, has Japanese wall hangings, a white paddle fan, and a private doorway to the garden. Upstairs, the Blue Room (also known as the honeymoon suite) has a canopied Charleston four-poster bed with a rice pattern, a Roman-style tub, and a balcony overlooking St. Mary's by the Sea Catholic Church. The South West Suite, under the eaves on the third floor, has the only air conditioner in the house. *729 Truman Ave., Key West 33040, tel. 305/ 294–1894. 5 rooms with bath. Facilities: heated Jacuzzi. No children under 16. MC, V. Moderate.*

The Arts and Nightlife

The Arts The Keys are more than warm weather and luminous scenery—a vigorous and sophisticated artistic community flourishes here. Key West alone currently claims among its residents 55 full-time writers and 500 painters and craftsmen. Arts organizations in the Keys sponsor many special events, some lasting only a weekend, others spanning an entire season.

The monthly *Island Navigator,* Monroe County's only countywide general-interest newspaper, is free at banks, campgrounds, and convenience stores. Its monthly community calendar lists cultural and sports events.

Three free publications covering Key West arts, music, and literature are available at hotels and other high-traffic areas:

The weekly *Island Life,* the most current and complete, is published by Ocean Gulf Corp. *517 Duval St., Suite 200, Key West 33040, tel. 305/294–1616. Subscription by mail: $12/year.*
Entertainment Key West, a biweekly, and *Solares Hill,* a monthly community newspaper, are published by Solares Hill Co., Inc. (4 Key Lime Sq., Key West 33040, tel. 305/294–3602). In the Upper and Middle Keys, the weekly *Free Press* is available at hotels, motels, and retail outlets. *Box 469, Islamorada 33036, tel. 305/664–2266. Subscription by mail: $3/month.*

Theater **Jan McArt's Cabaret Theater at Mallory Square.** In a brick wrecker's warehouse built in 1879 and restored in 1986, Jan McArt has established a 300-seat theater for equity and nonequity musical productions. (McArt also operates Jan McArt's Royal Palm Dinner Theater in Boca Raton.) *410 Wall St., Box 4866, Key West, tel. 305/296–2120, 800/346–3240 (FL), or 800/356–8217 (US). Closed Mon. AE, MC, V.*
Red Barn Theater. This nonequity, 95-seat theater in its 10th year performs dramas and musical comedies, including plays by new playwrights. *319 Duval St., Key West, tel. 305/296–9511. Closed Mon. and sometimes Tues. No credit cards.*
Waterfront Playhouse. This mid-1850s wrecker's warehouse was converted into an 185-seat nonequity community theater that specializes in comedy and drama. *Mallory Sq., Key West, tel. 305/294–5015. Open Dec.–May. No credit cards.*
Tennessee Williams Fine Arts Center. A 490-seat theater built in 1980 on Stock Island, BS, the center presents chamber music, dance, jazz concerts, plays (dramatic and musical) with national and international stars, and other performing-arts events. *Florida Keys Community College, 5901 Junior College Rd., Key West, tel. 305/294–6232. Open Nov.–Apr. MC, V.*

Nightlife
Key Largo

Coconuts Restaurant and Bar. The soft island music during dinner changes to top 40 after 10 PM. The outdoor bar at the marina is popular with the under-30 crowd. To find Coconuts from U.S. 1, turn OS at the Texaco station at Laguna Avenue, then left at the first intersection onto Caribbean Boulevard and continue about 100 yards. *MM 100, OS, in the Marina Del Mar Resort and Marina, Key Largo, tel. 305/451–4107. Open noon–4 AM. AE, CB, DC, MC, V.*

Key West

Cafe Exile. When everyone else on Duval Street closes, Cafe Exile is still going strong. You can get an espresso or capuccino coffee here 24 hours a day. The Rum Runner is the most popular drink. There is jazz nightly 8 PM–1 AM; local musicians join the group. An adjoining indoor nightclub, Backstreet at Exile, is open 10 PM–4 AM. *700 Duval St., Key West, tel. 305/296–0991. Food service 8 AM–5 AM, bar service 8 AM–4 AM. No credit cards.*

Capt. Tony's Saloon. While tourists flock to Sloppy Joe's, a predominantly local crowd enjoys old-style Key West nightlife at this bar a block away in an 1852 structure first used as a morgue and ice house. Later it was Key West's first telegraph station. Old business cards and T-shirts cover the walls and ceiling. Coral Reef, the house drink, contains a secret rum-based formula. Live country and rhythm-and-blues entertainment is featured nightly; Jimmy Buffet got his start here. *428 Greene St., tel. 305/294–1838. Open 11 AM–4 AM. No credit cards.*

Havana Docks Lounge. A high-energy disco club popular with young locals and visitors, this lounge is in the old William R. Porter Docks Shipping Office, now part of the Pier House hotel. The Havana Docks deck is a good place to watch the sun set when Mallory Square gets too crowded. *1 Duval St., Key West, tel. 305/296–4600 or 800/432–3414 (FL). Open Sun.–Thurs. 4 PM–2 AM, Fri.–Sat. 4 PM–4 AM. AE, MC, V.*

Margaritaville Cafe. This place is owned by Key West resident and MCA recording star Jimmy Buffett, who performs here several times a year. The menu, which changes often, includes Jimmy's mother's recipes. The house special drink is, of course, a margarita. *500 Duval St., Key West, tel. 305/292–1435. Open 11 AM–4 AM; closed Sun. noon–4 AM. Live music Tues.–Sun. Cover charge for special events. AE, MC, V.*

Sloppy Joe's. Named for its founder, Capt. Joe Russell, Sloppy Joe's started as a speakeasy. Ernest Hemingway liked to gamble in a partitioned club room in back. After Hemingway's death, the original manuscript of *To Have and Have Not*, sections of *Death in the Afternoon*, *The Fifth Column*, and notes for *A Farewell to Arms* were found among personal papers he had stored at the bar. Decorated with Hemingway memorabilia and marine flags, the bar is popular with tourists and is full and noisy all the time. There is live entertainment from noon to 2 AM by local and touring groups. *201 Duval St., Key West, tel. 305/294–5717. Dress: shoes and shirt required. No reservations. All customers must show proof of age at night. Open 9 AM–4 AM. $1 cover charge after 8 PM. No credit cards.*

The Top Lounge. Located on the seventh floor of the La Concha Holiday Inn, Key West's tallest building, this is one of the best places from which to view the sunset. The Top serves deli-style lunch and complete dinners and features live entertainment. *430 Duval St., Key West, tel. 305/296–2991 or 800/227–6151 (FL). Open 11 AM–2 AM. AE, CB, DC, MC, V.*

Index

Personal Itinerary

Departure *Date*

Time

Transportation

Arrival *Date*   *Time*

Departure *Date*   *Time*

Transportation

Accommodations

Arrival *Date*   *Time*

Departure *Date*   *Time*

Transportation

Accommodations

Arrival *Date*   *Time*

Departure *Date*   *Time*

Transportation

Accommodations

Personal Itinerary

Arrival *Date*   *Time*

Departure *Date*   *Time*

Transportation

Accommodations

Arrival *Date*   *Time*

Departure *Date*   *Time*

Transportation

Accommodations

Arrival *Date*   *Time*

Departure *Date*   *Time*

Transportation

Accommodations

Arrival *Date*   *Time*

Departure *Date*   *Time*

Transportation

Accommodations

Addresses

Name

Address

Telephone

Name

Address

Telephone

Name

Address

Telephone

Name

Address

Telephone

Name

Address

Telephone

Name

Address

Telephone

Name

Address

Telephone

Name

Address

Telephone

Name

Address

Telephone

Name

Address

Telephone

Name

Address

Telephone

Name

Address

Telephone

Name

Address

Telephone

Name

Address

Telephone

Name

Address

Telephone

Name

Address

Telephone

Fodor's Travel Guides

U.S. Guides

Alaska
Arizona
Atlantic City & the
  New Jersey Shore
Boston
California
Cape Cod
Carolinas & the
  Georgia Coast
The Chesapeake Region
Chicago
Colorado
Dallas & Fort
  Worth

Disney World & the
  Orlando Area
Florida
Hawaii
Houston &
  Galveston
Las Vegas
Los Angeles, Orange
  County, Palm Springs
Maui
Miami, Fort Lauderdale,
  Palm Beach
Michigan, Wisconsin,
  Minnesota

New England
New Mexico
New Orleans
New Orleans (Pocket
  Guide)
New York City
New York City (Pocket
  Guide)
New York State
Pacific North Coast
Philadelphia
The Rockies
San Diego
San Francisco

San Francisco (Pocket
  Guide)
The South
Texas
USA
Virgin Islands
Virginia
Waikiki
Washington, DC
Williamsburg

Foreign Guides

Acapulco
Amsterdam
Australia, New Zealand,
  The South Pacific
Austria
Bahamas
Bahamas (Pocket
  Guide)
Baja & the Pacific
  Coast Resorts
Barbados
Beijing, Guangzhou &
  Shanghai
Belgium &
  Luxembourg
Bermuda
Brazil
Britain (Great Travel
  Values)
Budget Europe
Canada
Canada (Great Travel
  Values)
Canada's Atlantic
  Provinces
Cancun, Cozumel,
  Yucatan Peninsula

Caribbean
Caribbean (Great
  Travel Values)
Central America
Eastern Europe
Egypt
Europe
Europe's Great
  Cities
Florence & Venice
France
France (Great Travel
  Values)
Germany
Germany (Great Travel
  Values)
Great Britain
Greece
The Himalayan
  Countries
Holland
Hong Kong
Hungary
India, including Nepal
Ireland
Israel
Italy

Italy (Great Travel
  Values)
Jamaica
Japan
Japan (Great Travel
  Values)
Jordan & the
  Holy Land
Kenya, Tanzania,
  the Seychelles
Korea
Lisbon
Loire Valley
London
London (Great
  Travel Values)
London (Pocket Guide)
Madrid & Barcelona
Mexico
Mexico City
Montreal &
  Quebec City
Munich
New Zealand
North Africa
Paris
Paris (Pocket Guide)

People's Republic of
  China
Portugal
Rio de Janeiro
The Riviera (Fun on)
Rome
Saint Martin &
  Sint Maarten
Scandinavia
Scandinavian Cities
Scotland
Singapore
South America
South Pacific
Southeast Asia
Soviet Union
Spain
Spain (Great Travel
  Values)
Sweden
Switzerland
Sydney
Tokyo
Toronto
Turkey
Vienna
Yugoslavia

Special-Interest Guides

Health & Fitness
  Vacations
Royalty Watching

Selected Hotels of
  Europe

Selected Resorts and
  Hotels of the U.S.
Shopping in Europe

Skiing in North America
Sunday in New York

Help us evaluate hotels and restaurants for the next edition of this guide, and we will send you a free issue of Fodor's newsletter, <u>TravelSense</u>.

Title of this guide:

1 Hotel ❏   **Restaurant** ❏   *(check one)*

Name

Number/Street

City/State/Country

Comments

2 Hotel ❏   **Restaurant** ❏   *(check one)*

Name

Number/Street

City/State/Country

Comments

3 Hotel ❏   **Restaurant** ❏   *(check one)*

Name

Number/Street

City/State/Country

Comments

General Comments

Please complete for a free copy of <u>TravelSense</u>

Name

Number/Street

City/State/Zip

Business Reply Mail

First Class Permit N⁰ 7775 *New York, NY*

Postage will be paid by addressee

Fodor's Travel Publications

201 East 50th Street
New York, NY 10022